ROBERT SHAW

ROBERT SHAW

AN ACTOR'S LIFE ON THE SET OF *JAWS* AND BEYOND

CHRISTOPHER SHAW MYERS

CITADEL PRESS
KENSINGTON PUBLISHING CORP.
KENSINGTONBOOKS.COM

CITADEL PRESS BOOKS are published by

Kensington Publishing Corp.
900 Third Avenue
New York, NY 10022

All Kensington titles, imprints, and distributed lines are available at special quantity discounts for bulk purchases for sales promotions, premiums, fund-raising, educational, or institutional use. Special book excerpts or customized printings can also be created to fit specific needs. For details, write or phone the office of the Kensington sales manager: Kensington Publishing Corp., 900 Third Avenue, New York, NY 10022, attn Sales Department; phone 1-800-221-2647.

10 9 8 7 6 5 4 3 2 1

First Citadel hardcover printing: June 2025

Printed in the United States of America

ISBN: 978-0-8065-4432-8

ISBN: 978-0-8065-4434-2 (e-book)

Library of Congress Control Number: 2025930761

The authorized representative in the EU for product safety and compliance
is eucomply OU, Parnu mnt 139b-14, Apt 123,
Tallinn, Berlin 11317; hello@eucompliancepartner.com

For my mother, who rarely smiled
for a photo but laughed an awful lot.

Contents

PART IV: War & Suicide

PART V: *JAWS* & Mrs. Shaw

PART VI: Leave Them Laughing

Author's Note

I grew up listening to the laugh-out-loud stories of my uncle, the actor Robert Shaw (who played Quint in *JAWS*); my mother, Joanna Shaw (Robert's sister); and my grandmother, Doreen Avery Shaw (whom I knew as Ouma). This is their story.

I have tried to capture, as best I can, what I heard from those three, supplementing it with my own research and a trove of information my mother kept in her closet for decades, including personal letters, audio recordings, playbills, and scrapbooks. I have used the same techniques in telling their story that they taught me: Rather than describe every aspect of their lives, I have focused on a few defining moments, and rather than gloss over those events, I have filled in details and crafted dialogue to capture how they talked, how they thought, and what they saw.

Robert Shaw was one of the most colorful characters in Hollywood. He was as good a writer as he was an actor, and even more interesting in person. Joanna Shaw knew him better than anyone, living or dead; they were as close as any brother and sister could be. She is the reason Robert wrote his best-known play and was nominated for a Tony Award, and he is the reason Joanna fought apartheid in South Africa, got her PhD in America, and sued her college for discriminating against women.

Robert and Joanna's story includes their childhood years in Orkney and Cornwall, where their father committed suicide and they witnessed the fire bombings of World War II; their formative years in London and America, where they began families and helped shape each other's careers; and their time together on the set of *JAWS*, revealing what really happened when the cameras were not rolling.

Despite the trauma in their lives, I never heard anyone laugh as hard as Robert and Joanna when they were talking about their childhood homes. Even well into their adult years, they were still like kids whenever they got together. In telling their story, I hope to capture some of the joy they felt in life and to find my own way home.

Prologue

[Spring 1974]

They were cut from the same cloth, the men in Paddy's Bar. Sometimes it was a group of farmers or laborers in coarse clothes. Sometimes it was landowners or professionals, only slightly better dressed. Sometimes it was another group altogether, or a combination. It didn't matter. The talk was always the same. No one ever felt the need to say anything, yet someone always did.

Robert Shaw entered through the back kitchen and made his way along the narrow hall. Shelves lined the wall with necessities for the locals: tea and sugar, loaves of bread, paraffin oil. He passed the dining room on his left, where families were eating dinner and exchanging gossip. Then he ducked into the small taproom on his right. With its low ceiling and stone walls, the room had a cozy feel. Several Irishmen sat enjoying their drinks at a wooden bar that ran along one side. At a table in the corner, Robert's friend, Jack, sat nursing a drink by himself.

Behind the bar, a black-and-white TV broadcast the day's news: Another IRA bombing in Dublin, inflation was at 25 percent, Richard Nixon was being impeached. Robert ducked under the partition and turned it off. "Enough bad news," he growled. He did not bother to ask if anyone was watching. Despite having achieved what few people could ever hope for—an Oscar nomination for acting and a Tony nomination for writing—Robert was not satisfied. Many of his peers had achieved greater recognition despite far less talent (or so he thought). Although he could seem arrogant and conceited at times, his eyes always seemed to sparkle.

1

Robert poured two shots of Irish whiskey and handed one to Jack, who had moved to the bar. With his bulbous nose and penchant for funny stories, Jack was popular at Paddy's. He and Robert toasted and downed their shots in a gulp. Robert poured two more.

Paddy emerged from the kitchen, apron in hand, and joined Robert behind the bar. "Drinkin' all my whiskey, Mr. Shaw?"

"Just keeping you in business, Paddy."

"Aye, I do well enough."

"I know you do." Turning to the locals, Robert asked, "Who wants another round?" Silence greeted him. "It's on me."

Everyone's hand went up, and Robert began pouring pints of Guinness. "When are you going to sell me the bar, Paddy?"

"You couldn't afford it."

"Ah, but that's a temporary problem."

"All those private school bills getting you down, Mr. Shaw?" one of the Irishmen asked.

"How many kids does he have again?" another said.

"Eight, I think. Or is it ten?"

"Don't forget the Rolls-Royce," someone chimed in.

"How does everyone know more about my business than me?" Robert asked with a grin.

Just then, the front door opened and a gust of wind swept through the bar. Conversation halted as an old woman made her way to a table. She folded her coat, placed it on the bench beside her pocketbook, and sat down.

"Ah, here's the reason," Robert said. "Good evening, Mrs. Gallagher. How is the switchboard today? Any good calls?"

"Could be," she said. "Could be an important one for you, Mr. Shaw."

"Then let me buy you a drink. What would tickle your fancy?"

"A cup of tea, thank you."

Robert got busy while the Irishmen turned their attention to Jack. "What's an Englishman like you doing in western Ireland?" one of them asked.

"Enjoying myself," Jack said. "Where else can you fish all day and then pull up here for a drink?"

"You mean, where can you drink all day?"

"What happened to your wife?" someone asked. "Haven't seen her this year."

"And you won't see her again," Jack replied.

"Murder her, did you?"

Jack smiled. "Remember the first summer we visited Tourmakeady?"

"Aye."

"I fell in love with this place. Next summer, I told my wife, we must come back."

"And?"

"It took some doing, but she agreed. This year, though, she said it's either Ireland or me."

"Made you choose, did she?"

Jack raised his glass. "Here's to being single."

Everyone laughed. Everyone except . . .

"I don't find that funny," Mrs. Gallagher said. "It's not easy finding a good woman, you know."

"Nor a good home," Jack shot back.

Robert stepped between them, looking every bit the polished waiter. He placed a white cloth on the table before her, smoothed it out, and set down the tray. "Your tea and sugar, my dear," he said. "Now please share your important news."

Mrs. Gallagher appeared not to hear. She picked up a spoon, fished two cubes of sugar from a jar, and dropped them in her tea. Everyone watched as she pulled the cup to her nose, smelled the aroma, and sighed. She took one sip, then another. Finally, satisfied, she looked up and said, "Your agent called."

"Oh? What did he say?"

"I put it through to your secretary."

Robert suppressed a laugh and pulled up a chair. "I appear to have two choices, then," he said, resting his chin in his hands and giving her his sweetest smile. "I can either learn the news when I get home, or you can tell me now."

"Hmm."

"Was it about *JAWS*?" he asked, leaning forward.

"Aye."

"And?"

Mrs. Gallagher paused for a moment. Then: "You got the part!"

"Bloody hell!" Robert stood and clapped his hands in glee.

The Irishmen were unimpressed. "Aren't you already a movie star?" one of them asked.

"No! Americans don't know the difference between a movie star and a real actor. I've only had supporting roles."

"You going to be as big as Peter O'Toole?"

"O'Toole?" Robert fairly spat out the word. "Yes, I am going to be as big as Peter O'Toole. Bigger, in fact. Bigger than O'Toole, bigger than Connery, bigger than all them buggers."

"I don't see how you could be bigger than O'Toole," the Irishman persisted. "He was born in the next county. Even a Cornishman can't top that."

"Have you seen even *one* of his movies?" Robert asked.

"No, but I haven't seen yours either."

"Nearest theater is forty miles away," someone added helpfully.

"O'Toole was born in England, not around here," someone else said.

"Not true. I was there at his birth."

Everyone laughed, and Robert began pouring more pints.

"When do you leave?"

All eyes turned to Mrs. Gallagher. "He needs to be in Marble Vineyard in three days."

"That's in the United States," Robert said. "*Martha's* Vineyard, actually. It's a six-week shoot." He stood and raised his glass. "Gentlemen, I will see you back here in June." Turning to Paddy, he added in his best Godfather accent, "If this is as big as I think, I'll be making you an offer you can't refuse!"

Several weeks later, everything that could possibly go wrong with *JAWS* was unfolding: The studio was over budget, the shark was not working, and no one was happy with the script's key speech about the USS *Indianapolis*. Half a mile offshore, Robert was at the end of *Orca's* bowsprit and hanging on for dear life. An hour earlier, the North Atlantic Ocean had been almost completely calm. Now, it was tossing him about like he was a toothpick.

A barge that had been dubbed *Garage Sale* was anchored nearby. Although larger and sturdier than the *Orca*, it was also bucking up and down in the waves. A film crew was spread across its flat deck, desperately trying to keep their equipment dry. Their goal was to capture a few more seconds of precious film before the weather turned even worse.

Beneath the waves, scuba divers worked on a steel platform. A giant mechanical shark was bolted to the top, just visible above the waterline. Cables running from the platform to the seafloor looked like beams of sunlight cutting through the murky water. Suddenly, one of the cables snapped, and the entire apparatus, thirty feet from base to shark, began to tilt. To the film crew, it looked like the shark had suddenly leaped out of the water. Then they heard the sound of splintering wood, and everyone groaned: The shark had collided with the boat. A hole opened in its side and water began pouring in.

"Save the actor," someone yelled.

"Forget the actor, save the equipment," someone else shouted.

The crew scrambled to save both, but when the boat began to roll over, Robert leaped overboard. He was a good swimmer, but the water was cold, and his Quint costume quickly became waterlogged. For a brief moment, he wondered if this was how it would all end, but before he could dwell on it, scuba divers propelled him toward the barge, where strong arms pulled him on board.

With water still pouring from him, Robert flopped down next to the director. "Steven, what the hell is going on? This was supposed to take six weeks!"

"I thought so too," Spielberg said. Handing him a towel, he joined Robert in watching the *Orca* slide beneath the waves, leaving a trail of bubbles.

Robert shook his head. "When are we going to be done?"

"I wish I knew. When we have every shot I need, we'll be done."

A man behind them had been speaking on a walkie-talkie. Now he interrupted. "Excuse me, Mr. Shaw. This might not be the best time to tell you, but your agent called. He said you need to get out of the country again, as soon as possible."

"Goddamn taxes," Robert swore. "They're killing me. I'm going to owe the IRS more than you're paying me to make this bloody film!" He took a deep breath and turned back to the director. "When will that thing be fixed?"

Spielberg turned to his production manager, and all three peered over the side. They could see the platform resting on the ocean floor. About fifty feet away, the shark had broken off and was lying on its side. Meanwhile, the *Orca* was caught between its anchors and its moorings, hovering midway between surface and seafloor, looking like a ghost ship.

"It'll be a couple of days, maybe more," the production manager said.

"My career is going down with that boat," Robert lamented.

"Mine too," Spielberg said. "You think they'll let me make another movie if this one fails?"

Robert rubbed his neck. "All right, Steven, we're in it together, then. You get that bloody thing working. Let me know when I need to be back."

The following day, Robert stepped up to an immigration booth and handed the agent his passport. Behind him was a sign: Welcome to Canada. The man looked at the paperwork and studied Robert's face. Then he smiled.

"Welcome back, Mr. Shaw. Good to see you again."

"Thanks."

"Tax troubles still chasing you?"

Robert professed shock. "Not at all! You know me, I just love Canada! The geese, the moose, the fresh air!"

The man laughed and stamped the passport. "Okay. I'll see you again soon."

That night, Robert sat by himself in a hotel bar overlooking Montreal. Below him, Notre Dame Basilica was lit up. He usually enjoyed the site but not tonight. In one hand he held a drink, in the other, a cigarette. Spread across the bar were his bills. He thumbed through them with growing disgust, then crumpled them into a ball and tossed it in the trash.

PART I

THE DOCTOR'S CHILDREN

Here lies One Whose Name
was writ in Water.

— Gravestone: John Keats

Chapter 1

The Inquest

[Winter 1940]

"Mrs. Shaw, did you murder your husband?"

The question should not have come as a surprise, but Mrs. Shaw stiffened. Then, drawing herself up like the Edwardian lady she saw herself to be, she said, "If I understand correctly, that is what we are here to determine." A few chuckles could be heard in the courtroom. A handful of observers sat in the back, mostly older women hoping to find something to entertain them. Suddenly, their day seemed more promising.

The judge scowled. He was a disheveled man in his fifties, with robes that hung loosely around his large body and stains that were undoubtedly from his lunch that day. His double chin jiggled when he spoke, and a small nose seemed oddly out of place on his large, jowly face. To top it off, he wore a powdered wig. He had intended the wig to give him an air of authority, but when Mrs. Shaw saw it, all she could think was, *A hog in a waistcoat is still a hog.*

By contrast, Mrs. Shaw was an attractive woman in her mid-thirties, with curly black hair, eyes that were both penetrating and intelligent, and cheekbones that hinted at her Celtic origin. Although born into Britain's middle class, she had married a doctor from a highly respected family in Cornwall. This, she believed, gave her status. She did not see how she could take the man before her seriously.

At the same time, she was no fool. Her appearance was appropriate for the occasion: She wore a dark dress, gray stockings, and black shoes. Her only nod to fashion was her hat, which had a red ribbon around it and a feather stuck in one side.

Her somber clothing, however, was lost from sight beneath her heavy overcoat, which she kept on. The courtroom was cold. The one source of heat was a stove in the corner, which gave off only enough heat to keep the judge warm, along with the two men beside him. England was at war. Germany had sunk a British destroyer, Hitler was planning the invasion of Scandinavia, and the British government was begging the United States to intervene. Rationing had begun, and coal for stoves such as this was in short supply.

A police officer stood at rigid attention to one side, wearing the standard uniform of the day: bobby hat, navy pants, and a jacket speckled with buttons and insignia. On the other side was a short man in an ill-fitting suit with large glasses that enveloped his face. He placed a sheaf of papers in front of the judge, and the two began going through them together. Every now and then, the young man pointed to something and they whispered.

Mrs. Shaw waited patiently. Finally, the judge looked up. "It was a simple question, Mrs. Shaw," he said. "Did you or did you not kill your husband?"

"I did not," she answered.

He nodded. "Thank you for gracing us with a direct response. Now let us get to the facts. Your name is Doreen Avery Shaw?"

"It is."

"And your husband was Thomas Archibald Shaw?"

"He was."

"In reading the police report," the judge continued, "I see that your neighbors reported a commotion on the night of your husband's death. Can you explain that?"

"Of course," Mrs. Shaw said. "The commotion was because my husband was drunk. As to why my neighbors felt the need to report it, I can only assume they are a bunch of nosy busybodies."

There were more snickers in the room, and the judge began to think he was losing control of his court. "Young lady," he said sternly, "you will address me as milord in this courtroom."

Mrs. Shaw looked at him coldly. "Do you think of me as young?"

"Of course. You are obviously a young woman."

"My husband is dead," Mrs. Shaw said. "I have five children to raise by myself, no money, and our country is at war. I do not feel young."

The judge softened a little. "Nevertheless, you will address me as milord."

"Yes, milord," she responded.

"Very well, let us get on," he said, satisfied. "Are you saying, Mrs. Shaw, that your husband was the cause of the commotion?"

"Of course!" The judge looked at her and Mrs. Shaw added, "Milord."

"Thank you. And what caused the commotion?"

"Have you ever lived with a drunk, milord?"

"I have not," he said. "My wife and I enjoy a sherry now and then but only on occasion."

"Then you are fortunate, milord," Mrs. Shaw said. "And ignorant." (More chuckles.) "I should have thought a man in your profession, milord, a man who spends his days in a room such as this, milord, would be familiar with what a drunk is like." She paused. "Who did you say reported the commotion?"

"I did not say. The police questioned several of your neighbors."

"Which ones, milord?"

"That is not relevant." The judge was beginning to suspect he was being mocked by the woman's repeated use of *milord*, but he could not reverse himself now; it would only make him look more foolish. "The fact is that several of your neighbors reported loud arguing on the night of your husband's death," he continued sternly. "And further, it was said that such a commotion was not uncommon in your household."

"Poppycock," Mrs. Shaw said. "If there was any commotion that night, it was when my husband fell in the mud. And that was in the yard behind our house, not inside. He was trying to avoid being seen by me, I imagine. And rightly so! He was in a disgraceful state. But I did not hear him fall, nor did I hear him come in, milord. In fact, I did not speak to my husband that night; it was my daughter who discovered his body in our bedroom."

"But you confronted him on other occasions, did you not?"

"Why do you say that, milord?"

"The same neighbors, your *nosy* neighbors, as you refer to them"—now it was the judge who drew some appreciative chuckles—"reported there were numerous occasions when loud noises could be heard in your home."

Mrs. Shaw thought for a moment. "They are correct in that. When my husband was sober, he was a gentleman. But he was subject to bursts of anger when he had been drinking, which was all too often. Did those neighbors tell you how he would stand outside our house at night, yelling for me to open the door and most likely waking them up as well?"

The judge and the young man looked back at the papers. Mrs. Shaw did not wait for them to find their answer. "Did they tell you why I left him and moved to Cornwall?" she continued. "Did they tell you how he followed me, appeared on my doorstep, and begged me to take him back?" The two men continued to shuffle through the papers. "And did they tell you," Mrs. Shaw finished, "how I would find him in the gutter some mornings, bruised and bloody and unable to remember how he had gotten there?"

The judge looked up. "Mrs. Shaw, you have answered my question. I understand how others would have heard noises coming from your house. Allow me to pose a different set of queries."

"By all means, milord."

"Why did your husband take morphine that night? He was a doctor. He must have known what he was doing."

"I do not presume to know my husband's mind, milord."

"I am asking you to speculate."

"You are asking me to guess. I am not a psychiatrist, not that those people know anything about anything. They only make matters worse. But if you are asking me to guess, milord, I would say that he took morphine to sleep it off."

The questioning went on like this for over an hour. The judge posed his questions and Mrs. Shaw answered them, always thoroughly, always with an attitude bordering on arrogance. The police officer barely moved throughout the proceedings, while the judge and the young man continued to look through the documents and whisper. Only when the judge had exhausted every conceivable question did he render a decision.

"Mrs. Shaw, I could easily recommend this case be investigated as a murder. You and your husband are known to have fought, sometimes violently. Several witnesses will attest to this, and I am sure we would find others, should we look further. You have not tried to hide your contempt for him. The fact that you left him and traveled from Orkney to Cornwall, a considerable distance, indicates the level of antipathy you felt."

The judge paused. Mrs. Shaw remained silent.

"However," he continued, "I must conclude that nothing connects you directly to his death. He was by himself at the pub, and the coroner's report states that he almost certainly took the morphine of his own accord. I therefore conclude that you are blameless."

The judge paused. Mrs. Shaw remained silent.

"At the same time," he continued, "I cannot rule this an accident, as you have suggested. Your husband was a doctor, he administered morphine on a regular basis, and he understood the effects of mixing it with alcohol. With his years of training, I do not believe he would have forgotten, even in an inebriated state, about its effects."

The young man placed a form on the table. The judge scribbled a few words and looked up. "I conclude that Thomas Archibald Shaw, on the evening of twenty-third January 1940, knowingly ingested a large amount of morphine after consuming large quantities of alcohol. It is my judgment that he was in a depressed state, having concluded he could not stop drinking and rightly believing that you would leave him again and take the children with you. I am therefore led to the conclusion that he took the morphine on purpose, to end his own life."

The judge met Mrs. Shaw's eyes. "I rule this a suicide. Case dismissed. You may go."

Mrs. Shaw stood. For a moment it appeared she would say something more, and the courtroom fell silent. But she turned instead and made her way to the back of the room. Halfway up the aisle, she passed two women on a bench.

"Do you think she killed him?" one of them whispered.

"Without a doubt," the other replied.

Mrs. Shaw did not pause on her way out.

Chapter 2

-‹‹‹◆›››-

The Shaws

[1926–1936]

Doreen Avery Shaw—mother to Robert Shaw and four other children of equally volatile temperament; wife to a drunk; born in Piggs Peak, Swaziland but raised in Cornwall, England; a woman of considerable intellect who laughed at herself as easily as at others—enjoyed reading her newspaper every morning. It gave her solace to learn about the ongoing incompetence of politicians, the inability of athletes to perform flawlessly, and the misfortunes of ordinary people who otherwise bored her. She read every article from the comfort of her sitting room, glasses dangling from her neck, a cup of tea by her side, and an ashtray slowly filling with cigarette butts.

Doreen was considered a tough woman, even by Cornish standards. She smoked a pack of cigarettes a day (and lived to be ninety-four), could praise or insult you equally well (often in the same breath), and never gave an inch to anyone who dared engage in small talk with her.

She had two great assets in life. The first was her birthplace. Doreen's father was a mining engineer in Swaziland after the Boer War, helping Britain secure its assets and expand its empire. She was a Cornishwoman at heart—both her parents were from Cornwall and she spent nearly her entire life there—but she liked to say she was Swahili. It confused people, which gave her an opening with them; more important, it placed the Avery family at the vanguard of the British Empire.

Her second great asset was her missing finger: the ring finger on her left hand. Doreen lost it as a young woman while working in a hospital. The doctors said they must amputate her entire arm, the infection was spreading so fast, but Doreen refused. She told them she would rather die. They argued with her (they were the experts, after all), but she was adamant. The surgeon removed only her finger as a result, and true to form, Doreen survived.

A disfigurement like this, a stump on her left hand, might have proven traumatic to some women. Not to Doreen. It became a source of amusement for her. She began shaking hands with people using her left hand; women wore white gloves in those days (proper women, that is), and unsuspecting guests were always caught by surprise. For further amusement, she would then waggle her glove in front of them, showing how the cloth for the missing finger flopped back and forth.

Thomas Archibald Shaw was a Cornishman through and through. He was born into a wealthy family in St. Austell, where they had a half dozen servants and a large house overlooking the sea. His father, Mr. Shaw, was a doctor, known throughout Cornwall for his excellence. He was called "Mr. Shaw" out of respect. In his day, the term *Dr.* denoted a surgeon who had learned his profession through apprenticeship. Mr. Shaw, however, had attended medical school and practiced a higher vocation: internal medicine.

Thomas was the eldest son. According to the unwritten rules of English society, this meant he would follow in his father's footsteps and become a doctor, but he had other ideas. He applied to Cambridge University instead, intending to pursue a career in teaching. It was not meant to be. The Great War was still raging in Europe (as World War I was then called), and being an upper-class boy who was trained in military affairs at his boarding school, Thomas was commissioned an officer and sent to France. There, he led grown men into battle at the absurd young age of eighteen. The records show that his artillery unit fought bravely in the battle of La Motte-au-Bois in the Nieppe Forest, where Britain finally pushed Germany out of France.

Life was never the same after that. When he returned, his father urged him to reconsider his choice of a career, and this time Thomas agreed. Instead of Cambridge, he attended Guy's Hospital in London, where he became Dr. Shaw. His only remaining rebellion was to become a surgeon rather than practice internal medicine.

Thomas and Doreen met at Truro Hospital in Cornwall. He found Doreen attractive and irreverent. Her self-mockery was a refreshing change from his family's austere manners, and he could not stop laughing at the pranks she played with her missing finger. For her part, Doreen was swept away by Thomas's charm and good looks; that he came from an upper-class family did not escape her attention.

The two were married and moved to Lancashire, England, where Mr. Shaw helped his son acquire a medical practice. Four children were born in quick succession: Robert, Elisabeth, Joanna, and Alexander (called Sandy by his family). Each came into the world in their own house, delivered from their mother's womb into the waiting hands of their father, who gave them an immediate spanking.

The children did not remember much about Lancashire. They had vague memories of a factory whistle that blew every morning; of women walking past their house on the way to work, their wooden shoes clip-clopping on the cobblestone street; of servants and a cook.

It was Orkney that they all remembered. Dr. Shaw acquired a practice in Stromness, and the family departed England for a more rugged way of life. The Orkneys are an archipelago in the North Sea, closer to Norway than to London. The earliest settlers were Picts and Celts, but most of the ruins scattered across the islands are Viking. One had to be tough to survive in Orkney. What Orcadians call a light wind, the rest of the world calls a gale. What Orcadians call a successful harvest, the rest of the world calls a failed crop. Winter nights last all day.

The Shaws were very young when they arrived—Robert was six; Elisabeth, five; Joanna, three; and Sandy, two—and though they only lived in Orkney for six years, it came to define how they thought of themselves.

Their parents found a house on Victoria Street called Seafield House, and the children discovered a new way of life. Everything around them was made of stone: the houses, the garden walls, even the streets. Their kitchen overlooked Stromness harbor, where fishing boats came and went all day long. Beyond that was Graemsay, a small island just outside the harbor, and beyond that Scapa Flow, where the German navy had been scuttled after the Great War. Parts of those ships still poked above the water, a ghostly reminder of the past.

Life in Stromness moved at a leisurely pace. The shops on Victoria Street served a dual purpose: They sold goods, but they were also where people gathered to exchange gossip. Benches could be found in front of most shops, each with its own personality. At the tailor shop, women gathered to complain about their husbands and children or to discuss the latest fashions coming out of Paris (even though none had ever been). The saddler's shop smelled of leather, and farmers discussed more important matters than their womenfolk (like the weather and sheep shearing). At the chandler's shop, captains and sailors spun fanciful stories of their adventures at sea. (And who could challenge them? No one else was out there.)

In the middle of it all, Dr. Shaw set up his practice. He chose the front room of their house for his surgery, with its two windows facing Victoria Street. On any given day, the people of Stromness could do their shopping, catch up on gossip, and linger outside Seafield House to watch the local doctor remove a child's tonsils, mend a broken bone, or attend to some other ailment. Dr. Shaw always welcomed their attention, smiling and waving.

Despite the easygoing lifestyle, the Shaws were not well received at first. Orcadians consider anyone who has not lived on the islands for at least three generations to be outsiders. Adults called them "ferry loupers," meaning they should leave on the next ferry, but the children were less subtle. They called them "those English kids." It was their accents that set them apart. Coming from England, the newcomers sounded condescending.

Robert was the one to break through. At six years old, he was already the leader in the family. When the local kids excluded them, he formed his own team; using Liz, Joey, and Sandy as his base, he recruited a few stragglers and they began playing their own games. When the others objected, he challenged them to a match.

"Why should we play with you?" they asked.

"Because we will beat you," Robert answered.

Who can turn down such a challenge? The game commenced at once, and though no one could remember who won, it did not matter. The Shaws had been accepted. Soon, they looked down on outsiders the way they had been looked down upon.

It did not take long for Mrs. Shaw to become popular with the other mothers and fathers in Stromness—they enjoyed her quick wit and self-deprecating manner—but their children were less enthusiastic. When Robert and the others brought friends over to play, Mrs. Shaw would offer her hand in greeting. Then, as they backed away in horror at her missing finger, she pretended to be upset. "What have you done with my finger?" she demanded, pulling off her glove and showing them the stump. The Shaws tended to play at other people's houses in those days.

It was during their first winter in Orkney that they learned how tough one had to be. When the winds turned and blew cold air down from the Arctic, the fog could become so thick that it would pick salt water right out of the ocean and deposit it onshore. It was called *sea haar*, and anyone caught outside risked a severe rash. On those days, from the safety of their kitchen, the Shaws listened to foghorns guiding the boats back to harbor; their eerie blasts sounded like cows bellowing at an approaching storm. Sometimes they could hear the rhythmic creaking of oars, and occasionally a sailor's chant would reach them, rising and falling at his relief to be safely home.

Spring brought heavy rains. Robert began setting track-and-field records at Stromness Academy; Elisabeth formed a girls' club, restricting it to the smartest girls in school and pointedly excluding her younger sister; Joanna became known as the bad girl in school and decided never to smile for a photo, thinking it phony; and Sandy, who was still the adorable baby, learned he could get away with almost anything.

That summer, Robert discovered an abandoned fishing boat on the beach, and he organized a group of boys to build a swing. They pried four beams loose, dug holes with pickaxes and shovels from their parents' sheds, and dropped the beams in. Then they secured the beams with rope from the hold, laid another beam across the notches, and fashioned a swing out of driftwood.

Robert made a great show of the opening ceremony. The local kids had all heard about the swing by now and gathered to watch. The boys lined up behind Robert, while fishing boats moved around behind them. Robert addressed the crowd, flourishing his arms like a carnival barker. "This is the first playground ever to have been built in Stromness," he said. Pointing to the boys, he added, "And it could not have been accomplished without the hard work of these good lads." The onlookers laughed and clapped while the boys shifted back and forth, looking at the ground sheepishly, obviously pleased.

Robert took the inaugural ride. He pushed back and swung into the air to cheers. Back and forth he went, stretching his body each time to gain more height. On the fourth swing, the structure collapsed. Heavy beams smashed to the ground, narrowly missing his head, and Robert was flung onto the rocks with a cry of pain.

"My leg is broken," he howled.

Back home, Dr. Shaw examined his leg and laughed. "It's just a sprain," he said, and wrapped it in gauze. Turning to Mrs. Shaw, he added, "Boys will be boys."

"Yes, and that is the problem."

Robert limped around for a week. When his father's pushchair was not in use, he had Joey and Sandy wheel him around the neighborhood. Up and down Victoria Street they went, with Robert waving to onlookers and looking like a regent gracing his realm. Only Liz refused to help; she believed Robert was exaggerating his injury to draw attention to himself (and indeed, she was correct).

Like all families, alliances formed among the Shaws. Robert was always nasty to Elisabeth, but he doted on Joanna and Sandy. Elisabeth fought constantly with Robert and looked down her nose at Joanna. Joanna fought back against her older sister as best she could, worshipped Robert, and became like a second mother to Sandy. Only Sandy seemed impervious to it all—he got along with everybody.

Robert and Joanna became inseparable during those years. It was their love of reading that brought them together, combined with their mutual enemy (Liz). They began a habit of visiting the local library in Stromness every Friday afternoon, where the librarian was delighted to share her knowledge of books with them. She was an elderly woman with a large bosom and thinning hair, and she walked them up and down the musty aisles, explaining the various literary genres and telling them what she had read as a girl.

After their first visit, Robert turned to Joanna. "Let's read the same books."

"Why?"

"So we can discuss them, of course."

As a result, Joanna read all the boys' stories of her day from an early age, the predecessors to books like *Harry Potter*—which replaced middle-class schoolboys with middle-class magicians—and all the popular adventure stories, with boys abandoned on desert islands, the forerunners of books like *Lord of the Flies*.

As they grew older, the two moved on to the classics, reading Chaucer, Dickens, the Brontë sisters, and all the other great authors. Whenever a novel had a particularly dreary opening, as in *Moby Dick* or *Tom Brown's School Days*, Robert would tell Joanna where to start, so she would not be put off. Both benefited from this routine, sharpening their literary skills and constantly challenging each other to think in different ways.

Robert's first experience with acting occurred in Orkney. A troupe of actors came through Stromness, parading up Victoria Street in outlandish costumes and banging on a variety of instruments. One by one, children poked their heads out their doors. One by one, children fell in behind the actors, following them up the street. As Mrs. Shaw watched her own children skip merrily away, she could only shake her head. "Like rats after the Pied Piper."

The actors charged a penny in the afternoon for the children's performance and then five pence in the evening for the adults. When the

Shaws arrived home at the end of the day, Robert was beaming. "I've won a prize," he said, "and I must go back to claim it."

"What have you won?" Mrs. Shaw demanded.

"I don't know. I have to go back and find out."

"It will be nothing much, I am sure. They are a third-rate group," she said. "Very well, be off, but come home at once. Your father and I are attending the second house."

Robert did not come home at once. That evening, as his parents made their way up Victoria Street, Mrs. Shaw could not stop cursing him. Dr. Shaw was unperturbed, however. "I expect he's gone up and around the Khyber Pass," he said. "He'll be waiting for us at home, I am certain of it."

They took their seats near the front, and the first half was as dreadful as Mrs. Shaw had expected. That, however, was not the worst of it. When the interval came, the manager announced a "special surprise," and to her mortification, Robert appeared on stage. His shoelaces were undone, his tie was wound behind his back, and there was lipstick smeared all over his face. Mrs. Shaw gasped in horror. Children were supposed to dress properly in those days.

The audience, however, loved it. They began cheering when an acrobat picked Robert up and tossed him to another acrobat. Each time Robert landed, he took a bow, and the audience cheered and laughed even harder. The more Robert exaggerated his movements, the more the audience cheered, and the more they cheered, the more he exaggerated everything.

Later that evening, when they got home, Mrs. Shaw was still furious, but Robert was unrepentant. "You don't understand, Mother," he explained. "You should see what they have behind the stage. All that lovely powder and paint."

Mrs. Shaw would never forget that day, and she never forgave her son. Even years later, even when Robert had become a successful actor, she would still say to people, "Do you know what drew him to that miserable profession? It was the powder and paint! Have you ever heard of such rubbish? Powder! And paint!"

Joanna's first experience with sexism also occurred in Orkney. The St. Ola ferry came by their house every morning, and she and Robert began going down to the wharf to watch the activity. It was all so fascinating. Sailors leaped off the ship as it pulled in and secured it to the dock with ropes. Planks were laid down for both passengers and animals to disembark, and giant hooks swung overhead, laden with cargo.

The kids soon began offering their services to the sailors, hoping to earn some money. They were more hindrance than help, but one of the men usually gave them a penny or two for their efforts. When that happened, they raced to the local store to buy sweets for themselves and sometimes cigarettes for their mother. (No one ever questioned young children buying cigarettes in those days.)

But when their parents discovered what they were doing, they forbade Joanna from talking to the sailors. Robert, however, was still allowed to go, and Joanna was furious, thinking she had been singled out for being a girl. Even so, she might have accepted this, had Robert not continued to go and keep all the sweets for himself.

It was the beginning of a lifelong crusade for women's rights, but it was not until Joanna was much older that she understood why her parents had treated her that way. It was when her own daughter complained that she was placing more restrictions on her than on her brother, older by only a year. Joanna was shocked, but then she realized her daughter was right—she *did* put more restrictions on her. She thought her daughter was more vulnerable. It was then that she decided we should all be just as scared for our boys.

And where was Wendy in all this? Robert and Joanna never forgot the day she was born. They did not know anything about pregnancies. Their mother claimed she played rounders with them the night before, a primitive form of baseball. The next morning, Elisabeth heard a commotion and went downstairs to investigate. When she came back, she said, "Mummy has a baby down there."

Sandy groaned and rolled over in bed, but Robert and Joanna leaped up in excitement. They dressed quickly and ran outside to tell the neighbors. When some of them asked whether it was a boy or a girl, they just looked at each other. They did not know.

Everyone was jealous of Wendy after that. She was the only one in the family who could say she was from Orkney. For the rest of their lives, on all those forms one has to fill in to say where they were born, the others always had to write "England" . . . even though *they* were the true Orcadians.

They were so free, the doctor's children. In a society where most people were farmers or fishermen, the Shaws were at the top of the British class culture, in that time and place. And they were a close-knit group, four energetic kids who excelled in school.

Their parents were happy, too, at least for a while. Dr. Shaw had the prestige of being the only doctor in the area and was much beloved. Mrs. Shaw had plenty of cheap domestic help and was a marvelous hostess. Everyone in Stromness considered them the ideal family, wonderful neighbors, a true asset to the community. But it was all about to change.

Chapter 3

-⟪⟨◆⟩⟫-

Riches to Rags

[1936–1939]

It was during their parents' bridge parties that the Shaws first became aware of their father's drinking problem. They were part of the privileged class in those days, as there were only three professional families on the island: a banker, a lawyer, and their father, the doctor. The kids were sent off early to bed on those nights, but from their upstairs perch, they eyed the lavish plates of food hungrily: almonds and raisins, cucumber sandwiches, bread, and cheese.

Of course, there was also scotch and soda—plenty of good fine scotch for the Orkney elite. They all drank heavily. The talk and the laughter went on into the night, growing louder and louder. One voice always rose above the others, though: Dr. Shaw was the biggest drunkard of the lot.

They soon discovered the bridge parties were not his only source of drink. When it came to alcohol, Dr. Shaw was an equal opportunity drinker, just as happy in the local pubs, with the farmers and fishermen, as with the Orkney elite.

It did not change how his children viewed him. He was a larger-than-life figure to them, radiating energy and good cheer. Dr. Shaw threw himself into everything he did. He was an avid hunter and fisherman and often disappeared for days, flying to Scotland or Norway from the small airport in Stenness. He had been an amateur boxer in college and cordoned off a part of their backyard, which he turned into a boxing ring, and taught Robert and Sandy how to box. He took all of them fishing every spring, showing them how to bait a hook, troll from the back of the boat, and clean a fish (only Robert and Sandy did that).

With his slicked-back hair, dark mustache, and fiery eyes, Dr. Shaw was a dashing figure. Everybody loved him. He could sew up a boy's cut, distract the child with a story, and tell the parents a funny joke, all at the same time, without ever missing a stitch.

"So good of you to drop in, Dr. Shaw," his patients would greet him.

"Won't you stay for a cup of tea, Dr. Shaw?" they would say.

"I do hope we see you again soon, Dr. Shaw."

They called him the Lighthouse Doctor because he never missed an appointment. Even in bad weather, he would anchor his boat and swim ashore. He kept extra medical bags in strategic locations for this purpose: On Hoy, he had a bag in a small cave above Ore Bay; on Ronaldsay, a local farmer allowed him to use the shed behind her house; on Rousay, he kept a bag at the fire station.

He often brought the kids with him, especially when he traveled by boat, which was often. With the cold wind blowing in their faces on Scapa Flow, he would regale them with stories. He had a gift for accents, something he passed down to Robert and Sandy, and his favorite stories were about the Great War, where he had fought alongside the Italians. In a broken Italian accent, he would say, "I hope they are our enemy in the next war. They are quite useless as allies, but I believe they would make a very decent enemy."

While Dr. Shaw tended to his patients, his kids played outside, exploring Viking ruins, searching for cockles, and occasionally swimming in the bay. They never thought to bring a towel or bathing suit with them: Kids in Orkney felt comfortable swimming naked and drying off in the air.

One of their more memorable trips was the day he fetched a patient from Kirkwall Hospital. It was Mrs. Porteous, the baker in Stromness. She had developed a bad case of gout, brought on by her profession and resulting weight gain. Everyone piled into the boat, and Dr. Shaw guided them past Graemsay and over to Scapa Beach. There, he tied up the boat and walked to the hospital. It was nearly an hour before he returned. Mrs. Porteous had refused to walk the short distance back, and so he was forced to organize a car service.

The woman was in an ugly mood. Without a word, she planted herself in the middle of the boat, draped a pile of blankets over herself, and ordered her doctor to "cast off!"

The ride home was not much fun. Mrs. Porteous offered up a steady stream of complaints: her legs hurt, the nurses were incompetent, the food was awful. Each grievance emerged from the mound of blankets like the braying of a donkey. Dr. Shaw remained silent in response, and the kids followed his example; no one wanted to aggravate her further.

The tide had gone out when they got home, which meant they would have to walk through the mud to their boat slip. Mrs. Porteous took one look and said, "I cannot possibly walk through that awful muck."

"We have no choice," Dr. Shaw replied grimly. "I'll help you."

"Don't be daft, man," she snapped. The kids looked up in surprise; people in Orkney did not speak like that. "There is no way someone in my condition can make it through that, that . . ." She pointed, at a loss for words. "You must take me back to the hospital."

Dr. Shaw looked stricken. Evening was falling, a light rain had begun, and the prospect of going back to Kirkwall, only to return empty-handed, did not please him. "Very well," he said, "I shall carry you on my back." Before Mrs. Porteous could protest, he leaped out of the boat and backed up to her, putting his hands over his shoulders. Reluctantly, she climbed onto his back and fixed her arms around his neck.

The two set off, and the kids scurried to the front of the boat, exhilarated by their father's chivalry. Dr. Shaw's first few steps were strong and confident. He lifted his boots straight up and brought them straight down, as experienced boaters will do. He knew how to get through muck like this. The steady pattering of rain, accompanied by the soft sucking sound of his boots, felt like a soothing end to a difficult trip.

His next few steps, however, were more labored. His boots no longer pulled out of the mud so easily. Dr. Shaw began swiveling back and forth, trying to wrench himself free, while Mrs. Porteous hung on for dear life, occasionally emitting soft yelps like a frightened puppy. Then he stopped altogether, breathing hard.

"What are you doing, you bampot?" the woman shrieked. "Keep moving. Keep moving, I tell you." She began swatting him and digging her knees into his side, as if he were a horse. Dr. Shaw jumped in surprise. He threw his entire body into it now, swinging wildly from side to side. Mrs. Porteous began to lose her grip. First one arm slipped off his neck, then the other. Finally, heaving a sigh, she toppled backward.

The children heard a loud plop and saw mud fly in the air. The only parts of Mrs. Porteous that were still visible were her arms and legs, sticking straight up in the air as if seeking assistance from heaven.

Dr. Shaw was horrified. With the weight gone from his back, he wrenched himself free and turned to help. Wedging one arm behind her and another around her waist, he pulled with all his might. The woman did not budge. Shifting positions, he got his arms behind her neck and tried to pull her into a sitting position. For his effort, he lost his balance and fell on top of her.

Mrs. Porteous screamed. Dr. Shaw swore. And the two began flailing about helplessly. Each time one seemed about to regain their footing, the other dragged them both down again. From the kids' perspective, it looked like a Buster Keaton movie, and they burst out laughing.

Mrs. Shaw had been making dinner at the time, but when she heard the commotion, she came down to investigate. Seeing her children laughing at two adults, she began to scold them. But when she looked again and saw her husband and the local baker performing such a comical dance in the mud, she also burst out laughing. With tears rolling down her cheeks, she was unable to render either discipline or assistance.

Discipline in the Shaw family was strictly one-sided. Dr. Shaw tended to ignore transgressions, or even encourage them, while Mrs. Shaw ruled with an iron fist. One example was the morning Sandy refused to eat his breakfast. She had made scrambled eggs, one of their favorites, but for reasons that only a five-year-old can explain, he decided they were disgusting.

An argument ensued. Mrs. Shaw insisted he eat. Sandy refused. They went back and forth for a while, until she turned her back. The matter was settled, as far as she was concerned. Sandy had other ideas, however, and he slid the eggs into his milk. They floated to the top of the glass, but Mrs. Shaw pretended not to notice.

"Well done," she said. A look of triumph began to spread across Sandy's face. "Now drink your milk." The smile faded.

Another argument ensued, and for a second time she seemed to relent. "Very well, be off to school." Her words hung in the air, until she added, "Your milk will be waiting for you when you get home."

That was a miserable day for Sandy; the thought of drinking egg-laden milk clearly did not agree with him. When they returned home, a glass of milk was waiting for him on the table. He began to protest again, but the fight had gone out of him. Mrs. Shaw sat him down firmly. "Drink," she ordered.

Robert, Liz, and Joey drew in closer, looking like a mob at a hanging: horrified but unable to look away. Sandy raised the glass to his lips. He took a reluctant sip. At first it seemed he would vomit, but then his face brightened. "They've melted," he exclaimed.

"What has melted?" Mrs. Shaw asked.

There was no response. With two quick gulps, Sandy finished the milk and was out the door.

What was so maddening about their mother was not so much her nasty wit, or her constant criticism, or even the way she sowed dissent among her children, turning one against the other. What was truly maddening was the capricious nature of her discipline. They never knew what to expect. Sometimes she would berate them, sometimes she would praise them for the exact same thing, and sometimes she would play a trick on them, as she did that day when she switched the soggy milk for a fresh glass without telling anyone.

Dr. Shaw's drinking grew steadily worse during their Orkney years. What started with the bridge parties became a daily routine. He began disappearing at lunchtime and would not reappear until late at night. They could hear him stumbling up Victoria Street, singing loudly. Sometimes he came up to their bedroom. The children slept on the top floor together, and they could smell the liquor on his breath. Robert always seemed ready to speak with him.

"Howsh it, son?"

"What?"

"I say, howsh it? Howsh your life, howsh the sheep, howsh everything?"

"Everything's good, Dad."

"That's not wot ah mean. Howsh school?"

"School's good, Dad."

"No, thatsh not wot ah mean either."

But it was the small incidents that worried them the most. "Let's go for a hike on Birsay," he said to them one day. They piled into the boat eagerly and set off. The Brough of Birsay was on the north part of the island, a haven for birds with a beautiful lighthouse on top and a breathtaking view of the ocean. Dr. Shaw steered them past Yesnaby and Skara Brae, then spotted Lord Kitchener's memorial. Kitchener was the hero of the Boer War. He had led Britain to victory but had also built concentration camps that killed thousands of Dutch civilians. After the war, his ship had run aground in sea haar, with all hands lost.

Dr. Shaw stood up and saluted. "Don't talk to me about atrocities in war," he said in an Irish accent (Kitchener was born in County Kerry). "All war is an atrocity."

They tied up the boat on the southern shore and hiked up Birsay, crisscrossing back and forth. Halfway up, they stopped by the ruins of a church, where the kids leaped from stone to stone. Dr. Shaw pointed to one section. "That was the nave where the Vikings gathered for worship," he said.

"I thought they were heathens?" Liz asked.

"Hmm, I thought so too," he said. "They must have found Christianity here. Orkney has a way of doing that."

They paused at the lighthouse and watched its beam circling, then flopped down on a grassy embankment. It never failed to fascinate them. Millions of birds flocked on that side, popping up unexpectedly above the cliff as the wind shot them upward. Everyone was feeling relaxed when Liz said, "Dad, why do you spend so much time with your patients? We waited nearly two hours yesterday."

Dr. Shaw laughed. "What an interesting question," he said. Then, adopting a thick Orkney accent, he said, "It wos like this, you see. Ae wis in this hoose, the one o'er by Marwick, not too far from ere, in actuality. Tide was oot like it is tooday, and I had a fair tam crossing the small firth. Do ye remember?"

The kids smiled—it was exactly how the older Orcadians talked.

"Then I tied the boat and made me wae across't. There, Ae treated their wee bairn—twas a peedie cut but the beuy was bawling sich, and so Ae couldna deal wid it quick like I usually do. Just as Ae wis leavin', Mrs. Rae appeared and offered me a cup o' tea. You know one canna leave a house in Orkney when they offer you a cup o' tea. One canna insult them sich."

He stopped, pleased at deflecting his daughter's question so deftly. Robert surprised him with his own Orkney accent. "But, Fither, Ae doot thee enjoyed simply biding time wid de Rae's. We hae observed how thee linger and observe on their lovely gairdeens and such, it is true, but Mr. Rae, wis he naught thar as well?"

Dr. Shaw gave his son an odd look. "Is there a pint to yer observation?"

"Ae was just pondering as to wot else wis offered wid the tea. Wis there a wee bit o' whiskey, perhaps?"

Dr. Shaw stood up. The wind grabbed his jacket, nearly tearing it off, but he ignored it. "Better drowned than a duffer," he said. Then he walked toward the edge of the cliff and followed a path jutting onto a narrow peninsula. Far below, the ocean pounded against the rocks.

Seeing him there, a feeling of dread came over Joanna. It was the first time she thought he might die. The quote from *Swallows and Amazons* was popular with both their parents, and indeed with their entire generation. Better to die than be a duffer, it meant. Joanna did not think that way; she wanted both her parents to live, duffers or not.

After a few moments, Robert jumped to his feet and followed his father. Sandy got up to follow, but Liz grabbed his arm. "Sit," she ordered. Then: "You, too, Joey," as Joanna began to stand.

The three sat and watched Robert approach their father. He said something, and Dr. Shaw looked down and laughed. Then the two flopped on the edge of the cliff, arms behind them, their feet dangling over the edge. Neither seemed bothered by the height.

The others strained to hear what they were saying, but the wind carried their words away. It seemed like an eternity before they returned. The trip home was a somber one. Dr. Shaw did not tell any stories, and the kids remained quiet.

"What did you say to Daddy?" Joanna whispered to Robert at one point, but he only shook his head.

Mrs. Shaw was not one to hold back her criticism: She told her husband exactly what she thought of him. Where she came from, it was called "Cornish honesty." For his part, Dr. Shaw began having bouts of rage, which were followed by apologies and repentance and, in turn, more bouts of rage.

The bridge parties ended. The neighbors began avoiding them. Children were no longer allowed to play at their house. Robert and the others were forced to entertain each other. He and Sandy played war games while Liz and Joanna played skipping games. The boys were not very good at skipping, and the girls did not like pretending to fight. A gloom set in.

But it was when their father's patients stopped calling on him that they realized how bad it was. The Shaws were no longer part of Orkney's elite. Without any warning, they had fallen from riches to rags. One somber morning, six years after their arrival, Mrs. Shaw marched the children out of the house. They walked to the ferry, dragging their luggage behind them. They would be moving in with their aunt, who lived in Cornwall.

Dr. Shaw arrived as they were boarding the ferry. He had disappeared that morning but now wanted to say farewell. They heard him before they saw him; he was waving his hands and shouting from across the pier. It was obvious he was drunk.

Mrs. Shaw lined them up in front of her. "Say goodbye to your father," she told her children.

"Goodbye, Daddy," they said.

Dr. Shaw swayed back and forth in front of them. He put a finger in the air and began counting: "One, two, three, four." Then he paused, looking puzzled. Licking his finger, he counted again. "One, two, three, four."

"Where's Joey?" he asked.

Joanna raised her hand. "I'm here, Daddy."

"Where's Joey?" he asked again.

"Right here," she said more loudly.

Then she looked at Robert. "Don't bother," he whispered.

Mrs. Shaw turned in disgust. Up the gangway they went, leaving their father on the dock still trying to figure out how many children he had. They went to the railing and peered down. He looked up and waved. They waved back.

The *St. Ola* drifted backward slowly, churning water, then turned and moved out of the harbor. Their father disappeared from view. The ship entered Scapa Flow, and they watched the Old Man of Hoy appear on its western cliff, then transform back into a rocky outcrop. The wind picked up in Pentland Firth, and the ship began rolling in the heavy sea, but still the kids clung to the railing. They could see waves breaking on the shore below their house, they could see Brinkie's Brae on the hill above their house, and they could even make out the stone walls of Stromness Academy high above that.

A plume of diesel fumes spewed over their heads, twisting and turning and looking like the grim reaper pointing the way home. Orkney began to turn from a colorful green into a dull gray, the hills and rocks and grass turned hazy, and finally, the islands disappeared altogether. It would be a long time before they would see them again.

Chapter 4

The Cocks

[Fall 1939]

At 120 feet long and weighing 200 tons, the *St. Ola* was built to withstand Pentland Firth. Located at the junction of the North Sea and the Arctic Ocean, the Firth is a constantly churning body of water buffeted by gale-force winds and dangerous currents. The ship had never foundered, but this fact was lost on most passengers, who immediately made their way below deck.

Mrs. Shaw and her children remained above deck, along with a few other hardy passengers. She found a chair and made herself comfortable with Wendy, while the other kids wandered around. Near the stern, they found a couple hiding beneath a blanket, giggling at the skuas who were darting between the gulls and trying to steal their food. On the leeward side, a flock of sheep was cordoned off behind ropes, swaying back and forth with the rolling ship. When one of them slipped and found itself unexpectedly on the other side of the rope, it wobbled about until a passing sailor returned it roughly to its pen.

In Thurso, they boarded a train and began a three-day journey south. When the train stopped to discharge passengers or switch engines, vendors clambered on board. Mrs. Shaw always purchased a cup of tea and cigarettes. Through the grimy windows, Scotland and England flew by.

In London, they got a black cab and drove to Paddington Station, where they caught the *Cornish Riviera*—the express train to Cornwall. Mrs. Shaw got a bunk for herself and Wendy, and Sandy curled up at their feet, while Robert, Liz, and Joanna fell asleep in the coach car, resting on each other's shoulders.

They were in Cornwall before they knew it. Truro Cathedral began making its appearance, guiding them in to a tiny station. Stepping off the train, they heard a shout: "Doreen!" A man was waving to them, dressed in overalls and suspenders with heavy boots on his feet. His dark beard was scruffy, but his smile was cheery.

"Hello, Tom," Mrs. Shaw said, extending her hand. He pushed it away with a laugh.

"You're not going to fool me with that finger of yours," he said. "Do you think I've forgotten?" Then, turning to the kids, he said, "I haven't seen you birds since you were babies. Let me see if I can remember your names." He pointed to Sandy. "You're Robert, aren't you." Before Sandy could protest, he turned to Liz. "And you must be Joey,"

Soon they were all laughing. "Children," Mrs. Shaw said, "this is your foolish Uncle Tom." But she was smiling.

They were soon on their way. Mrs. Shaw sat in front, with Wendy on her lap and Sandy next to her. Joanna squeezed into the back seat between Robert and Liz, and immediately began to feel sick. Uncle Tom navigated through Truro, avoiding horses and carts, and then they were on the open road.

"Tough times, Doreen?" he asked.

"No more than usual," she answered.

A light rain began to fall. With each turn, the roads got narrower. Hedges began appearing on both sides of the car, so high they could not see over them. Cornwall could not have been more different from Orkney's wide-open terrain.

"Almost there," Uncle Tom called out cheerily.

"I feel claustrophobic," Liz complained.

"I think I'm going to be sick," Joanna said.

"What is this mad world?" Robert asked.

"Almost there," Uncle Tom repeated, less cheerfully.

They finally came to a turn with two enormous oak trees guarding a narrow lane. Their uncle guided the car through the opening and came to a stop in front of an enormous stone house. "Welcome to Treworyan," he announced.

The Shaws got out and looked around. Treworyan sat on a small rise, giving them a view of rolling hills and farms. As they looked back, the two oak trees were momentarily lit by lightning. "The gates of hell," Robert muttered. Somewhere in the distance, a cow bellowed.

Aunt Aileen, who had been waiting patiently in the doorway, waved them in. "Why are you standing in the rain?" she called. "Come inside, all of you. Doreen, let me see the baby."

They unloaded their luggage and introductions were made. The Shaws were moving in with the Cocks. There was Uncle Tom, Aunt Aileen, and their cousin, Michael Cock. Aunt Aileen could not have been more different from their mother. Where Mrs. Shaw had sharp features and a stern expression, Aunt Aileen had soft features and a mouth that curled up. Where Mrs. Shaw aspired to the upper class, Aunt Aileen was proud to be the wife of a Cornish farmer.

When the kids were alone, Robert turned to his cousin. "Seriously?" he said. "Your last name is Cock?"

Michael showed no hint of embarrassment. "I know what you are thinking," he said. He was younger than Robert but taller, with long blond hair and a smile that lacked any hint of guile. "What you must understand is that around here, nobody sees it that way. It is just a word. Cock means a ruddy complexion, in Celtic." He grinned and pointed to himself. "And as you can see, everyone around here has a ruddy complexion."

"All right, then," Robert said. "Master Cock it is. We shall say no more of it."

Treworyan was typical of Cornish farms in many ways. Gas lamps were lit at sundown, each room had a fireplace, and running water was available from a pump in the back. The one thing that set it apart was something Uncle Tom had built. A series of pipes ran from the well to a storage tank in the attic, which could be released whenever someone used the crapper. The Cocks were one of the few families in Cornwall to have a flush toilet.

But there was only one toilet, and now there were nine people in the house. Aunt Aileen made a quick decision. "Michael," she said, "show your cousins the privy out back."

Michael led them to a small wooden shed wedged between the barn and the pigsty. Several pigs wandered over to investigate. "This is the loo," Michael said, pushing open the door and pointing inside.

"Why are there two seats?" Liz asked.

"We have extra farmhands during the busy season," Michael explained.

"That will come in handy," Robert said. "We'll go in pairs."

"Oh, gee, I don't think that will be necessary," Michael said. Unlike the Shaws, who had lived their entire lives bathing and dressing together on the upstairs floor in Orkney, without any supervision, Michael was an only child. He was used to his privacy.

"Of course it is necessary." Robert said. He was delighted to have another child to boss around. Pointing to the pigs, he asked, "Do they ever burrow under the floor and into the privy?"

Liz, Joey, and Sandy all jumped back, as if seeing the pigs for the first time. Michael scratched his chin. "I've never seen them do that," he answered. "I cannot say for certain that they would not dig underneath. I can only say I have never seen them do it."

"But pigs like to dig, don't they?" Robert persisted.

"Oh yes," Michael said, pleased to be asked something he knew about. "Pigs are natural diggers, they are. That is how they feed themselves when they are not on a farm. They dig for roots and such in the forest. So yes, I would have to say that pigs are, in fact, very good diggers."

"Then it's settled," Robert said. "We will use the privy in pairs. Michael, Joey, you two go first."

Michael's smile faded. "But I don't have to go."

"Doesn't matter," Robert said. "Joey will need someone to protect her from the pigs."

And so it was established, on their first day at Treworyan, that the children would go into the loo two by two, while the animals would not. *Exactly the opposite of Noah's ark,* Joanna thought, as she sat next to Michael with her skirt hiked up.

The following morning, they were awoken by a rooster at the crack of dawn. "Rise and shine," Aunt Aileen called out cheerily. The Shaws could see nothing cheery about it. They had never gotten up before 8:00 in Orkney. School did not begin until ten in the morning. They considered that a sensible hour.

The five of them made their way to Ladock School together, taking turns riding Michael's bike. Once again, they discovered they were outcasts—once again, it was their accents that set them apart, but this time it was their Orkney accents. The Cornish are as wary of outsiders as Orcadians, and neither group considers itself part of Great Britain. Just as people in Orkney say they are going to Scotland when they take the ferry south, as if that is a different country, the Cornish say they are going to England when they travel north.

They assimilated more quickly this time, thanks to Michael. And to their pleasant surprise, they discovered they were far ahead of the local children academically. As far back as the eighteenth century, Scotland had been ahead of the English in public schooling, as Sir Walter Scott so eloquently described in his novel, *Heart of Midlothian.*

Life at Treworyan settled into a routine. Uncle Tom and Aunt Aileen managed a dairy farm. There were cows, pigs and sheep, a few hens and roosters, and a field that rotated a new crop each year.

Laborers came and went during the day, but there was still plenty of work for everyone. Michael showed the boys how to operate a tractor, shovel manure, and mend a broken fence. He taught the girls how to milk a cow, and the boys eagerly joined. With their pails beneath the cows' teats, they tugged and pulled until the milk was flowing—some of it even landed in their buckets.

While Robert and Sandy worked outside, Liz and Joanna were usually given tasks inside the house. "Girls, please make up the beds," Aunt Aileen would say. After dinner: "Be good dears and clean the table."

"I feel like Cinderella," Joanna grumbled. She had never been singled out for different tasks in Orkney; Mrs. Shaw always divided chores equally between boys and girls. Still, Joanna might have accepted this had it not been for the incident with the boot. One afternoon, after the boys had returned from a muddy field, Aunt Aileen said, "Girls, please help the boys remove their boots. You'll find a bucket and a brush behind the back door, scrub them down."

"I'm not taking off their boots," Joanna protested.

"You will do as you are told, young lady," Aunt Aileen said firmly. "The boys have been working hard and must be exhausted."

Robert laughed. "I don't need any help," he said, and began pulling his boots off. Sandy, however, being the younger child, was delighted. He flopped on the sofa, propped his feet on the table, and looked at Joanna with a wicked grin, pointing to his boots.

Reluctantly, she began to pull them off, but Sandy squirmed this way and that, pretending to help but really making it more difficult for her. Finally, she hit him. "Be still!"

"Joanna, stop that," Aunt Aileen said. "I will have no hysteria in this house."

Joanna reacted with fury. Yanking Sandy's boot off, she turned and hurled it at her aunt. It came to a stop next to Aileen's foot. "I've been working just as hard as the boys," Joanna screamed. "I'd rather be outside than stuck in here with you!"

Aunt Aileen's mouth opened and closed wordlessly, while Mrs. Shaw held back a laugh. Robert, Liz, and Sandy simply looked on in surprise. After that, a tension set in between the two families. Mrs. Shaw became more and more frustrated that she was not in charge and began prodding her sister to make changes. She wanted to hang new paintings in the dining room; Aileen refused. She wanted to repaint the house in fresh new colors; Aileen refused.

The only area where Mrs. Shaw could exert any control was over the children. She had always subscribed to the idea of "divide and rule" and had taken turns picking on one child or another. In Treworyan, she found a new target.

"Adam and Eve and Pinchme went down to the river to bathe," she would say to Michael. "Adam and Eve were drowned. Who do you think was saved?"

"Pinchme," Michael always said, whereupon Mrs. Shaw would order her children to pinch him. They gleefully complied. Michael never seemed to get the joke, which only made them laugh all the more and pinch him all the harder. Like any mob, they were easily manipulated.

"Doesn't he realize we are going to pinch him again?" Joanna asked.

"I really don't know," Robert answered.

Years later, however, Joanna saw a movie called *Babe* in which the farmer reminded her of Michael: honest, sincere, and guileless. He only wanted everyone around him to be happy. And then it hit her: Michael must have known all along what Mother was doing, but he kept going along with it because it made everyone laugh.

In the months that followed, the Shaws came to love their new home. They enjoyed working on a farm, they learned to appreciate the rolling fields, and they especially loved Cornwall's beautiful walking paths, which seemed to go on forever. That fall, the trees turned lovely colors and dropped their chestnuts. The harvest brought extra laborers, and everyone threw themselves into the work. The field was harvested, the sheep were shorn, and the cows and pigs were prepared for market.

That Christmas, the two families celebrated modestly. Each child found a small present by the fireplace. The following day they were still feeling the effects of the goose Aileen had cooked when Michael poked his nose into the living room.

"Mum, Dad," he said, "I thought you should know. I was looking out the window just now, and an automobile has pulled up. I thought it must be someone from Treweager Farm, but then it struck me that I did not recognize the car. So I said to myself, I said, this car must be from somewhere else. I would recognize it if it was from Treweager, don't you think?"

"Yes, yes," his mother said impatiently, "what of it?"

"Well, you see, the car has stopped directly in front of our house. It is just parked right there, right there in front. I simply thought you should know."

Aileen went to the door, thinking someone was lost. That happened a lot, with all the narrow lanes around them. But when she flung it open, her eyes opened in surprise. "Oh my!" she exclaimed.

Everyone crowded behind her, curious to see what had startled her.

"Well, I'll be gobsmacked," Uncle Tom said, scratching his beard.

"The return of the native," Mrs. Shaw growled.

"If it isn't Thomas Archibald Shaw, as I live and breathe," Aileen proclaimed.

"Who?" Michael whispered.

Michael did not recognize the man, but the Shaws knew him well. Their faces reflected a mixture of surprise and concern, for standing before them was none other than their own father. His eyes looked dark and hollow in the dim light coming through the door, and with the rain matting down his hair, Dr. Shaw looked like he had been raised from the dead.

"Hello, everyone," he said.

PART II

RISING STARS

Freedom does not come from casting off one's chains
but from respecting the freedom of others.

— Nelson Mandela

Chapter 5

-⟨⟨⟨◆⟩⟩⟩-

Accents & Attitudes

[1939]

When Joanna was nine years old, her best friend asked what she wanted to be when she grew up. She did not have to think for long. "A teacher!" she said.

Olivia's hand flew to her mouth. "Oh, you mustn't do that! You would have to teach boys!"

The two girls had slipped through the kissing gate behind Ladock School, which kept the cows and sheep in while giving everyone else access to Cornwall's footpaths. Joanna laughed. She knew why Olivia did not like boys: She had no brothers. What she could not understand was why she did not like the idea of teaching. Then she remembered that everyone in Ladock was the child of either a farmer or laborer.

"You must find an in-service position," Olivia said. "That is so much better than becoming a teacher."

"A what?"

"An in-service position, silly. Don't you know what that is?" Joanna shook her head. "I don't want to marry a farmer," Olivia said, "they are dirty and smelly. I hope to be a lady's maid. That way, I will marry a boy who is clean. I suppose I could become a housekeeper. That is also a respectable position, but the trouble is all the keys she must carry. *And* all the responsibility. I don't care if they are called 'missus of the house,' it isn't worth the trouble. Do you know that if anyone in the house—*anyone*, I tell you—makes a mistake, it is the housekeeper who must make it right? Please tell me you will become a lady's maid and not a housekeeper."

"I don't know what a lady's maid is," Joanna said. "Do you mean a servant?"

"Of course! But do not call it a servant, they are so much more than that. You would live on an estate! Maybe even a castle! I wouldn't want to work in the kitchen—it is too hot in there. Of course, that would be welcome in winter, but there is plenty of warmth elsewhere . . . *if* you work for a lady. Whenever you are cold, you can always find an excuse to clean around the fireplace. I would never want to work for the housemaid, that can only lead to housekeeping, and I've already told you what that leads to."

"All those keys?" Joanna said, smiling.

"Yes, and all the responsibility and blame when things go wrong," Olivia continued. "And they always go wrong, you know. But a lady's maid . . ." Her voice trailed off as she dreamed of a pleasant future. "Of course, I would not *start* there. I would begin as a laundry maid, perhaps, or even a nurse maid. But think how much fun it would be to use all those secret passages. You can come and go wherever you please."

"Secret passages?" Joanna asked, still baffled. She had never imagined Olivia could be such a fount of knowledge on so foreign a subject. "In any case, I do not believe I will ever work for a wealthy family."

Olivia turned in horror. "You aren't planning to work for a lower-class family, are you?" She was close to tears. "Please do not let yourself be drawn into that, Joanna. Those houses do not have forty servants, or even ten! There is only one, and that means you would have to do everything: cook, clean, do the laundry, scrub the floors. From morning until night. Every day! Please, please, please, please tell me you will not do that!"

Joanna put her arm through Olivia's and turned them back to the school. "I believe I can safely say I will never become a servant for a lower-class family," she said.

Olivia wiped her forehead in relief. "Please don't scare me like that!"

[2019]

Eighty years later, Joanna was asked what had driven her brother to such heights of fame. She answered a different question. "There was something out of kilter in both Robert and Mother," she said. "They both had competitive streaks that bordered on obsession. They took over a room as soon as they entered. Each of them always had to be the center of attention. And they both liked to poke at people."

"Poke?"

"Yes, poke. To get a reaction. And they kept on poking until they got one. People tended to like them at first, because they were so full of energy. But when they got to know them, many of those same people pulled away. Their energy could be overwhelming.

"Of course," Joanna continued, "it was those same traits that made them both succeed so well. We all know how well Robert did, but Mother was equally successful, in her own way. Women did not have a career in her day; some were nurses or teachers but most were housewives. That was the world back then. And Mother became a widow at an early age, thrown into poverty just as the country went to war. Resources were scarce.

"And yet, she not only survived, but she put each of her children firmly on the path to success. Everyone around us was a farmer, or some such thing, but Robert attended RADA, Liz went to Oxford, I attended Cambridge, Sandy went to a prestigious medical school, and Wendy became known throughout England for her work with autistic children."

"What did your mother do to accomplish all of that? Did she read to you every night?"

"Oh no, she was not that type of person. She liked to keep to herself, reading her newspaper."

"Did she help you with homework?"

Joanna laughed. "Absolutely not."

"Did she discuss your studies with you?"

"No, she was never interested in that sort of thing."

"What, then? What did she do?"

Joanna thought for a moment. "She gave us our accents," she finally said.

"Your accents? Is that all?"

Joanna nodded, then she thought some more. "Our accents and our attitudes," she added.

"I don't understand. Are you telling me that the only thing your mother did for you was to give you your accents and your attitudes? She did nothing more than that?"

Joanna shrugged. "What more is there?"

Chapter 6

-≪≪◆≫≫-

The London
Acting Scene

[1945-1953]

World War II ended a few days short of Robert's eighteenth birthday. Like all boys his age, he had tried to enlist but was ruled ineligible for medical reasons. With high school behind him, he moved to London and took a job as a teacher. He hated it. The students were unruly and not very bright. The silver lining was that he could afford a tiny flat in the city—but he hated that as well. The room was filthy and overrun by mice.

London, however, was fascinating. The city had been nearly wiped out by the Blitz: Poverty was everywhere, and people still had a look of shock on their faces, having lost friends and loved ones. But there was also a sense of renewal. The Marshall Plan was in place, construction was everywhere, and Londoners were beginning to recover their optimism.

Best of all, Robert had long ago been bitten by the acting bug, and he was now able to see some of the greatest actors in history who performed regularly in local theaters. For very little money, he watched people like Laurence Olivier, John Gielgud, and Alec Guinness that year.

A year later, with some money saved and an additional amount left to him by his grandmother, he applied to the Royal Academy of Dramatic

Art (RADA). That was the most prestigious acting school in the country, and perhaps in the world. His aunt, however, who had been left in charge of distributing the money, thought acting was a ridiculous profession— like everyone in Cornwall. She insisted he try for Cambridge. Whether Robert failed the exam on purpose, as he later claimed, or simply had a bad day, no one ever knew. But fail he did, and off to RADA he went for an audition.

Robert was only nineteen years old, but he had the proper accent and attitude. He was confident. Nevertheless, he paused for a moment in front of RADA's imposing façade. The front door was massive, made of solid oak, with gargoyles looking down from above it. Gathering his courage, he knocked. It took nearly a minute before the door swung open. Robert blinked in surprise. Standing before him was a man who looked more like a cadaver. He was emaciated, with layers of wrinkles on his face and a spiderweb of wispy gray hair on his head. He wore a tuxedo, polished black shoes, and white gloves. Robert could not tell if he was a butler or an eccentric member of the staff.

"I, um, I am here for the exam," Robert said.

The man crooked his finger and beckoned Robert inside. He found himself in a large atrium, surrounded by wood panels and a stone staircase circling upwards. The man climbed the stairs, one slow step at a time, and Robert followed.

"I say, your name isn't Jeeves, is it?" Robert asked, trying to lighten the mood. There was no response. "All right, then."

At the top, the man opened a door and motioned Robert in. He entered an enormous room, with a ceiling twenty feet high, a floor made of polished wood, and one wall covered in mirrors. The room was empty, except for three people seated at a table: There was a man in the middle, and two women, one on each side. Behind him, the door closed, and Robert felt suddenly awkward. He was about to perform for these people, but he had no makeup, no stage props, and no supporting cast.

"Robert Shaw?" the man asked.

"Yes, sir."

"What have you brought us to read?"

Robert stepped forward. "'As I Walked One Evening,' by W. H. Auden."

"A poem?" The man asked, surprised.

"Yes," Robert said. "A very good poem."

The man tilted his head. "We are accustomed to hearing candidates read from the theater. Nevertheless, let us hear what you have."

Robert pulled a crumpled piece of paper from his pocket. He had written it out the night before, and though the ink had begun to run, he knew it by heart.

> As I walked out one evening,
> Walking down Bristol Street,
> The crowds upon the pavement
> Were fields of harvest wheat.
> And down by the brimming river
> I heard a lover sing
> Under an arch of the railway:
> "Love has no ending."

The three judges listened carefully, occasionally jotting down notes or whispering to each other. When Robert finished, the man said, "That was, shall I say, interesting. Why did you choose that particular poem?"

"It is one of the best poems ever written, in my humble opinion."

"Why is that?"

"Several reasons," Robert answered, never at a loss when it came to sports, politics, or poetry. "First, it is about mortality. Young people lose sight of that; it feels as if we will live forever." He smiled. "Do you remember those days?"

They stared back at him.

"But the poem doesn't stop there," Robert continued quickly. "What I find truly interesting is that it examines the idea from several different perspectives. In the early stanzas, the speaker is walking down the street—I believe he represents Death. In the middle, we see the world through the eyes of the lovers, full of hope. But in the end, it is the city clocks who tell the story. The circle is complete, time has won the battle."

There was a pause, then one of the women spoke. "What else have you brought to read?"

"Am I required to perform two readings?" Robert asked.

"Yes," she said. "That should have been clear from the application. We need to hear you recite something from the theater."

Robert was prepared for this, but he feigned surprise. "I suppose I could perform Marc Antony's soliloquy from *Julius Caesar*," he said.

"Please do."

Robert bowed his head. When he looked up, he had become Marc Antony—the man who was outraged at the murder of Julius Caesar but who hid his rage so he could convince the crowd to avenge Caesar's death. Robert did not stutter this time, as he had done when he performed it as a teenager. Instead, he employed every technique he had learned since then: All the tricks he had picked up while reading to his siblings during air raids and everything he had learned from Mr. Wilkes, his high school drama teacher.

When he finished, the three judges bowed their heads and conferred. Robert stood patiently. Finally, the man looked up. "That was not especially inspiring, Mister Shaw, but it is good enough. You will have a position here in the fall."

Robert knew when to make an exit. "Thank you," he said, and turned to leave. Outside the door, the gaunt figure was waiting for him and escorted him onto the street. As Robert descended the last step, he heard someone say, "Congratulations."

Turning, Robert found the gaunt figure still watching him. "Thank you," he said. The man raised a hand in silent acknowledgment. Slowly, the door swung shut.

RADA turned out to be more like an army boot camp than a school. That was not by accident. Just as an army must toughen its soldiers for battle, so must acting school. Nothing compares to the horrors of war, of course, but an unhappy audience is no picnic.

At home during holidays, Robert shared his experiences with an amused family. They laughed with him as he described the ridiculous exercises they were forced to do, like pretending to be mimes or prancing around a stage dressed only in black tights. They frowned with him when he explained how the RADA teachers would embarrass students in front of everyone. "They believe actors need to be able to take a punch. Some of the students look like they're going to have a nervous breakdown."

"Anybody who has a nervous breakdown must have something wrong with them," his mother pointed out.

But Robert also admitted he was learning some things, like how to project his voice, how to use body language to convey emotion, and how to bring an entirely new character to life. Two years later, he graduated and joined the Royal Shakespeare Company. His acting career had begun, but it was anything but glamorous. For several years, he was forced to take whatever small roles he could get, working long hours for very little pay.

Robert had always been the star of the family, the golden child who set athletic records in school and was lauded for his acting. Joanna had done equally well—she was the top student in her class, the captain of the girls' field hockey team, and the leader among her friends—yet somehow, she always took a back seat to Robert. He was the oldest child, had the biggest personality, and more important, worked hard at drawing attention to himself.

But when he failed Cambridge and went into acting, his star had fallen. Acting was considered a loser's path, both within his family and in their circle of friends. People in Cornwall only saw films in a grubby little cinema in Truro, long after they had come out. To the Shaws, however, that grubby cinema was one of the highlights of their life. For fourpence they could sit in the front row, and so they scoured every conceivable hiding place for pennies, searching in telephone booths, under cushions, and in wishing wells. Then they laughed hysterically at the Marx Brothers, sneered at Shirley Temple films (but saw them nevertheless), and watched in awe as Laurence Olivier portrayed Henry V.

Robert's star had dimmed in their backwoods corner of English society, while Joanna achieved something few girls even dreamed about in those days: scholarships to both Oxford and Cambridge. It appeared *she* was the one going places.

It began during her final year of high school, when she was selected for special university training. The government paid for a limited number of poor children to attend elite universities, and high schools across the country, eager to get one of their pupils into these programs, assigned extra help to their top students. To qualify, a student had to first pass an entrance exam and then an even more challenging interview process.

And this is where their mother's training came in. In America, people pride themselves for succeeding in spite of their humble beginnings, but the British are the opposite: They aspire to have descended from royalty. To succeed in Britain, one only needs to have the right accent and the right attitude.

Joanna aced her exams and was granted interviews at both Oxford and Cambridge. She came away from both schools with a scholarship. The decision on Oxford versus Cambridge was made for her, however. "You and Elisabeth have been fighting for too long," Mrs. Shaw said. "Oxford is not big enough for the two of you." And so it was decided that Joanna would attend Cambridge University in the fall. The only question was what to do with the remainder of the school year.

"Stay home and finish school," Aunt Aileen advised.

"Come to London and try your hand at acting," Robert suggested.

"I don't care," Mrs. Shaw said.

In the end, her French teacher prevailed. She found Joanna an au pair job in Paris and told her to learn proper French. It turned out to be a terrible mistake. The family lived in a poor neighborhood on the outskirts of the city. Joanna had to perform the most menial chores, even cleaning their sanitary napkins. The saving grace was the cook's son, who took her to see the sights of Paris on her days off. The cook also looked out for her, but her way of helping was to give Joanna extra food and wine on the sly: Hence she became fat and drunk during her stay.

After a month, she quit and decided to move in with Robert until school began. She knew he was working in Stratford but did not know the address. She set out to find him. First, she caught a train to Calais, then boarded a ferry to cross the Channel, then took a train from Dover to London. There, she switched to another train and got off in Stratford. Arriving in the middle of the night and finding no taxis at that hour, she walked the last four miles to Wilmcote, dragging her suitcase behind her. The only thing she knew was that Robert was living over a cheese shop.

Meanwhile, Robert was dreaming happily that night. He had just performed the role of Angus in *Macbeth* at the Memorial Theatre. It was a small role, but the audience applauded him when he said, "Now does he feel his secret murders sticking on his hands." Robert delivered the line in a near-perfect imitation of Banquo's ghost, and the audience understood he was transforming Angus into the conscience of the king. The director was also impressed and bought Robert a pint of ale afterward at the Rose and Crown.

Robert was still reliving all the congratulations when his dream was interrupted. He opened one eye. Hearing nothing, he fell back asleep, and now the audience was applauding even louder. From his spot on the stage, he looked into a sea of happy faces. They were standing and cheering. "Encore! Encore! Encore!" they chanted, stamping their feet.

Robert sat up suddenly. He had definitely heard a noise this time. His eye focused on a crack in the wall, and he studied it for a moment, thinking it must hold the answer. Then he realized someone was banging on the door below his room. He stood and threw open the shutter.

"The cheese shop is closed," he yelled.

"Robert, let me in," someone yelled back.

He paused. That was unexpected. "Who's there?"

"Robert, you idiot, it's me. Joey. Let me in, it's bloody cold out here!"

"Joey?" Robert blinked. His eyes focused and he smiled. "It is Joey! Good of you to drop by. What brings you to this part of the world?"

He was met with silence. "All right, all right. I'll be right down."

Joanna poured herself into the kitchen. She was cold and tired and hungry, and it took her a few minutes to recover. Soon, however, she was making breakfast for the two of them while recounting her misadventures in Paris. Robert listened, occasionally interjecting a comment. In the end, he had only one real question: "Did you learn French?"

"*Oui, monsieur. J'ai tout à fait maîtrisé la langue, en fait.*"

"*Trés bien!*"

That fall, Joanna attended Cambridge and was assigned to Newnham College, one of two campuses that allowed women (out of twenty-four). She was shocked to find that the men outnumbered women by 20 to 1. To her further surprise, most of those men despised intellectual women. They called them "bluestockings," meaning they dressed like an old maid. It reminded her of a movie she had seen, *It's a Wonderful Life*, in which the film's beautiful actress became a dowdy librarian in the bleak alternate world and wore blue stockings! The fate of all intellectual women, apparently. But Joanna also discovered there were plenty of men who were interested in her—a pleasant surprise after coming from an all-girls high school.

She got her first taste of London during those years. Robert had moved back to the city, and Cambridge was only an hour away by train. Travel was cheap for students, and she spent many weekends in his small flat. Robert always gave her his bed for the night while he crawled into the bathtub.

Robert's career did not get off to a fast start. He was working with some of the greatest actors in English history, but his brash personality tended to push them off. During one exchange with John Gielgud, he demanded more face time as the other actors looked on in surprise. On another occasion, after seeing Gielgud in a performance in London, he told the older actor exactly what he thought of the play, including its strengths and weaknesses. It was a thorough analysis, but no one likes to be taken apart by a junior member of the crew. Gielgud did not invite Robert to perform with him again.

Yet, Robert's personality could work *for* him just as easily as *against* him. During Joanna's second year at Cambridge, Robert got his first break. Alec Guinness was so impressed with him that he offered Robert a role in his upcoming performance of *Hamlet* in London's West End. Robert would play Rosencrantz. He invited Joanna to opening night.

Joanna brought her best friend with her, and the two gaped at the lavish set design. Guinness had chosen Spanish architecture for the play, believing England was influenced by Spain in those days. As the curtain was raised, however, a problem developed with the lighting. The stage took on a ghostly appearance, and the spotlight was unable to focus on the proper actor when they were speaking.

It got worse. When Robert made his appearance, he was wearing a patch over one eye. He thought it would give Rosencrantz a sinister appearance, but in the darkened theater he looked ridiculous. The audience burst out laughing.

After the play, Joanna went backstage with her friend, where they found a despondent Guinness apologizing profusely to his cast. He took all the blame on himself. Then everyone went across the street to a cafeteria to await the reviews. Over the years, this would become one of Joanna's favorite activities: hanging out in a grubby café with Robert, waiting for the newspapers to arrive. It was always the same. Actors huddled together until long after midnight; some paced back and forth nervously while others bolstered themselves with drink. When the reviews finally arrived, there was either great rejoicing at the reviewer's brilliance or tremendous anger at their stupidity!

That night, the reviews were not good. The set design was said to be fanciful, the production wooden, and the actors robotic. One reviewer even poked fun at Robert's eye patch. Joanna's friend made the mistake of agreeing, and everyone just stared. Slowly, Robert raised his eyes and fixed them on her. Joanna had seen that look too many times; she grabbed her friend and beat a hasty retreat. "We really must be going," she said. "Our train is leaving."

In her third year at Cambridge, Joanna received a postcard. The postman gave her a funny look as he handed it to her, because it was really just the side of a Weetabix box, torn off and with a message scrawled on the back.

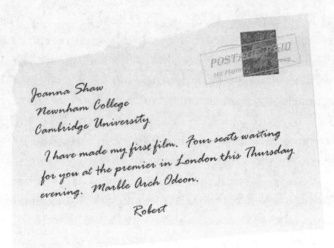

Joanna Shaw
Newnham College
Cambridge University

I have made my first film. Four seats waiting
for you at the premier in London this Thursday
evening. Marble Arch Odeon.

Robert

This was just the beginning of her embarrassment, though. Joanna invited several friends to join her, and they all sat in the cinema waiting for Robert to appear. They waited . . . and waited . . . and waited . . . Finally, Robert came on screen halfway through the movie, for all of five seconds. Joanna's friends did not even see him, and they made rude remarks all the way home.

She did not care. Joanna enjoyed the movie—it was *The Lavender Hill Mob*. She loved seeing her brother on screen, and she even got to speak to Guinness this time. He was the star of the movie and was extremely gracious. He told her how he had based his character on a cartoon that he liked called *The Everyman*. Joanna noted his whimsical smile, and she also noticed how he kept looking at her brother. Guinness was obviously infatuated with Robert.

That summer, Robert invited Joanna to a party in London, which Guinness had organized for Robert's twenty-fourth birthday. She found herself seated at a table with the two men, and listened in interest as they talked about Shakespeare, the theater, and other topics. Guinness then asked Robert if he was a member of the Shaw family.

"Of course," Robert said.

"I mean George Bernard Shaw's family."

"Oh. No, I am afraid not."

Guinness gave him a retiring smile and said, "I only ask because I got my start in theater when John Gielgud thought I was part of the brewing family. Can you imagine? He thought I might provide some financing for his play. The man was quite disappointed to learn my mother was a whore and my father one of her clients."

Joanna nearly choked on her drink, but Robert did not bat an eye. "Yet you somehow went to a fancy boarding school," he said.

"I did not say my father was a poor client," Guinness replied.

"I saw George Bernard Shaw recently," Joanna said, and the two men turned. "Yes," she continued, "I was bicycling with a friend, and we came to a sign for Ayot St Lawrence. I always claimed Shaw was my uncle but only on Tuesdays and Thursdays. The rest of the week, I was honest." Guinness chuckled and Robert raised an eyebrow, wondering where his sister was going. Joanna ignored him.

"We found his house," she continued, "and went around to the garden. It was surrounded by a brick wall, but we were able to climb to the top. And there he was, looking exactly like the pictures one sees. He was sitting in a chair, with a long white beard and a blanket over his knees."

"You are fortunate to have only seen him," Guinness said. "I had the misfortune of meeting him once, and the man would not stop talking. I am accustomed to writers who have something to say, but Shaw was the most boring individual I ever met."

"In any case, he is not a relative," Robert said.

"I only ask because I thought perhaps you might have inherited some of his writing ability, Robert. I do like the poems you have shared with me."

"Oh." Robert considered this. "In that case, I change my answer. I am descended from Shaw, but only on Tuesdays and Thursdays, as Joey said."

Guinness leaned forward and put a hand on Robert's knee. "You don't have to be descended from royalty to make it in this business," he said. "The only question, Robert, is what is your ambition? Do you truly want to be both an actor and a writer?"

Robert took Guinness's hand and placed it on the table. It was a subtle move, making it clear he was not interested but without making a fuss.

Guinness leaned back in his chair, as if nothing had happened. "I like to think of the stage as a canvas," he said. "An actor like Olivier fills it up with his personality. You can always see the man behind the character."

"I find Olivier rather interesting, actually," Joanna said.

Guinness ignored her. "He is like a concerto soloist, always taking the spotlight, always projecting. You cannot help but be drawn to the man. But are his characters honest? Gielgud disappears into the canvas. A serious actor needs to add just the right touch of color to make the character real. I prefer to imbue my roles with an inner truth. And I prefer a writer who can set that up properly, who can give me something that works on a blank canvas."

The two men continued to banter. Both were confident, never at a loss for words. But they were also very different. Robert was animated and lively, while Guinness was thoughtful and probing. They flitted from topic to topic, laughing at each other's jokes and applauding each other's intellect. Afterward, as they walked back to his flat, Robert explained that Guinness's marriage was one of convenience, homosexuality being illegal in Britain. He said it was common in the theater world.

Robert was not interested in men, but neither was he bothered by it. He and Joanna had grown up in a world where everyone was white, Protestant, and heterosexual—or so they thought at the time—and the result was neither of them ever gave much thought to the differences between people. In their world, no one was ever told they did not belong. Belonging was assumed.

The only prejudice they had grown up with came from their mother, who did not like the Welsh. "Taffy was a Welshman. Taffy was a thief," she used to say. Mrs. Shaw told them Welshmen were all short, never looked you in the eye, and could not be trusted. Years later, however, Joanna took a trip to Wales to see for herself. She searched high and low for short, dishonest Welshmen who would not look her in the eye, but all she found were tall, good-looking Welshmen who were kind and generous. One of them came running after her when she left her bank card in an ATM. Had the Welsh evolved, or was Mother wrong?

Joanna received her Cambridge degree the following year. She was fortunate to graduate, because she rarely studied and only managed to get through her exams at the last minute. The problem was the ratio of men to women. She was simply boy crazy during those years. In the end, she received a degree in English literature, but it would be more accurate to say she majored in boys and only minored in literature.

Nevertheless, Joanna had her Oxbridge diploma—the term for an Oxford or Cambridge degree—and that opened a lot of doors in those days. Her star, it seemed, was still brighter than Robert's.

Chapter 7

-‹‹‹◆›››-

A Wild Ride

[1953–1955]

"**W**hat's that?" Robert asked, pointing to an ad. He and Joanna were in a café, a newspaper spread out between them, sipping coffee and trying to find a job for her.

"What, a nanny position? Do you remember the last time I did that?"

"You don't follow me," Robert said. He circled two words at the end of the ad: *South Africa*. "I don't think you'll be cleaning sanitary napkins down there."

"But I'm looking for a teaching position."

"And I was looking for an acting job when I came to London. I didn't get it right away, but look where I am now."

"Where are you?"

"Well, I'm nowhere yet," Robert had to admit. "But I'm on the right path. The point is, I wouldn't be anywhere if I hadn't taken a chance."

The more Joanna thought about it that day, the more she liked it. Their mother had painted a wonderful picture of that part of the world, even though she had left when she was four years old. To hear her talk about it, she had spent her entire life in South Africa. Joanna could almost see the blue hills and green valleys, hear the elephants trumpeting, and smell the markets full of exotic fruits and vegetables.

She applied for the job and was given an interview. She was twenty-three years old and ready for an adventure, and once again, her accent and her attitude, now coupled with an Oxbridge degree, did the trick. She was hired on the spot.

A week later, Joanna said goodbye to Robert and sailed out of Southampton, bound for Cape Town. She had taken a job with the Morgans, a wealthy English family who were moving to Pietermaritzburg, where Mr. Morgan would become principal of Michaelhouse, an elite boarding school in KwaZulu-Natal. During the day, she looked after the children in their first-class cabins. In the evenings, she went back to her own third-class quarters, where she discovered that all the stories about the *Titanic* were true: The upper decks were full of snotty aristocrats while the lower decks, though crowded and dirty, were full of people laughing and dancing.

She hooked up in a shipboard romance that week with a South African, Georges Boerstra. Georges was a typically big Afrikaner, not exactly handsome but appealing to her in a rugged sort of way. Joanna got along very well with him despite their different languages and the history of war between the British and the Dutch. On the night they entered Cape Town, the two sat up all night to get a view of Table Mountain, with its twin peaks. Georges had climbed those peaks and was eager to point them out to her. But it turned out they were on the wrong side of the ship and never noticed as they entered the harbor.

When the ship docked, they bade farewell, and Georges went to his family in Pretoria while Joanna made the long car trip to Pietermaritzburg with the Morgans. The family moved into a large mansion next to the school, where Joanna was given the help of a local African woman to care for the children. She soon learned her first lesson about South Africa: The Morgans treated Joanna with great respect, but they displayed only contempt for the African. Their prejudice was based on their aristocratic background; they looked down on anyone who did not speak the proper English. But Joanna saw the same attitude among South African whites, which was more troubling. Parents routinely turned their children over to black nannies and then taught the children to despise the very people who cared for them so lovingly. This came during the children's most formative years; Joanna decided there must be a lot of schizophrenia among the white population.

But she was enjoying herself too much to brood about it. Joanna was one of the few young white females at Michaelhouse, surrounded by a host of eager men. There was tennis and gin every afternoon, lots of both in true South African style.

The Morgan children were adorable, especially three-year-old Benjy, who became the love of her life. But her favorite duty was tutoring Caroline, the oldest daughter. She had to pass a difficult entrance exam in order to get into Roedean School, an elite boarding school for girls in Johannesburg. Joanna was able to handle the English and math easily enough, and together she and Caroline studied South Africa's history, which was fascinating.

The problem began with the practice tests. Caroline kept giving creative answers that were incorrect, but rather than accept the right answer, she would come up with a creative explanation for why her bizarre response was better. No matter how many times Joanna corrected her, Caroline refused to give the right answer.

Joanna began to despair, but then she remembered another young girl who had done the same thing: herself. She had also resisted giving the obvious answers, and it was only when the headmaster warned her she would end up marrying a farmer that she fell into line. She applied the same logic here. "Do you want to be stuck here at Michaelhouse for the rest of your life?" she asked Caroline.

"I don't know," the girl replied lazily.

"It would mean living with your brothers for a very long time."

"Oh. Then no!"

Caroline began writing the boring but correct answers after that. She learned how to be dull and passed with flying colors. Joanna had learned a valuable lesson in psychology, but with Caroline gone, and the older boys in boarding school, she was left alone with Benjy and the parents. Dinner conversations became awkward. She had little in common with them.

Joanna was saved when a letter arrived from Georges inviting her to spend time with his family in Pretoria. It turned out Georges was rich—the only reason he had spent so much time in third-class was because he liked Joanna. His family owned a baking factory with more than a dozen establishments around the city.

It was an awkward introduction. Herr and Frau Boerstra were skeptical at first; women in South Africa were not independent and never pursued a career. But they laughed at Joanna's stories about the war, and it seemed they were getting along well. Herr Boerstra told her about the baking business and how he wanted to pass it on to Georges. Frau Boerstra puttered about, setting the table, serving meals, and cleaning up afterward.

Near the end of the week, Georges took Joanna to a quarry for a swim and a picnic. It was a lovely day, with a milky-blue sky and wisps of clouds. The water was refreshing, and they splashed about merrily until a group of Black South Africans came for a swim on the other side.

"I better get you out of here," Georges said.

"Why, what's wrong?"

Georges pointed, and then used a word that is not acceptable, then or now. "How can these goddam ***** spoil our day?"

Joanna was shocked. "How can you say that?"

"What?"

"They are just here for a swim, like we are. Why does it matter to you?"

At dinner that night, Georges related the story to his parents, including Joanna's reaction. The table fell silent. She looked from one Boerstra to the other, but no one would make eye contact with her. The silence continued until Frau Boerstra began to speak. She spoke so quietly that Joanna could barely hear her, but it became clear what she was saying. She was describing the other girl her son liked: the girl who came from the same background, the girl who wanted the same things . . . the girl who understood their system.

That was the end of that. Joanna left the next day and never saw Georges again. She had lost a chance at a rich guy but was not disappointed.

She could never be the Dutch Frau who waited on her husband, and she would never be on their side of apartheid.

Back at Michaelhouse, she went back to her duties, back to the tennis and gin, back to the eager young men. But everything seemed different now. The discomfort she had been feeling had moved to the center of her thoughts. If she was going to stay in South Africa, Joanna decided she must do something to fight apartheid.

She began by speaking to the chaplain at Michaelhouse. She told him what she had seen and how she felt about it, and asked for his advice. The chaplain talked about the mission schools, which had formed a hundred years earlier to bring Christianity to Africa, but many had been converted into schools to educate Blacks in the same curriculum as the whites. He had a friend at one of those schools, Adams College, in Durban, and arranged an interview.

Joanna got a lift from a staff member at Michaelhouse. The woman had always been friendly with her, but she spent the entire trip trying to talk Joanna out of leaving. Joanna ignored her and focused on the beautiful scenery—they were driving through the foothills of the Drakensburg mountains. On one particularly steep incline, she saw a tire roll past the car. *How odd*, she thought, but before she could say anything, the car lurched and nearly went over the cliff. It was their own tire she had seen. The woman managed to stop in time, and they peered over the edge together, shaking with fright, as the tire bounced into the ravine.

"This is an omen!" the woman exclaimed. "You must not leave Michaelhouse!"

Joanna agreed it was an omen, but she thought it meant she must do something more with her life. A passing African family helped them retrieve the tire, and they finished the journey without further incident.

At Adams, Joanna was introduced to the principal of the school, Jack Grant, who had been a West Indian cricketer in his day. Within five minutes, he had offered her a position. Once again, her accent and attitude helped her secure a job—although it didn't hurt that Grant was also a graduate of Cambridge.

Joanna took an immediate liking to the man. Grant was enthusiastic and explained how Adams was promoting change. Apartheid was designed to separate the country into four races, and to keep Blacks at the bottom of the hierarchy. The Bantu Authorities Act had created standardized tests, which were given to both white and Black students, but the tests were designed for the white curriculums. The resulting scores were then used to justify apartheid.

That was why it was so important to teach Black students with the white curriculum. Graduates of Adams were scoring just as highly as the white students and many were in positions of leadership as a result—including Adam Luthuli, president of the African National Congress, and Anton Lembede, who had founded the ANC Youth League.

The following day, Joanna resigned from the Morgans. It was not pleasant. Mrs. Morgan broke down and cried. "If I had to choose between looking after my children and cleaning my house," she sobbed, "I would prefer to clean the house."

Mr. Morgan was kinder and wished her well. "I knew we could not keep you in this position for long," he told her.

Joanna gave up the gin, the tennis, and the eager young men, but she found something more satisfying. She was using her first real teaching job to do something important. She entered a diverse environment: Her boss was a dark-skinned Zulu, her roommate was a white Afrikaner, and the teachers were all a mixture of white and Black, African and European, Zulu and Xhosa.

She began teaching English literature and discovered her students were eager to learn. They ranged in age from eighteen to forty, and every one of them had saved their entire lives to get a real education.

And to her delight, Joanna did not have to give up romance. She began dating one of her colleagues, an uncharacteristically tall light-skinned Zulu who was very handsome and athletic. Their friendship began as tennis partners at social events, and soon they were spending all their time together. This would have been unheard-of outside Adams, and even within the campus it was frowned upon, not because the others thought it wrong but because they feared for the young couple.

And indeed, her colleague broke it off after Joanna spotted him in Durban one day. She was with some girlfriends and waved to him, but he ignored her and hurried away. When she later confronted him angrily, she was shocked at what he said. "Joanna, if you and I were ever seen together outside of Adams, you would be all right. But I would be thrown in jail, and I would be beaten every day for the rest of my life."

It was another tough lesson in apartheid.

Her other love affair that year was platonic—it was with her boss, who was old enough to be her father. Mr. M'tchali was a very tiny Zulu, wiry and agile, who also loved English literature and recognized at once that Joanna had no sense of race. They took to one another at once.

M'tchali's favorite activity was discussing teaching assignments while sipping on vodka and orange juice. He chose vodka because it had no smell and always kept a bottle in the bottom drawer of his desk. Joanna resisted at first, but M'tchali's charm was overwhelming, and she usually joined him. They were sometimes interrupted by a noise in the hall, which would cause her boss to leap into the closet, lest he be caught drinking. He always took his drink with him and never spilled a drop, which had Joanna gasping with laughter.

Adams was filled with interesting personalities. Joanna's roommate was a white South African who taught Afrikaans literature. Her roommate's husband was a math teacher who preferred discussing William Blake to Pythagoras, and so he got along very well with Joanna. Everyone at the school was extremely nice, with one exception: Frank Wilson. Joanna only called him Wilson!—spoken through clenched teeth—because he was nasty to everyone. Yet for reasons unknown, he became attached to Joanna and would not leave her alone. She decided it was the lack of attractive women at Adams, or perhaps it was because Wilson! had tried for a spot at Cambridge but did not get in.

Ironically, the only people who tolerated Wilson! were the African teachers. Mr. M'tchali explained it to Joanna one day. "Yes, Frank is a nasty person," he admitted, "we see that. But he is nasty to everyone. He treats everyone the same way, white or Black, and that is a refreshing change."

Joanna gained a lifetime of experience during her first year. Teaching was everything she hoped for: stimulating, enlightening, and challenging all at once. Her second year, however, did not go so well. The Bantu Education Act had just been passed; the government was taking further steps to prevent schools like Adams from destroying their system.

Many of the Black teachers at Adams objected to the term *Bantu*, which means "native," but Mr. M'tchali saw it differently. "After all," he said, "we *are* the only natives in this country." Yet even he saw the change coming, especially after Hendrik Verwoerd, the Minister of Native Affairs, gave a speech about what the government wanted to accomplish. "The Bantu must be guided to serve his own community in all respects. There is no place for him in the European community above the level of labor."

Inspectors began arriving that fall: serious-looking men dressed in white suits and straw hats. They carried large briefcases that they slammed down on their desks when they walked into a classroom unexpectedly. They began interrupting teachers in midsentence, instructing them on what to say, and perhaps more important, what *not* to say.

That semester, Joanna was teaching two courses, one in English and one in divinity. She was not especially knowledgeable about divinity, despite having attended a Church of England school, but M'tchali needed someone to teach it. With two inspectors in the back of the room, Joanna's students sensed the danger and desperately tried to help, only asking questions they knew she could answer. The men were not fooled.

"Stop right there," one of them said. "You obviously don't know anything about religion. This class is over; let's move on."

They followed her into English class, where Mr. M'tchali had asked her to teach *The Wind in the Willows*. Joanna was well read and had devoured all the classics, but this was one book she had never picked up. Like teachers throughout the ages, however, she was able to teach it by staying one chapter ahead of her students. She began with a discussion of the previous assignment, but one of the inspectors stopped her. He walked to the front of the room, picked up the book, and opened to a random chapter. "Teach this," he ordered.

It was a later chapter, one she had not yet read. Joanna could not admit that, however, not after the prior class, and so there was only one thing left to do: She began reading the chapter out loud to the class, so they could discuss it together. It was *Mr. Toad's Wild Ride.*

> In the inn yard, Toad saw a beautiful motorcar whose owners were inside, having lunch. He could not resist trying it out. He turned the starting handle, hopped in behind the wheel, and drove off in a cloud of dust. As he sped along, he chanted a little song about how clever he was.
>
> Toad's next appearance was as a limp and miserable prisoner in the dock at the Magistrate's Court. He was charged with dangerous driving, stealing a motorcar, and worst of all, "cheeking" the police. The Magistrate took a serious view and sentenced him to twenty years' imprisonment . . .

A problem began to emerge as Joanna read. Like all great children's literature—books like *Alice in Wonderland*, *The Tale of Peter Rabbit*, and *The House at Pooh Corner*—this one was so marvelously written, with such sophisticated humor and deep insights into human behavior, that she began to giggle. Soon, the entire class was laughing. Even one of the inspectors found it funny; he laughed as hard as anyone.

The other inspector, however, only scowled, and the more everyone laughed, the deeper his scowl became. When the class was over, he went into Mr. M'tchali's office and ordered him to demote Joanna to the high school. "She won't do as much harm there," he said.

This might have been disheartening, but Joanna discovered the high school students were as dedicated as those in college. They varied in age—some were in their forties—and one of them, a great big man who went by the name of Father Ben, gave her the nickname of Little Miss Shaw. Soon, everyone called her that.

Working at the high school had an unexpected benefit that spring. It was located directly across from the campus parking lot, which was why

Joanna was the first to spot four cars pull up one day. They were large black vehicles in perfect condition: a sharp contrast to the battered cars of the Adams teachers that exhibited the usual wear and tear of driving on dirt roads.

Joanna went to the back door of the school and peeked out. The heat of Kwa-Zulu Natal had already built up, and a rush of hot air greeted her, sending bits of trash scurrying up the hall like riderless horses. Her students pressed their noses against the window to see who was visiting.

Doors were flung open and a group of large men emerged from the vehicles. They were much like the cars, tall and black and shiny, wearing matching dark suits and sunglasses that hid their eyes. One of them opened a back car door, and another man stepped out. He was in his mid-thirties, well-dressed, and well-fed. He looked like the others, with one important difference: There was an enormous smile on his face.

"So this is where Albert Luthuli was educated," Joanna heard him say.

She walked over and introduced herself. "My name is Joanna Shaw."

"And I am Nelson Mandela," the man said, shaking her hand warmly. "I have come to thank you for your service to South Africa."

As students gathered around her, Joanna's face fell. "In that case, you might be better off speaking with the other teachers. I believe the government is trying to deport me."

"Why is that?"

"Because of the way I read *Mr. Toad* to my class."

Mandela gave her an odd look. "Who is Mr. Toad?"

"A toad," Joanna said, keeping a straight face.

Mandela studied her for a moment, then burst out laughing. "I assumed as much. But how can a small animal be responsible for you leaving Africa?"

And without thinking, Joanna found herself relating the incident with the inspectors: how she could not admit that she had not read the chapter and how she began laughing as she read it to her class. "Even one of the inspectors found it funny," she said.

Mandela was now laughing as well. "Please tell me the full story."

"Mr. Toad was the owner of Toad Hall," Joanna began, "the most beautiful house in the forest. But he left it unguarded one day, having become infatuated with a shiny new motorcar . . ." She glanced at the vehicles behind them, and Mandela followed her gaze.

"Please continue," he said with a smile.

"Mr. Toad was thrown in jail for reasons that were not entirely his fault," Joanna continued, "and by the time he escaped, his house had been taken over by some very nasty animals—weasels and stoats and the like. He was locked out of his own home."

"This seems very familiar," Mandela murmured.

Joanna told him how the other animals had helped Toad recover his house, and how Mr. Toad had then become the leader of all the animals of the forest. When she finished, Mandela leaned in to her.

"Let me tell you a secret," he whispered. "I was born in an African-only hospital, attended an African-only school, and I live in an African-only neighborhood. *I* am Mr. Toad. *I* have been locked out of my own country. Education is the only way we will change that."

Then Mandela straightened and spoke so that everyone could hear. "Miss Shaw, I believe you have discovered the key to our struggle. Everyone must laugh more often."

And he was gone, moving down the line and shaking hands. With each person, he had the same look on his face—everyone's story was of interest to him.

Shortly after this encounter, the government revoked Joanna's visa, and she was forced to leave South Africa. Her involvement in the fight against apartheid was brief, but Mandela's was not. He was accused of treason and went to prison for three decades. When Joanna saw him emerge many years later, she barely recognized the man she had met. He was no longer young, no longer well-fed, and his hair had turned completely white.

One thing about him had not changed, though. His smile was the same: enormous and warm and generous. He shared it with the world in the same way he had shared it with the teachers at Adams College that day. Nelson Mandela had been on a wild ride, but it had not changed him.

Chapter 8

Ye Olde
Cheshire Cheese

[Summer 1955]

*I*t was not until Joanna was back in London and sitting on top of a double-decker bus that she realized how alien it felt. She had experienced the same feeling when she first arrived in South Africa. Everything had seemed so strange then: the colonial wealth next to the village poverty; the smell of human beings on a bus, because African households did not have running water; the savannas teaming with animals, and the markets teaming with people. Yet, as soon as she became used to it, England had felt like the dream, like it could not possibly exist.

Now it was happening in reverse. Looking down on all the shops, all the traffic, all the white people milling about on the sidewalks . . . it suddenly felt like South Africa could not possibly exist.

She found Robert's flat in the north of London. It would be the third time in five years that she would be moving in with him, but times had changed. Robert was now married to Jennifer, a fellow actress who had given up her career to raise a family, and they had two daughters. Their apartment was tiny—the only bathroom was shared by all the tenants—but Jennifer welcomed Joanna graciously and cleared out a closet for her.

Joanna assured her she would be leaving as soon as her visa to America came through. Liz had written to her about an opening at her college in Lancaster, Pennsylvania, where she now lived with her husband and two boys, and Joanna decided to get another year or two of international teaching experience before settling down in Britain.

That summer, she divided her time between three activities. In the mornings, Joanna was a substitute teacher in the London public schools. In the afternoons, she helped Jennifer with the girls, often taking them to the park for long walks; she fell in love with them and looked forward to the day when she would have her own. In the evenings, she usually went out with Robert. He had already become bored with Jennifer, she discovered, and was always making excuses to get away. Whenever Joanna had a date, he would tell the fellow she was ill; then, when she returned from work, Robert would say her date had canceled.

One evening, they went to a cinema in Leicester Square together to see Robert's latest movie, *The Dam Busters*. He assured Joanna his part was bigger this time and kept nudging her as they watched. "Here comes my scene," he kept saying. But each time, it turned out his scene had been cut. Just about the only time he was on camera was on an airplane, next to the star of the film, Richard Todd—and even then, Robert's face was covered by an oxygen mask. They both had a good laugh about it afterward, and Joanna was glad to see Robert could still laugh at himself.

A few days later, arriving home from work, Joanna found a note on her closet:

> *Your date canceled. Come join us at*
> *Ye Olde Cheshire Cheese*
> *— Robert*

Making her apologies to Jennifer—again—Joanna caught the Underground to St. Paul's and made her way through the labyrinth of alleys in the oldest part of London. The passages were so narrow that she could touch both sides by stretching her arms. Inside the pub, she searched for Robert in one room after another. She ducked beneath the annoying sign that read Gentlemen Only Served in This Bar. Robert was not there. She poked her head in the next room, where one plaque said that Charles Dickens had entertained friends there and another told of how Samuel Johnson had written his English dictionary in the same place. Robert was not there either. She went up the narrow stairs to the second-floor bar—no Robert. She went down the narrow basement stairs, being careful not to bang her head on the overhang, and checked in the various nooks and crannies—no Robert. Finally, she went down one more flight of steps into the sub-basement, with its bar along one wall and picnic tables scattered about.

"Joanna, over here," someone called.

It was Barbara Jeffords, Robert's close friend from Stratford. Next to her was Diane Cilento. Joanna knew both women well, because Robert had dated each of them before meeting Jennifer, and there were also two men at the table, whom she did not know. It turned out they were all actors performing with Robert that summer in the West End production of *Tiger at the Gates*, starring Michael Redgrave.

The two men were flamboyant. One of them leaned forward eagerly and shook Joanna's hand while the other appeared to be asleep. The eager man's name was Gaston, although he did not explain why he had a French name yet spoke with an English accent. "May I offer you a cigarette?" Gaston said.

Joanna took a mentholated filter-tip and lit up. Smoke drifted toward the ceiling, mixing with a half dozen other wisps of smoke and filling in the spaces between the ancient beams.

"Where's Robert?"

"Playing tennis with Vanessa," Barbara said. "I've found someone willing to put up with the way he plays."

Joanna laughed. "He used to upset chessboards when he was losing. Does he still do that?"

"No, but only because one cannot overturn a tennis court. To be honest, he doesn't lose very often. I don't really mind. The problem is when it affects his acting."

"What do you mean?"

"He overdoes everything. Every word he says, every flourish is exaggerated. He thinks about winning, even when he has a small part in the production."

"Reveal the character but hide the actor," Gaston said. "Robert has learned the first but not the second."

"The star of the show doesn't like that, you know," Diane said. "Michael has it in for him. Robert did the same thing to Richard Todd, and look where it got him."

"*The Dam Busters*?" Joanna asked. "But he didn't even have a speaking line."

"Because he kept taking the spotlight away," Barbara said. "They cut his parts. But Robert can steal a scene even if it is only his eyes that are showing." She changed the subject. "I understand you've been in South Africa. What was that like?"

"It was"—Joanna searched for the right word—"seductive," she finished.

"Oh my," Gaston said, leaning forward. "Do tell us more."

"If you're white," Joanna said, "you can have a jolly good time of it. But to do so, you must accept that Blacks are inferior."

"Oh. I was thinking you meant something else by seductive," Gaston said, disappointed.

"There was plenty of that as well," Joanna said. "Lots of gin and tennis, in true South African style. And lots of eager young men."

Gaston laughed a little louder than he should have and began hiccupping. Next to him, his companion roused himself and burst out laughing.

"Did you have any romances?" Diane asked. "Anything you can share?"

"Yes, two. The first was with an Afrikaner, a big, rugged man who introduced me to his family. But they resented me for being English."

"Why?"

"I suppose for the same reason the South resents the North in America: because they both lost. Anyway, it ended badly. I told them what I thought about how they treated Blacks, and they practically threw me out of the house."

"Good for you," Barbara said.

"And the other romance?" Gaston asked, recovering. He handed Joanna another cigarette, and blew a circle of smoke above her head. "Did you have anything resembling an Italian romance, perhaps?"

"Gaston is teasing Diane," Barbara explained. "She just married an Italian and is madly in love."

"He was not Italian," Joanna said, "he was Zulu. A lovely, tall man who taught me how to play real tennis. We were inseparable for a while, but he broke it off very suddenly."

"Whatever for?"

"He said he would be thrown in jail if we were ever discovered."

"So, both romances ended for the same reason," Diane said. "Apartheid."

"I suppose."

They were interrupted by Robert and Vanessa Redgrave, who burst into the sub-basement dressed in tennis whites, twirling their rackets and beaming with perspiration and delight.

"Let me guess," Barbara said. "From the expression on your face, Robert, you have beaten your young opponent."

"Handily," Robert said, unable to hide his grin. He looked about. "What the devil are you doing in this smoke-filled cellar? It is delightful outside. We should all be in a street café."

"Robert, my dear," Diane said, "we are quite happy down here. Among other topics, we are discussing what an actor must do to achieve success."

"Oh, well, then, let us join you." Robert got two drinks and handed one to Vanessa. They slid into open spots at the table.

"Gaston has offered the opinion," Barbara said, "that an actor should expose the character while making himself invisible. What do you say to that?"

"Of course! But I will offer a corollary," Robert said, raising his glass. "Whatever the role, no matter how large or small, the actor must think of himself as the star. When he is speaking, he must command attention."

"God knows everyone needs to be entertained these days," the man next to Gaston said, rousing himself. "Do you know the bloody RAF is carrying nuclear bombs? Right now, over our heads. They could blow up the whole world at any moment."

"Those are Valiant aircraft," Robert pointed out.

"We are doomed."

"Every age has its dangers," Robert said. "We're not the first ones to think the end of the world is near."

"Every age does not have nuclear bombs," Gaston pointed out.

"No, but does it matter if you are in a village and a horde of cavalry sweeps through and kills everyone? Even Charles Dickens thought the world was going to shit." Robert adopted a Victorian accent. "'I say, Charles, what do you think of the world these days?' 'Why, I believe the world is going to shit. What do you say?' 'I believe you are correct, Charles.'" Robert turned to Joanna. "Isn't that right, Joey? You're the literary expert."

"I am hardly an expert," Joanna said with a smile, "but I do agree that every age believes the world is going to shit."

"There you have it," Robert said. "Now, let me propose something."

"You're too late for that," Barbara said, "Diane and I are both married."

Robert ignored the chuckles. "I propose, " he said, "that there is something even more powerful than the atom bomb."

"What?"

"Family!"

"Is that why you married Jen?" Diane asked. "To have a family?"

"To have a dozen children."

"Why, Robert," Barabara said with mock surprise, "I do believe you have revealed your secret." Everyone paused. "You are afraid to be alone."

"Barbara, my love," Robert replied, "if everyone who wants a family is afraid to be alone, then we must all be afraid. Don't you think?"

"But you started so young."

"What are you going on about? You and Diane are younger than me."

"But we are mature women. You are still a child."

Robert raised his glass. "To children."

"In any case," Diane said, "the world is not ready for a dozen baby Shaws. They would be like tigers at the gate."

"Speaking of which," Gaston said. "Let us toast our upcoming adventure in New York."

"Who's going to New York?" Joanna asked.

"Our play has been picked up for Broadway."

Joanna turned to Robert. "I didn't know that."

"Not all of us are going," Barbara said.

There was a moment of silence, and Joanna saw a momentary flash of anger in Robert's eyes. "What am I giving up?" he asked. "A small part in a small play."

"You're giving up Broadway," Diane said. "Giving up a chance for a bigger stage."

Robert scoffed. "Do you know that in France, at the end of every performance, they call the playwright onto the stage for applause. The French understand art. In England, we applaud the actors. In America . . . well, I don't know what they do there."

"You don't believe in Broadway?"

"I will tell you what I believe," Robert said. Everyone smiled. "I believe there is a hierarchy in the world, and acting is not at the top."

"Please educate us," Barbara said.

"I shall happily do so. The lowest form of art is painting. A painter merely puts on canvas what he sees in the world. He does not *create* anything. He merely *recreates*. Like a photograph."

"What about impressionism?"

"That is just a photo that is out of focus." Everyone laughed. "And above painting," Robert continued, "is music. That is more creative, but it is just a series of concentric circles, notes going round and round, always returning to where they began. We all like closure, so it feels satisfying to us."

"Shakespeare wrote his own music," Vanessa pointed out. Looking at her, Joanna realized how young she was and also that she was obviously smitten with Robert, despite their difference in age. She looked at him the way she had seen Alec Guinness stare at Robert: stealing glances, unable to look away.

"There, you see," Robert said. "Is Shakespeare known for his music? Of course not."

"And what is next on your hierarchy?" Diane asked.

"Acting," Robert said. "Playing a role. More challenging than painting or music, but it is still not creating. It is more like an interpretation of someone else's work."

"But if acting is not at the top, what then?"

"Writing, of course," Robert said. "The writer creates. He educates. He pulls characters out of thin air, gives them a personality, shows how they interact with each other, and then turns everything upside down when someone new enters the room."

"But other than France," Gaston pointed out, "the writer toils in the background, lonely and frustrated, while the actor gets the applause."

"That's right," Barbara said. "Until you've written something special, why not focus on being a good actor?"

"But I *have* written something special."

"What?"

"*Off the Mainland*. I've found a producer."

"I said something *special*," Barbara said, to more chuckles.

Vanessa spoke up. "Robert, if you are going to write something special, then you must do what Charles Dickens did. He has a plaque upstairs because he wrote about the poor. England is owned by a few wealthy families. We are all descended from either royalty or from peasants, and there is little we can do about it. We must all do something to change this."

"But you are descended from royalty," Gaston pointed out.

"Do you mean my family?" Vanessa's father, Michael Redgrave, was the star of the play and was the man who did not like Robert stealing his spotlight. "A family of actors is hardly royalty."

"That is all well and good," Barbara said. She turned to Robert. "But we are all going to New York, and you are not going with us. It would be so much fun if you could join. All you have to do is apologize to Michael."

Robert shook his head. "That would mean changing who I am."

Chapter 9

-⟪⟪◆⟫⟫-

Pregnant in
an Outhouse

[1955–1956]

A few weeks later, Joanna's visa came through, and she was off to America. Robert found a cargo ship willing to take on passengers, so she hitch-hiked to Liverpool and set sail. In Lancaster, Pennsylvania, she moved in with Liz and her husband, Bob Russell, along with their two boys. Bob was blind, but it did not slow him down. He was a professor at Franklin & Marshall, a graduate of Oxford and Yale, and a jack-of-all-trades. Despite his lack of sight, he performed carpentry around the house, as well as the plumbing and electrical work. He had even taken apart the engine in their car, simply to learn how to put it back together. He would write his memoir a few years later, *To Catch an Angel*, which became a bestseller.

But as for the teaching position Liz had promised, there was none. She had exaggerated the opportunity, being homesick and wanting someone from the family to visit. Fortunately, teachers were in high demand in those days, and Joanna quickly found an opening at an all-girls high school in Maryland.

Her students could not have been more different from those in South Africa, but they were intelligent and polite and rarely gave her trouble—all except one. Joan Tunney was a tall, dark-haired girl who would have been pretty if she was not always scowling. She had a good mind when she was paying attention, but that was rare. Joanna tried to draw her out in class. "What did you think of *Great Expectations*?" she asked.

"I liked it very much," Joan replied. "I know how Pip must have felt, stealing food to help a convict. The man might have killed him, but Pip did it anyway."

"Very good. Do you think it helped prepare him for what he would find after leaving home?"

Joan answered a different question. "I never wanted to trespass on our neighbor's property. The convict was trespassing, that was not right. My father told me never to go into our neighbor's yard, and I was always careful not to."

At the end of the term, Joanna gathered the final exam papers, but she could not find Joan's. The girl swore she turned it in and refused to take a makeup exam. After speaking with the headmistress, Joanna was forced to fail her.

A few days later, there was a knock on her office door, and she looked up to find the largest man she had ever seen standing there. He was as wide as he was tall, nearly filling the doorway. "I'm Joan's father," he said.

Joanna gulped. "Mr. Tunney, please come in."

Tunney was impeccably dressed in a suit and tie, with sharp features, curly dark hair, and an angular chin. He might have looked handsome, Joanna thought, if he didn't remind her of Joan. He sat across the desk and leaned back casually. "I've come to find out why you failed my daughter in your class."

"Yes, I'm very sorry about that," Joanna said. "She wasn't able to perform her work during the semester and then didn't even turn in a final exam. I had no choice."

Tunney sighed. "My wife and I are having similar problems. But failing her will only make matters worse, I'm afraid."

"What kind of problems?"

"Polly and I hug our children every day. We read to them, play with them. Joan's brothers all laugh easily. But for some reason, it is impossible to coax even a smile out of Joan. We've been through everything: therapy, counseling, expert advice."

Joanna imagined what her mother would say about therapy but kept it to herself. "She seems to be on the verge of exploding at times," she offered.

"She gets that from my father," Tunney replied. "He was an Irish immigrant, working on the docks of New York. If you didn't fight down there, you didn't work; and if you didn't work, you couldn't feed your family. It was a simple equation: 'the valiant taste of death but once.'"

"Are you quoting . . . ?"

"Hmm?"

"*Julius Caesar*?"

"Yes, one of my favorite plays."

"I didn't think a man like you would read Shakespeare."

Tunney pursed his lips. "What do you mean 'a man like me'?"

"I didn't mean it that way," Joanna said quickly. "I just don't meet many men of your size who can quote Shakespeare."

"I wasn't always this big. My father used to call me *skinny*. He taught me how to box so I wouldn't get beaten up in school. I never thought I would make a living from it."

"You're a professional boxer?" Joanna asked.

Tunney stared at her. "Do you know who I am?"

"Yes. Joan's father."

"You don't know I was once heavyweight champion of the world?"

"I'm afraid not."

"That's very refreshing. So many people, when they meet me, it is all they see."

For the next thirty minutes, they discussed several topics, and for the moment Joan was forgotten. Tunney had a wide range of interesting views, from Shakespeare to politics to international affairs. He was very articulate, and Joanna could not help but like him. When the conversation came back to boxing, he was equally animated.

"People never gave me credit," he said. "I was undefeated. Knocked out Jack Dempsey twice, but they still thought he was the better boxer."

"Why?"

"Dempsey was a bull, always charging. He never had a strategy, other than to attack. People liked that, I suppose. I was smaller but smarter. I only attacked when I had an opening."

"My father was an amateur boxer," Joanna said. "He taught my brothers to box."

"I would love to meet him."

"I'm afraid that's impossible. He died several years ago."

"I'm very sorry. He must have been quite young. How did it happen?" Joanna shook her head.

"We won't turn that rock over, eh?"

"We will not."

They left on good terms, and Joanna was exonerated when a student came forward and said he had watched Joan during the exam, and she had spent the entire time just staring at the paper and then turned in the blank pages. Joanna did not think about the girl again, or her father . . . until fifteen years later, when she got a phone call. She did not know who it was at first, but then she realized it was Gene Tunney, and he was apologizing for Joan: apologizing for her behavior, for asking Joanna to pass her, for how much danger Joanna had been in. He told her that Joan had murdered her husband recently with a meat cleaver in their apartment outside of London.

"I am so sorry," was all Joanna could think to say.

To herself, though, she thanked God it had not been her. At the same time, she also wondered what really happened in that apartment outside of London. She remembered Joan had been a troubled teenager, but she never thought of her as someone capable of murder.

Joanna made several friends that year, including an attractive redheaded American, Walt Myers. Walt was a veteran of the navy and an administrator at F&M. Joanna loved his smile, his humor, and most of all, his American accent. Walt was clearly smitten with her as well and spent nearly every weekend driving back and forth to visit.

Joanna was not planning to spend a lot of time in America, though, and she broke up with Walt at the end of the school year. That summer, she joined a group of friends on a field trip to Alaska, an early Peace Corps sort of project, to help the local Inuit build a summer camp.

The group set off in a small bus. There were three men, three women, two drivers, and one Anglican priest who would be their chaperone. They were all enjoying themselves watching America slide past, when Joanna began to feel nauseous. Thinking it was her usual car sickness, she opened a window and sucked in fresh air. It was not a pleasant trip. In Alaska, they took a ferry to an offshore island and began their tasks. In the fresh air, Joanna felt better again. She was assigned to a team building the out-house, and for the next several days, she hammered and sawed, occasionally looking up to find a family of seals watching her curiously.

On the third day, her nausea returned. She was just putting the finishing touches on the outhouse when it hit her, and she inaugurated the new structure by emptying her stomach into the pit. Now she knew something was wrong. She bade farewell to her friends, caught the ferry back to the mainland, and spent the next five days hitchhiking across Canada and America. The trip was made even longer by her frequent need to ask the driver to pull over so she could vomit.

In Lancaster, it did not take long for Liz to identify the problem. "You're pregnant!"

Joanna was shocked. It was worse than she imagined. Being unwed and pregnant in those days meant utter and permanent disgrace for a woman. Society had moved a long way from the suicides of unwed mothers in the nineteenth century, as depicted in novels like *Tess of the D'Urbervilles* and *Far from the Madding Crowd*, but it was still unacceptable. "A fate worse than death," it was called in the *Bridge of Sighs*, where the young woman had drowned herself.

She called Walt with the news, and he immediately proposed. But she was not ready to give up her dream of returning home and said no. For the next several weeks, Walt called every day and proposed again, and each time Joanna said no.

In August, she phoned her school and told them she would not be back.

In September, Joanna received a phone call from her old colleague, Wilson! He had heard the news and traveled to America to see her. He offered to marry her and take her back to England, where he had come into some money. "I can take care of all your needs," Wilson! said. Joanna was tempted—her situation was dire—but she still said no.

In October, Robert called to say he would be in New York for the Macy's Thanksgiving parade. He had landed a starring role on a TV show in England, *The Buccaneers*, and CBS was airing it in America. They were paying Robert's expenses to promote the show. Liz and Joanna both laughed. They had seen the show, and though it was similar to *Horatio Hornblower*, it was only for very young children. Nevertheless, Robert was basking in his new fame.

That November, Liz and Joanna went to New York for a family council. They met Robert at the Plaza and were shocked at the size of his hotel room. "My God, this is bigger than my house," Liz said. They ordered room service that evening. Robert had been wined and dined all week, including parties with scantily clad Buccaneer girls, and wanted to stay in.

After dinner, Robert ran a bath and laid out his clothes for the next day, being unaccustomed to the American practice of showering in the morning. Then he asked Joanna to keep him company, and she made herself comfortable in a chair. Robert lay there for a while, his eyes closed, luxuriating in the steam. Then he asked, "What's the matter with Liz?"

"What do you mean?"

"Something is wrong, I can always tell. It's not just your pregnancy."

Joanna thought for a moment. "It might be her cooking."

"Hmm?"

"You know the young man who has been calling on me?"

"You mean the father of your unborn child?"

"Yes, that one. His name is Walt."

"Nice chap?"

"Very nice. But that is not the point."

"Well get on with it, then."

Joanna laughed. "Walt has been spending a lot of time with us, and he prides himself on his cooking. He and Liz have become rather competitive about it, because, you know, Liz also believes she is a good cook."

"Which she is not," Robert said.

"Yes. But frankly, neither is Walt. Once again, though, that is not the point."

"So, what is the point?"

"The point is that Bob got a letter from Yale recently, his alma mater. They were doing some sort of survey and wanted Bob to fill out a form, so he asked Walt for help."

"What does this have to do with Liz's cooking?"

"One of the questions was 'How good a cook is your wife?' Bob's answer was 'not very good.'"

Robert's eyes flew open.

"Walt was delighted," Joanna said, "and let it slip out over dinner. Liz was absolutely furious."

Robert sat up.

"Would you mind handing me the phone," he said. Joanna stretched it across the tub. "Dial 0, will you, please." Then Robert put a finger to his lips for her to be quiet. When the operator came on, he said: "This is Robert Shaw in room 811. Would you be so kind as to ring my other line for me." He paused. "That's right, I am not able to get to the bedroom just now, and I must speak to my sister."

He waited a moment, then began speaking in an American accent, high and thin and nasal. "Hello, is this Elisabeth Russell? Oh good, I was told I could find you here. I am a reporter from *Good Housekeeping* magazine. Have you heard of us?" Another pause. "Wonderful, wonderful, we do appreciate your support. The reason I am calling is because our staff has learned, through some of your associates at Franklin & Marshall, that you are an exceptionally good cook. Is this true?"

Joanna heard a delighted clucking in the other room.

"Wonderful, wonderful. Would you be so kind as to tell us about some of your dishes? It is for the magazine, you understand. We would like to include some recipes in the article."

More clucking came through the door. Robert nodded thoughtfully, occasionally asking a question. After a minute or so, he said, "Listen, Mrs. Russell, this is all wonderfully interesting. But tell me, do you enjoy a glass of wine with your dinner? Our readers like to match the proper wine with their meals. Can you recommend anything?"

Robert listened for another minute, then said, "Now I must ask you a rather personal question. I hope you will not be put off. Once again, it is for the benefit of our readers. They are interested in all aspects of cooking." He paused. "Do you and your husband ever do it while preparing a meal? On the kitchen table, perhaps?"

Now there was only silence through the door. Robert looked at Joanna and shrugged. Then Liz burst in, shaking with rage. She looked from Robert to Joanna, then back to Robert. Joanna waited for her to explode. Robert had been doing this sort of thing to her for a very long time. But she turned to Joanna instead. "You told him, didn't you!"

The next morning, Robert disappeared early. Liz and Joanna ate a leisurely breakfast, then made their way to Broadway. Barriers already lined the streets, and crowds had formed. Mothers held babies in their arms, fathers carried children on their shoulders, and a few enterprising youths had placed boards on top of trash cans, so they could see over the crowd.

It was a windy day and bitterly cold. Liz and Joanna huddled together for warmth, occasionally catching glimpses of marching bands. At one point, Mighty Mouse floated by, looking rather disheveled. They later learned that he had struck a lamppost.

"Robert will be in front of Macy's at 10:47," Liz said, reading a brochure someone handed her. They pushed their way to the front of the crowd just in time to see him come by in a car with Roy Rogers. Several hours later, the three of them were walking up the deserted street, arm in arm, while street cleaners began the process of restoring Broadway to its previous condition.

"Did you see me out there?" Robert asked. He was in high spirits. "I was with Roy Rogers! He had his guns with him. He showed them to me; they were gold plated!"

"Yes, he is just as popular as you with eight-year-old boys," Liz scoffed.

Robert laughed, and Joanna brought the conversation back to her issue. "Must I remind you that I am pregnant, and I do not know what I am going to do."

"I do recall something about that," Robert said. "I think it is wonderful."

"What are you talking about," Liz said. "This is horrible. She isn't married."

"One needn't be married to have a child," Robert said. Then he turned serious. "Joey, if you want to have an abortion, I will pay for it."

"Absolutely not," Liz said.

"Since when do you have a say in this?" Robert asked.

"Does anyone care what I think?" Joanna said.

"I'm not saying she should do it," Robert said to Liz. "I'm only saying I will pay for it if she chooses."

"She's five months pregnant."

"Abortions are legal in Britain until six months."

"I'll tell you what she must do," Liz said, with sudden inspiration. "Joey must stay with me and have the baby. She will stay indoors, so that no one sees her. Then she will fly home and never return." She took Joanna by the arms with growing excitement. "I will raise the child as if it is my own. But you must never come back. No one must ever know, not even Mother."

"Especially not Mother," Robert said.

Joanna understood what Liz was thinking. She had two boys, but she desperately wanted a girl and had had two miscarriages. Just then, they heard a shout from across the street. A young woman was waving to them.

"My God, it's one of my students," Joanna exclaimed.

"Hello, Miss Shaw," the girl yelled, "I was wondering why I hadn't seen you in school this year." She made a circle around her belly. "Now I understand why!"

Robert burst out laughing, but Liz was incensed. "Did you hear that?" she hissed. "This is exactly what I mean. You must do as I say, Joey. Give the child to me. Go home and never come back."

It is moments like this that often shine a light on a seemingly intractable problem. Joanna suddenly knew what she would do. She had been obeying her older brother and sister ever since she was a little girl . . . but this was her life. *She* would be the one to live with the consequences. In that moment, she knew she could never give up her child, certainly not to be raised as a second-class citizen in someone else's family.

"Liz, I am not going to give you my baby," she said. Robert began to say something, but she cut him off. "And I am not going to have an abortion."

"What, then?" they both asked.

"I am going to marry Walt and have my baby."

There was a moment of silence. Then Robert said, "Good for you! You said he was a nice chap."

Back in Lancaster, Joanna called Walt and told him the news. There was a moment of silence. Then he said, "Wonderful." Walt was as shocked as anyone; he came from a deeply religious family and was having his own misgivings about marrying a pregnant woman.

They were married the following week at a church in York, Pennsylvania. Walt chose York because it was far enough away that he thought no one would recognize him. But when they got to the altar, he discovered the minister was an old school friend.

"Good to see you, Walt," the minister said.

"You won't tell anyone, will you?"

"Of course not."

It was not a very romantic start to their marriage, and neither of them were sure they would make it, but they agreed to try. If things didn't work out, at least their child would be legitimate. Sixty years and seven children later, they were still trying.

Chapter 10

Kings & Heirs

[Fall 1961]

Robert Shaw was an unusual man in many ways. He was an actor of growing importance, yet he preferred to be thought of as a writer. He loved nothing more than talking sports, yet he moved easily in the British theater world. Most unusual of all, however, was that he was involved with two different women, and both were pregnant with his child.

He and Joanna were sipping drinks in the Algonquin Hotel while waiting for Robert's colleagues to arrive. Rehearsals were underway for *The Caretaker*, Harold Pinter's new play that would be opening at the Lyceum Theater in October. Robert was in a good mood. He had written two novels by this point and would now be starring in his first Broadway play.

Joanna was also in a good mood; she could get used to these fancy New York hotels. Robert had treated her to the Plaza last time, but she liked this one even more. The Plaza was opulent, screaming of wealth— "airs and graces," Robert called it—but the Algonquin had a more subtle charm. It oozed sophistication. With its low ceilings, dark paneling, and plush sofas, one could imagine sipping tea in a British outpost at the turn of the century. Guests of the Algonquin were intellectuals with no need to show off (and by making this point, they were doing just that).

Robert bounded outside when the taxis arrived. Joanna watched through the lobby window as doors were flung open and men and women sidled onto the street, hugging and kissing. She had grown used to this—even Robert did it. It was like a carefully choreographed dance: First, they would kiss each other on both cheeks, smacking lips loudly; then they would step back and look each other up and down admiringly; lastly, they would take turns remarking on how they had simply *adored* their latest play . . . or film . . . or novel . . . with the words *marvelous* and *darling* sprinkled in generously.

It reminded Joanna of J. M. Barrie's play, *Peter Pan*. He had named the family Darling, not only poking fun at English parents (Barrie was a Scotsman) but also at the actors who portrayed them.

"And who can blame them?" she decided. In Cornwall, Robert had performed before classmates and parents, who all had low expectations. But now he was in front of audiences in London and New York, doctors and lawyers, teachers and businessmen . . . sophisticated people who paid good money and expected to see something special. The pressure was enormous. She could see the toll it took on her brother on those rare occasions when Robert let down his guard. When seen like this, all the cooing was understandable, necessary even. These people needed constant boosts to their confidence—they had to truly believe they were special in order to get up in front of an audience, night after night, no matter what had gone wrong previously.

The group came bursting into the lobby, laughing gaily, and glided into their seats. The men wore slacks and jackets with button-down shirts open at the collar. The women wore dresses and had on plenty of jewelry and makeup. Joanna's only nod to fashion was a little lipstick, but these women smelled like a perfume counter at Macy's. Buttons were loosened and cigarettes lit; fingers signaled a nearby waiter for drinks; introductions were made, and everyone settled into their seats comfortably, ready to howl with laughter.

There was Harold Pinter, the playwright, along with his actress wife, Ada. There were Donald Pleasence and Alan Bates, who would be starring with Robert in the fall. And there was one other woman, an attractive

American actress who did not give her name, apparently assuming Joanna already knew her.

"Tell me, Robert, darling," the young actress said, stirring her drink with the tip of her finger, "which girl are you going to marry? Jen or Mary?"

Joanna cringed, but Robert was in his element, brash and confident, ready to parry every thrust. "Whichever gives me a boy," he said, laughing loudly. Heads turned across the lobby. Everyone could see these were important people . . . and British, no less. "You can punch above your weight in America when you have a British accent," Robert liked to say.

"I suppose you could attempt to defend that remark," Pinter said with a smile. "But I don't believe you will. Robert, your position is indefensible. I shall put it to you simply: You must marry the woman, not the child."

"Hear, hear," Ada said, raising her glass. Joanna looked at her more closely and realized she was the only one in the group who did not seem happy. Her smile was wan and haggard.

"I don't know if that's true," the young actress said. "Men come and go, but children are with you forever." She blew a ring of smoke into a dark corner above her head.

"I'm in love with Mary, to be truthful," Robert said, "but I hate the idea of divorce. Still, I have three *girls* . . ." His voice trailed off.

"Why do you say it like that?" Joanna asked sharply, and the group turned to her. It might prove interesting to have Robert's sister with them this evening, they were thinking.

"Say it like what?" Robert asked.

"Like having girls is a bad thing," Joanna said. "They'll be the ones supporting you in your old age, you know. Boys don't do that."

"I agree," the young actress said. "Every man should have girls. It's the only way you will be adored forever."

"A man is not a man until he has a boy," Robert said. "You should know, Joey. You have four boys; you've proved your manhood."

The group paused, wondering if there would be a family spat. Half of them thought it might spoil the evening, while the other half desperately wanted to see it. But Joanna only laughed. She was used to Robert's needling.

"I have six daughters, you know," Pleasence said. "Does that mean I am not a man?" The group paused again, considered his words, and burst out laughing.

"What do you love about Mary?" Bates asked, turning serious. He was extraordinarily handsome, Joanna realized. She gazed at him for a moment, admiring his sharp, chiseled features and jet-black hair that curled across his forehead. Then she caught herself and looked away.

"I'll tell you what I love about Mary," Robert said. "She carries herself like a woman, but she's got the backbone of a man. She's my equal in every way. You know me—I'm not one of those men who just wants a woman to stay at home. I want someone with ambition."

"I don't think you understand men, Robert," Ada said. "*Every* man wants a strong woman; you're not the only one. But I don't believe it's because you want someone who is your equal. I believe it is to prove your masculinity, to show your male friends that you can handle a strong woman."

"Like *Taming of the Shrew*?" the young actress asked.

"Exactly."

"What if both women give you a daughter?" Bates asked.

"Then I'll have to keep trying until I get it right," Robert said.

"Robert, you are incorrigible," the young actress said.

"I will say this in Robert's defense," Joanna said. "I have four sons, as Robert so eloquently pointed out, and my husband could not be happier. I think you're right, Ada; it proves their masculinity."

"Where are the feminists when we need them?" Ada asked.

"I like to think of myself as a male feminist," Robert said. "Equal opportunity and equal pay for equal work and equal talent."

"Yes, but do you think women have equal talent?" Joanna asked.

Robert considered this. "Certainly, my sisters have talent," he said. "But I didn't know any other intelligent girls until I joined the theater."

"In other words," Joanna said, "the only intelligent women are those within your own personal circle."

"It's an affliction," Bates said. "We men grew up being told we were the center of the universe. You can't blame us for it; we had no choice but to try and meet expectations. And yes, some of us succumb to temptation and believe we are superior."

Joanna turned to Robert. "You can't be a male feminist if you don't believe women are as intelligent as men."

"Don't get hysterical, Joey," Robert said. "I didn't say that."

Joanna looked at him sharply. "Et tu, Brutus? Funny how that word only applies to women. Hysterical, from *hysterectomy*: Its roots are in women's problems."

"I hadn't thought of that," Bates said. "Words can be a weapon."

"There are a lot of phrases embedded in our language," Joanna said, "for the sole purpose of preserving a group's power."

"Such as?"

"Take *male chauvinism* and *butch feminism*," she said. "Both are disparaging terms—one coined by women and the other by men. But it goes much deeper. For a boy to be called a sissy is to put him down for being weak, like his sister. But for a girl to be a tomboy, that suggests she has the energy of a boy, and it is a compliment."

"I want my girls to be tomboys," Robert said.

"Not me," Pleasence said. "I like girls just the way they are."

"How do you think this came about?" Ada asked. "What is it about men that leads them to strut about so much?"

Joanna considered it. "Simplistically," she said, "I would say it goes back to the cavemen: The bigger and stronger you were, the more likely you were to survive. And equally important, the more likely those around you would also survive. Men are bigger and stronger, so when brawn mattered more than brains, they were the kings."

Robert raised his glass. "Here's to kings," he said.

"But as intelligence became important," Joanna continued, "it made them uneasy. No one likes to give up power. That's why women were denied education for so long. When you can keep a group in ignorance, you can control them. But ever since education was opened to women, it's obvious that men and women are equally intelligent."

Ada raised her glass. "Here's to queens," she said.

"Hear, hear," Bates said, clinking his glass against Ada's. "It must be hard to give up privilege. I should think any group in power would find it difficult."

"I saw it in South Africa," Joanna said. "The whites do all sorts of things to stay in power. But it's true everywhere. Whoever is in power wants to keep it that way. The rich do it, and perhaps even the talented." Joanna swept her finger in a circle around the group; they were the talented.

"You sound like a socialist," Pinter said.

"In theory," Joanna said, nodding. "I agree with William Morris: Blue-collar workers should receive the same pay as white-collar workers. I know it's naïve, but I was influenced by Victorian protest literature as a teenager. I have veered away since then, as it doesn't work in practice."

"'From each according to their ability, to each according to their needs,'" Pleasence said. "But in reality, it becomes work as little as possible and take as much as you can."

"Yes," Joanna said, "but in theory, they were right, don't you think?"

Pleasence nodded.

"So, what is it, Robert?" Ada asked. "Do you need someone to carry on your name?"

"That's part of it, yes. I don't think it's too much to ask. I want the Shaw name to be carried on. Joanna will only have Myers's and Liz will only have Russell's."

"There's still Sandy," Joanna pointed out.

Robert laughed. "Sandy will have nothing but girls, mark my words. You and Liz will be the only Shaws to have boys."

"A king needs his heir, is that it?" Ada asked. She turned to Joanna. "Why is it that we women change our names? Are we just feeding their superiority? Enabling them?"

"There's no such thing as an enabler," Robert said. "Everyone's responsible for themselves."

"Very well," Ada said. "Then it is agreed. Men are responsible for their own misguided feelings of superiority."

Robert laughed and raised his glass. "Here's to women coming out on top," he said with a smile. And the talk returned to lighter topics, as glasses clinked and drinks flowed until late in the night.

That October, Joanna returned to New York for opening night and was astounded at the transformation. The people from the Algonquin, who seemed so pleasant and normal, had become something else entirely: Pleasence was a revolting old man, an amoral bum who took advantage of Robert's character; Bates was nasty and sadistic, ridiculing the tramp and delighting in his misfortune; and Robert was his deeply troubled brother, Aston, suffering from electric shock therapy.

For Joanna, the highlight was Aston's soliloquy in the second half of the play, when he talked about a man—a doctor, he presumed—who had conducted some sort of examination. The doctor showed him some papers and spoke of a complaint. He indicated they would be doing something to Aston because of the complaint. Gazing into space, his jaw clenching and unclenching, Robert spoke in halting words:

> We've decided, he said, that in your interests there's only one course we can take. He said . . . but I can't . . . exactly remember . . . how he put it . . . he said, we're going to do something to your brain.

After the play, Joanna joined the group in a grubby café while they waited for the reviews. For the first time in her life, her gushing was genuine. She had loved the play. She had loved Robert's performance. And they were rewarded; when *The New York Times* arrived, Pinter read it aloud. The review likened the production to a Samuel Beckett play, noting the current of rage bubbling just beneath the surface. It spoke of the play's intelligence and compassion and how the audience laughed at the mess everyone was making, even as they were drawn into Pinter's angry protest.

"Well, I like that!" Pinter said. He continued reading.

> The play starts like a comedy, but the laughter is mordant and gradually turns into scorn, pity, and sorrow. Donald Pleasence delivers a superb performance as the derelict, Robert Shaw as the withdrawn brother, and Alan Bates as the wild extrovert . . . all conveying the ribald laughter and bitter grief that Pinter has poured into this play.

When he finished, the four men—Harold Pinter, Donald Pleasence, Alan Bates, and Robert Shaw—just stood and looked from one to the other. No one said anything. Their nervous anticipation had been replaced by something else, but Joanna was not sure if it was triumph or relief. Perhaps it was both.

"You were all magnificent," she said. "Simply marvelous!"

Chapter 11

-≪≪◆≫≫-

The Angel of
Broadway

[1958–1968]

When Joanna turned down the offer of marriage from Wilson!, he left Philadelphia and she assumed that would be the last of it. He did not return to England, however. Instead, Wilson! moved to New York and began dating the daughter of a real estate tycoon, Roger Stevens. Stevens was known as the "Angel of Broadway" because he financed Broadway productions, including hits like *West Side Story* and *Cat on a Hot Tin Roof.*

Even after moving into the Stevens' penthouse apartment, however, Wilson! continued calling Joanna. It did not matter what she said, it did not matter that she was now married to Walt—he would not leave her alone. Worst of all, he was now using the family's personal phone, and when Stevens overheard him talking to Joanna one day, he traced the call and rang her up.

"Is this Joanna Myers?"

"Yes."

Without further introduction, Stevens unloaded. "How dare you ruin my daughter's life," he screamed. "How dare you engage in an extra-marital affair with Frank Wilson. Do you know he is dating my daughter?

I believe you do, and yet you still encourage him. What kind of a woman are you? You are a disgrace, that's what you are, the way you interfere with other people's lives."

"But," Joanna said, "but, but, but . . ."

She was unable to get in another word. Stevens hung up abruptly, leaving her staring at the phone. She looked up to find Walt staring at her. "Wrong number," she mumbled.

Wilson! later broke up with the Stevens' daughter and returned to England but not before delivering one final missive to Joanna. She received a book in the mail one day, titled *W. B. Yeats and Tradition*. The author was Frank Wilson. On the inside cover, the dedication read:

> For Joanna, Perch' io non spero di tornar già mai.
> [Translation] For Joanna, Now all hope is lost.

In the fall of 1966, Robert and Joanna were in a hotel room, sipping cocktails, when they heard a news bulletin:

> Pope Paul VI has absolved all Jews, living and dead, for the death of Christ. Only those Jews who were present at the Crucifixion will now be held responsible. The pope added that despite this, he hopes that Jews will one day join Christians in celebrating the one true God.

"Did he just say the pope has forgiven the Jews?" Robert asked.

"Apparently," Joanna said.

"Jesus Christ, it should be the other way around."

She laughed. "That's an ironic way to put it."

Robert could not stop talking about it that day. "My God, it is the Jews who have been persecuted throughout history. What the bloody hell is the pope thinking? *He* should be the one who is being absolved, not the other way round."

The more they discussed it, the angrier Robert became. A year later, he published his fourth novel, *The Man in the Glass Booth*.

Joanna was taken aback when she read it. She was not sure if it was the height of creativity or complete madness. Robert had taken a story about the pope forgiving the Jews and turned it into a novel about a Holocaust survivor, Arthur Goldman, who pretends to be a Nazi general named Dorf. The hero/villain fabricates his own history in order to be put on trial—in a glass booth, for his own protection—so he can tell the world what happened in the concentration camps.

The story was interesting enough, but Joanna thought the characters were more like caricatures than real people. When Robert asked her what she thought, she demurred. "It was marvelous," she said.

Robert knew his sister too well. "Come on, Joey, tell me what you think."

She answered carefully. "The story is complex and interesting, but I thought it was a bit melodramatic. Your other novels were about real people, but this seemed almost fantastical. The trial of a Holocaust survivor, a glass cage, a man who believes himself a Nazi war criminal . . ."

Joanna paused. She had a sudden inspiration. "Have you thought of turning it into a play?" she asked. Robert shook his head. "The drama might work better on a stage. That is traditionally where larger-than-life figures belong. Imagine a glass cage in front of an audience, with a man undressing before their eyes. That could be very popular, hmm?"

A year later, Robert was in a London restaurant with two of his closest friends, Harold Pinter and Donald Pleasence, discussing the play he had just written. Their plan was to start in small cities in England, then go to London, and then, if everything came together perfectly, they would bring it to Broadway. While they ate and talked about their plans, two women were seated nearby, observing them. One of them was Antonia Fraser, who would become Harold Pinter's wife.

In the opening paragraph of her memoir, *Must You Go*, Fraser describes that meeting:

> The three men were Robert Shaw, Donald Pleasence, and Harold [Pinter]; they were discussing Robert's play, *The Man in the Glass Booth*, in which Harold would direct

Donald. My companion admired Robert Shaw intensely: the handsome redheaded star who was said to do his own stunt work and embodied machismo. Apparently I said thoughtfully, "I'll take the dark one."

When *The Man in the Glass Booth* opened on Broadway, Joanna was back in New York for another opening night. This time, however, it was not to see Robert on stage but to watch a play he had written. Robert would be sitting in the back of the theater, powerless to do anything after the curtain had gone up. Like writers everywhere, he would be biting his nails and praying the actors did what they were supposed to do and that the audience (and critics) enjoyed it.

Joanna arrived a little late and found Robert in the lobby, deep in a conversation with an older gentleman. He waved her over. "Joey, you look lovely," he said.

"I'm sorry I'm late. I was scrambling for a dress again."

"You're not late at all. You are precisely on time, as a good English-woman should be. Let me introduce you to Roger Stevens. Roger is one of the most important producers in New York. Some call him the Angel of Broadway, but I simply call him my angel."

Joanna stretched out her hand. "Hello, I'm Joanna Myers."

Stevens began to extend his hand, then pulled back. He turned to Robert. "I thought your sister's name was Joanna *Shaw*?"

"Yes, I sometimes forget to use her married name," Robert said. "She is a married woman now, aren't you Joey?"

Stevens turned back to Joanna. "Are you from Philadelphia?" he asked.

And then it hit her: The Angel of Broadway . . . *Wilson!*

"Are you Roger Stevens," she asked, "whose daughter was with Frank Wilson?"

"Yes," Stevens answered grimly.

Robert was delighted. He had not noticed the sudden tension, being distracted by others in the lobby who needed his attention. "This is wonderful," he said, "I had no idea you two knew each other. Roger, you must hear Joey's thoughts on the play. She was the person who inspired it. My muse." And Robert was off, glancing over his shoulder to give Joanna a thumbs-up.

Joanna looked at Stevens. Stevens looked at Joanna. She began to say something. He raised his hand. *There is nothing you can say to excuse your heinous crime*, he indicated.

They found their seats, the lights went down, the curtain went up, and Joanna sank into her seat, trying to make herself appear as small as possible. A hum of expectation filled the theater, but she did not hear it. All she could think about was the image of Roger Stevens, suddenly leaping onto his seat in front of everyone, pointing a finger at her, and screaming, *"J'accuse!"*

Joanna barely noticed when Donald Pleasence entered the stage and began one of the great performances of his career. She could not remember a single thing that happened in the first act. She fiddled with her playbill. She glanced at her watch. She looked at her shoes.

Intermission brought some relief. She and Stevens made their way stiffly into the lobby. He purchased two glasses of wine and handed one to her—always the gentleman. Still without a word to each other, they moved into a corner and sipped their wine.

Finally, Joanna blurted out, "I absolutely hated Frank Wilson."

Stevens looked at her coldly. "He told me you were in love with him."

Some of the wine in Joanna's throat came out her mouth. Some came out her nose. Some of it landed on Stevens's white tuxedo shirt, although she could not tell if it was from her mouth or her nose. She gasped in horror and began wiping it with her napkin, but Stevens brushed her away.

"Forget the shirt. Tell me why you hated Frank Wilson."

Joanna took a deep breath and told him the story of why she went to South Africa, why she taught at Adams College, how Wilson! was the only one on the staff that everyone hated, and how he had become infatuated with her for reasons unknown and followed her to America.

There is no bond so powerful as one forged by the mutual disdain of a fellow human being. Their feud was over. Stevens cleaned up his shirt as best he could, and they returned to the play. The second half was far more enjoyable for Joanna.

Afterward, she joined Robert in another grubby little café to await the reviews. Outside, taxicabs beeped their horns while the after-Broadway theater crowd milled about on the sidewalk. Inside, actors paced back and forth, or bolstered their spirits with spirits, or simply sat by themselves, brooding.

Robert was at a table with Harold and Donald. No one said very much. When the first paper arrived, Pinter leaped up. As the director, he had the honor of being the first to read it. "This is Clive Barnes, in *The New York Times*," he said to the group—and he read aloud:

> If you will pardon the frankness, this is going to be a diffi-
> cult notice to write. On the cover of the playbill for Robert
> Shaw's play, *The Man in the Glass Booth*, there is a diagram-
> matic picture of a man in a glass booth. The man is neatly
> split down the middle, and the drawing symbolizes the
> play in more ways than one . . . it is a fantastically effective
> vehicle for the bravura acting of Donald Pleasence and the
> subtly virtuoso directing of Harold Pinter.

"Well, I like that!" Pinter said. He read on, and with each paragraph, it got better and better. Barnes compared the play to an Alfred Hitchcock movie, he noted that it was engrossing and would be much talked about, and he even said that it would make a fine movie (as it one day would become).

For the second time in the span of a few years, Joanna found herself in a grubby little café with these three men after an opening night perfor-mance. For the second time, she saw a mixture of triumph and relief on their faces. And for the second time, all she could think to say was, "You were all marvelous."

Robert was rewarded with a year-long run on Broadway, a Tony nom-ination, and subsequent performances in several other cities, including one at The Old Globe theater in San Diego, where Leonard Nimoy, of

Star Trek fame, played the lead role of Goldman/Dorf. Nimoy would later say he was drawn to the play because it questions the need for vengeance, the need to say, "You and I are better than they" and "they started it"—when in fact "we are all we."

[1968-1974]

In the years leading up to *JAWS*, Robert and Joanna entered middle age. This changed them. Do any of us truly know our parents? We are all born long after their youth, after those carefree days when everything seems possible. As the years rolled by, both of them began experiencing the stresses of marriage, family, and finances. And there was another stress they had not anticipated: the increasing awareness of their own mortality.

Joanna began stopping at the local bars on her way home from work. Her kids were old enough to look after each other now, and her friends and colleagues provided lots of raucous laughter. It all seemed natural, the fruits of one's labor. Robert began telling people he could not go on stage without having a drink.

Robert confessed to Joanna that he was thinking of getting a divorce. Joanna told him the same thing. But she also knew her situation was different. Margaret Mead once wrote that everyone should have three spouses: the first for passion and excitement in youth; the second for career and raising a family; and the third for companionship and solace in old age. Robert could afford to have three wives—and indeed, that is what he did. Joanna could not afford it. She and Walt never had enough money, despite the fact that they both worked. They became trapped in a vicious circle: The more their family grew, the tighter the money; the tighter the money, the less they could afford to get a divorce; and the less they could afford to get a divorce, the more children they had.

At work, Joanna was surrounded by homosexual men. An all-women's school is a safe haven for them, and many of those men became her best friends. Yet, when she heard them canvassing for marital rights and rites, she would tell them, "Why bother? If you marry and adopt kids, all you will get out of it is the mess and pain of divorce. And the more kids you adopt, the more difficult it becomes."

One evening, Joanna was speaking to a married couple and shared her frustrations. To her surprise, they told her they were in the same predicament—fighting every day and considering a divorce. Joanna sympathized with them. "Our problem," she said, "is that Walt and I can't get a divorce because neither of us are willing to give up the children."

The couple looked at her in surprise. "We have the same problem," the man said, "but in our case, we can't get a divorce because neither of us wants to *take* the children."

In the spring of 1974, Robert and Joanna found themselves in a hotel room in New York, once again sipping drinks and complaining about their lives. Joanna made what she thought was an innocent comment: "You can't possibly understand what I'm going through, Robert. You don't have anything to worry about."

Robert gave her an odd look.

"That's right," she continued, "you have no idea what it's like to struggle. Men have all the advantages. I work as hard as my husband, and yet I get paid less. I have to run home after work every day to take care of the children. And in between, I'm the one who has to do all the cooking and cleaning."

"Do you do all those things?" Robert asked in amusement.

"Well, not the cleaning part," Joanna admitted. "Our house is a mess. But everything else. You were always the golden child. You never had to make a single sacrifice."

Robert suddenly turned cold. "You don't think I've made sacrifices?"

"What have you given up?"

"Freedom," he said. "The freedom to have a bad day. What happens to you when you have a bad day? You come back and fix it, right? I don't have that luxury. When I have a bad day, my picture is in the tabloids, and people say that's who I am."

"Yes, okay, I've seen that."

"My temper, my ego, my eagerness to compete and win . . . they all go hand in hand. I keep grabbing for the brass ring, but I can't get off the carousel. People want me on there for their amusement. Sometimes they clap; sometimes they boo."

"I don't boo."

"I know you don't, but others do. I wake up every morning knowing I have to deliver another great performance. It doesn't matter what I've done the night before. It's always a fresh audience." He shook his head. "I don't sleep well."

"If it's any consolation," Joanna said, "I'm in a lousy job, my marriage is a disaster, and Walt and I are completely broke. I'm drinking every day. At least you're making money."

"I'm not making enough money," Robert said. "You can get used to being rich as easily as being poor. I spend it faster than I make it." He thought for a moment. "Of course, I prefer getting used to being rich. But it sucks the life out of you. I haven't written anything in five years."

"You've won awards." Joanna pointed out. "Writing awards, acting awards. And you have a loving family."

"I push my kids as hard as I push myself. They don't take it well."

"No one takes it well," Joanna said, smiling.

"I don't know if my children even love me."

"Now that is the first untrue thing you've said. You'll never lose your children."

"I hope not."

Robert sighed. They stared at each other for a moment, lost in their own thoughts. When their eyes met again, they burst out laughing.

"Our life is really awful, isn't it," Joanna said, wiping away tears.

"I guess so," Robert chortled.

A few hours later, Robert made his final appearance on Broadway. It was Strindberg's *The Dance of Death* at the Vivian Beaumont Theater. In the afternoon, he had been morose and reflective. In the evening, he was full of energy and received a standing ovation.

Life has no script. Sometimes a downward spiral ends in a crash. Other times, it turns upward unexpectedly. That summer, the lives of

Robert and Joanna were turned upside down, though in different ways. It was the summer when Richard Nixon resigned; when a skeleton named Lucy was found in Africa, proving Darwin's theory of evolution; when personal computers were first introduced to the world.

And it was the summer when Robert filmed a movie on Martha's Vineyard. It should have been a minor horror film, but it became a masterpiece. It should have been Robert's ultimate triumph in life, but it hastened his death. While Robert struggled to achieve artistic perfection, Joanna visited him on the set of *JAWS*, witnessed the demons eating away at him, and tried to save him. But she could only save herself.

PART III

JAWS &
ROBERT SHAW

To be an artist means never to avert one's eyes.

— Akira Kurosawa

Chapter 12

-‹‹‹◆›››-

Stepped in Blood

[Early summer 1974]

Robert was on the veranda of his bungalow with Ned Lynch. It had been a long day of filming, and they were now relaxing and sipping drinks as the sun settled down behind Chappaquiddick Bay. Below them, the ferry that connected the two islands was making its last crossing, trailing a series of ripples across the dappled red and orange water. "Look how the light is filtered," Ned pointed out. "There's nothing like it. You don't find it any other time of day, not even the morning." He took a deep breath. "Everything is so crisp, I absolutely love it."

"Yes, sure," Robert answered.

Ned turned to his friend. "What's on your mind, old man? Enough wallowing in self-pity."

Robert smiled. Ned had a way of pointing out exactly what he was feeling. The two had known each other for twenty years, beginning on the set of *The Buccaneers* and progressing to the point where Ned was Robert's regular stand-in. His job was to make sure that everything was in its proper place before Robert stepped onto the set: that the lighting was just right, the camera angles were correct, and everyone understood what Robert would be doing in the scene. But Ned was also much more than that—he had become Robert's personal secretary, his valet, and arguably his closest friend.

And Ned was right: Robert was feeling lousy. *JAWS* was supposed to be his break into stardom, his first major role with a major studio, but the production had been nothing but a series of disasters. The shark was not working, the weather was not cooperating, and the extra salary Robert had negotiated, combined with his earnings on Broadway earlier in the year, meant that he would owe a boatload of U.S. taxes before it was all over.

But that was not the worst of it. The real disaster, in his mind, was that the monologue he was supposed to deliver—about the sailors on the USS *Indianapolis* who had been eaten by sharks during World War II— had gone through a dozen rewrites and was still not right. The original concept had come from Howard Sackler, whose play, *The Great White Hope*, had been on Broadway the same year as *The Man in the Glass Booth* (and to Robert's chagrin, had beaten him out for the Tony Award). Everyone thought Sackler's idea was great, and a dozen writers had tried expanding it—including Spielberg and Gottlieb, John Milius, and several other people whom Spielberg had asked for help—but no one had been able to put together the right dialogue, with the right level of tension and raw emotion, to make the scene truly special.

Robert thought the speech would elevate his character into something Shakespearean, but now he was afraid it would make him look like a buffoon. He said as much to Ned, but his friend only shrugged. "You'll figure out that little speech, Robert," he said.

"Even if I do, what does it matter if they can't get the bloody shark working?"

"Forget the shark, that isn't your problem. Other people are working on that; there's nothing you can do about it. Focus on your speech. That's where you have control."

"Ned, you don't understand movies."

"Oh? Then please educate me, dear fellow. I would love to learn how they make movies."

"Don't give me that. You know exactly what I mean. Sharks sell tickets. Shakespearean soliloquys do not."

"Methinks thou doth protest too much."

"Do you know how much money I made for *The Caretaker*?"

"Yes. Nothing."

"And do you know how much money I made for *The Birthday Party*?"

"Yes. Less than nothing."

"That's right. I had to pay for the marketing on that one. But this movie has a chance. IF they can get the bloody shark working."

They continued debating the subject until Ned suddenly stood up. "Robert, we are not getting anywhere sitting here by ourselves and going round and round in circles. I suggest we go and mingle with the natives."

Robert needed little encouragement. They made their way to the nearest bar and found several members of the film crew already there. In one corner, a Ping-Pong game was in progress, and they found a table nearby.

"Mind if I join you?" someone asked. They looked up to find the movie's producer, Richard Zanuck, standing next to them. Zanuck did not wait for a response. He slid in next to them and signaled someone for drinks.

"Cheers," he said, when the drinks arrived. "Robert, how are you feeling? You don't look so good."

"It's that mechanical beast," Robert grunted. "You need to get it working."

"Fair enough."

"And we're spending far too much money on this island. Building an entire town, renting out half the rooms. You're not going to have enough money to promote it properly."

"Fair enough."

"But other than that," Ned said, "everything is going swimmingly."

Zanuck laughed. Then he asked Robert, "What do you think of the *Indianapolis* speech?"

"You know what I think. It's awful."

"I read the latest version today," the producer said. "It seemed okay to me."

"I read it," Robert said. "It's okay if you want to give the audience a history lesson. But otherwise it's still awful."

"We have to explain what happened."

"No, we don't."

"What, then?"

"Richard, people don't give a damn about history. They'll open a book if they want that."

"What, then?" Zanuck repeated.

"They want to know how it *affected* Quint. What it did to him. How it ate away at him until he became the mean son of a bitch we see in the film."

"Steve tells me it's critical."

Robert shrugged, but before he could say anything further, the Ping-Pong table opened up. His eyes lit up. "Do you play?" Zanuck asked.

"Is the pope Catholic?" Robert answered.

"You're good, then?"

"I'm okay. You?"

"I'm okay."

They both grinned, and soon a fierce game was underway. Each smacked the ball as if their lives depended on it. Robert won the first few points and gloated. "I had no backhand when I started, Chief. Look at me now. You're a dead man."

"Shut up and give me the ball."

The crew watched with growing interest as the intensity rose further. When Zanuck won the final point, he raised his arms in triumph. "A rematch," Robert roared. "You must give me a rematch."

The producer only shook his head and walked away. Robert looked like he would physically grab him and drag him back to the table, but a member of the crew jumped in before he could do anything, and Robert became absorbed in another game.

"Not very competitive, is he?" Zanuck said, sitting next to Ned.

"He's been like that for as long as I've known him," Ned said. "I hope you don't find him rude."

"Of course he's rude. That's what I like about him. He's real."

"A lot of people hate it."

"Not me. He and I have the same flaw," Zanuck said. "We're competitive sons of bitches. But you know what? It's also what drives us, so I have no regrets."

They turned back to the game and watched as Robert pounded the ball, gloating when he won a point and cursing when he lost one. Then he became so frustrated that he smashed the ball with his paddle, crushing it. The bar fell silent. Robert looked up sheepishly.

"Sorry," he said. He left the smashed ball on the table and rejoined his companions. "I never lose two in a row," he lamented.

"I'll give you a chance to lose another one tomorrow," Zanuck said.

"That's the spirit!" Robert leaned over and motioned the producer to come closer. "What is this I hear about shutting down the production?" he whispered.

"Like you said, we're over budget."

"I know that, of course I know that. But, Richard, I've done enough films to know they always find a way to get them out."

"Have you ever made a movie on the ocean?" Zanuck asked.

"Well, no."

"Then don't be so sure. Look at it from the studio's point of view. We're making a movie about a shark, right?" Robert nodded. "But the shark doesn't work. And we have a hero who is obsessed with sharks, right?" Robert nodded. "But we can't explain why." Robert shrugged. "Meanwhile," Zanuck said, "the bills are piling up."

Robert took a long breath and looked him in the eye. "Richard, this picture has more potential than anything I've ever done, and that includes *The Sting*. You've got to keep it going." He flourished his hand in the air. "I am stepped so far in blood, returning is as tedious as to continue forward."

"That's from *Macbeth*, if I'm not mistaken," Zanuck pointed out. Robert nodded. "Remind me what happened at the end of that story?"

"It wasn't pretty, I'll give you that," Robert said, "but I know where this road leads. This picture will have a happy ending, I swear to you. But only if you keep it going."

Zanuck shrugged. "I'm doing my best."

Chapter 13

Wilder & Wilder

[The following day]

"Where are we off to tonight?" Ned asked. He and Robert were back on the veranda once again, enjoying another sunset and sipping on more drinks.

"I don't know about you," Robert said, "but I have a date."

"Oh? With whom?"

"Thornton Wilder."

"The writer? I didn't know you were friends."

"We are very good friends, actually."

"The man is a legend. What has he won, two Pulitzer Prizes?"

"Three, in fact. He is absolutely brilliant and one of my favorite people." Robert drew a crumpled envelope from his pocket and pulled out a letter, handwritten in multiple shades of colorful ink. "Let me read you something he wrote me."

"You just happen to have that with you?" Ned asked in surprise.

"Yes. Something wrong with that?"

Ned waggled his head. "Seems a bit unusual."

"Listen to this:

Querido Don Roberto. I have remained long under the spell of your taut and lacerating performances. The past two nights, Peter and I got up at five in the morning and wrote and wrote for hours, hellbent to emulate such a standard.

"He does seem to like you," Ned said. Robert continued to read.

I should apologize to you for my wooden stupidity about the party. I so love the gesture and ceremony of hospitality that I blundered in like a steamroller and rejoiced in dispersing the loaves and the fishes. But I'm not so repentant as I ought to be, because by table shifting I was able to spend another hour with you.

Ned put his arm on Robert's. "Old man, the fellow is in *love* with you!"

Robert chuckled. "You don't understand. He's seventy-five years old, more like an uncle to me."

Ned shrugged. "If you say so. By the way, who is Peter?"

Robert shook his head. "I haven't figured that out yet."

The Black Dog Tavern was new to Martha's Vineyard. Only the most seasoned travelers knew about it—they were the ones who came to the island every year, the ones who made it their perennial destination during the summer, the ones who thought of it as a second home. Thornton Wilder was one of those people. He liked to say he arrived before the blue fish were running north and never left before they were making their way south again.

Tonight, he was in his favorite spot at the table by the fireplace. A bottle of champagne and two glasses stood before him. Wilder liked this seat because it gave him a view of the entire room. With his white hair and round glasses, he had the appearance of a wise old owl surveying the world. A keen observer of human nature, his eyes radiated intelligence, curiosity, and kindness.

Across the room, a singer was belting out a tune. It was one of the
local musicians—unencumbered by a desire to become famous, the man
was happy to eke out a living and enjoy the beauty of the island all year
round. Tonight, he was singing Bobby Darin's version of "Mack the
Knife," slightly off-key:

> Oh the shark, babe, has such teeth, dear
> And he shows them pearly white
> Just a jackknife has old Macheath, babe
> And he keeps it out of sight
> You know when that shark bites with his teeth, babe
> Scarlet billows start to spread
> Fancy gloves, though, wears old Macheath, babe
> So there's never, never a trace of red.

It was into this setting that Robert made his entrance. He paused
at the door for a moment, observing the singer with some amusement.
He looked around the bar, taking in the various people, then spotted his
friend in the corner. "Started without me, have you, Thornt?"

"Making up for lost time," Wilder said. "I've been under house arrest."

"Oh? On what charges?"

"Disorderly fluid in the lungs. A wretched cold. I find it far more
difficult, in my old age, to shake these common ailments."

Robert sat down and poured two glasses of champagne. "Here's to
freedom from arrest," he said. They toasted.

"How's that delightful family of yours?" Wilder asked.

"Everyone's fine."

"And the movie? Will it be the jewel in your crown?"

"I used to think so," Robert said. "No longer. My guess is it will be a
summer thriller, nothing more. Maybe not even that."

"I thought your character had a Shakespearean quality to him?"

"I thought so too. Turns out he's missing something."

"No pearl in the oyster?"

"No spice in the stew."

"What is missing?"

"A heart and soul."

"That *is* a problem."

"You know better than anyone," Robert said. "All great characters need that one defining moment, that one scene where they unburden themselves. Where the audience finally sees them for who they are, with all their fears and foibles exposed to the world."

Wilder was no stranger to a great soliloquy. "Shall we work on it together?"

Robert's eyes opened wide. "Yes! Where would you begin?"

"I will share with you Wilder's Law number 173. Normally, I only dispense my own advice, but in this case, I will make an exception and quote from Billy Wilder."

"The other Wilder."

"Spiritually, we are cousins; otherwise, no relation. At least once, at every dinner party where our paths happen to cross, the man sits me down and explains that every story must start with a bang."

Robert chuckled. The thought that anyone, even Billy Wilder, would offer advice to Thornton Wilder struck him as funny.

"So tell me, Don Roberto, what is the bang that starts your soliloquy?"

Robert thought for a moment. "Literally, it is when the ship gets hit by a torpedo." He clapped his hands together. "Bang!"

"Okay, let's hear it."

Robert thought for a moment, then adopted his Quint accent. "Japanese submarine slammed two torpedoes into our side, Uncle."

"Where?"

"Middle of the Pacific Ocean. We just delivered the bomb, the atomic bomb. The first bomb, the one that blew up Hiroshima."

"And everyone went down with the ship?"

"Eleven hundred men went into the water. Ship sank in ten minutes."

"And there were sharks in the water?"

"Lots of sharks. The water was fairly crawling with them."

"Could the sailors see the sharks?"

Robert dropped out of character for a moment. "Yes, it was brutal. But do you want to know the worst part?"

"What could be worse than being surrounded by sharks?"

Robert went back into character. "The worst part, Uncle, was that no one knew we were there. The mission was so secret, no distress signal had been sent."

Wilder took a long breath. "So those men were in the water for a very long time," he said, "with nothing but sharks to keep them company." He got up and leaned against the table. "Don Roberto, you must write this speech yourself. *You* are the one who will deliver it, so *you* should be the one to write it. You have to feel it in your bones, feel what it meant to watch your friends being eaten like that. Those sharks robbed you of your joy, your humanity."

Robert nodded and raised his glass. "Cheers to that."

Several hours later, the two men left the bar arm in arm. Behind them was a small mountain of champagne bottles, along with much laughter and good cheer. As they stepped outside, they began singing, "Oh the shark, babe, has such teeth, dear, and he shows them pearly white . . ."

"What fun!" Wilder exclaimed.

"I love your stories," Robert said.

"I love *you*," Wilder said.

Robert unhitched his arm and took a step back. The usual twinkle was in his eye. "If my father had lived," he said, "I believe he would have been just like you."

Wilder's body sagged. "Is that how you think of me? As a father?"

"It's a compliment."

"I suppose every tiger has his spots. I just wish they didn't come in so many different shapes and sizes."

"Tigers don't have spots," Robert pointed out. "That's leopards."

"Not in my world."

Robert laughed. As he did so, he stumbled into a trash can, knocking it over with a bang. A police officer looked up. "Hey," he shouted, "I can't have drunks wandering around Vineyard Haven at this hour."

Robert started to respond, but Wilder grabbed his arm. "Please don't confront the man. He is correct, we are drunk. And he has a gun."

Robert grinned. "I would never challenge a keeper of the law." Turning to the policeman, he said, "It is true we have been drinking, Officer. But surely you can see we are in perfect control."

"Doesn't look that way to me."

"What must I do to convince you? Walk a straight line?"

"That's only if you're driving."

"Then allow me to improvise." Robert moved under a nearby streetlamp. He took a step forward. He took a step back. He took a step to one side, then to the other. Soon he was performing a little jig, hopping back and forth in perfect time to a silent beat. When he finished, he looked up and smiled.

"That's pretty good," the policeman admitted. "Can you do it in reverse?"

Robert reversed his steps perfectly. When he came to a stop, he spread his arms and gave a bow. Wilder clapped enthusiastically.

"All right," the policeman said. He was smiling now. "Move along, but please keep it quiet."

"Thank you, Officer. We shall endeavor to do so."

Robert and Wilder moved down the street, where Robert had a car waiting for him. They gave each other a hug. "Remember," Wilder said, "don't let your concerns eat you up."

"And don't you get into any more house arrests," Robert said. "You're too valuable to the art world." He paused. "One more thing." He pulled the envelope from his pocket and waved it in the air.

"What is that?"

"One of your letters. I've been trying to understand something."

"You have one of my letters?" Wilder said. "I am honored."

"You piqued my curiosity. Who's Peter?"

Wilder looked thoughtful. "I suppose I should explain," he said slowly. "Peter is a friend of mine. A very good friend. I've known him for years—we are like brothers. Like twin brothers. Peter is the type of person I can count on, the type who is always there when I need him." Wilder looked at Robert closely. "I keep him in a closet in my pantry and only take him out when I need him. When I need inspiration. Peter is *that* kind of a friend."

He paused. Robert stared at him.

"Do you have anyone like that in your life?" Wilder asked.

Robert did not respond, and Wilder gave him a wistful smile. Then he bowed, twirled his cane, and hobbled away. As he disappeared into the night, Robert nodded his head. "I believe I do."

Ned was still awake and reading a book when Robert burst in. "Ned, I've solved it," he exclaimed.

"Solved what?" But before he could answer, Robert tripped and sprawled on the floor.

"My God, you're drunk!" Ned said, rushing over to help him.

"It was the torpedoes," Robert mumbled.

"Yes, you'll drink anything."

"Thornton's fault, not mine."

"And with anyone." Ned helped him to the sofa. "Robert, old man, you have to stop doing this to yourself."

"You mind your table manners!"

"It's going to kill you!"

"Dammit, Ned, don't you understand? I *have* to do this!"

"Why?"

"Because it's my turn. Everyone else had their turn, this one is mine."

Ned shook his head. "I have no idea what you're talking about."

Robert lay back on the sofa and put his hands behind his head. "That's okay, Ned" he said. "You don't need to understand. I'll figure it out."

Soon, he was snoring peacefully.

Chapter 14

-⟨⟨⟨◆⟩⟩⟩-

We Have Our Picture!

[The following day]

Robert did not go to work the following morning. Instead of being picked up at 6:00 a.m., as was his usual routine, he ambled into the kitchen of the bungalow long after the sun had risen. Ned handed him a coffee. "Not going to work?"

Robert rubbed his head. "They don't need me today," he said. "And in any case, I've got some things I need to get down on paper."

"What's that?"

Robert waved him off and savored his coffee. Then he withdrew to the sitting room, where he had a desk with several pens and reams of paper. He spent nearly the entire day at that table, scribbling down thoughts, crossing things out, and then rewriting them. He captured what he and Wilder had discussed, reviewed prior versions of the *Indianapolis* speech, and wrote and crossed out and rewrote some more.

Throughout the process, his head felt like it was being attacked by hungry sharks. His body felt like it was being chewed up and spat out. *Perhaps it is for the best*, he said to himself more than once.

That evening, Ned drove him to Steven's Spielberg's house. The director had rented a log cabin for the summer, large enough for his senior staff to join him for dinner on most nights in order to plan out the next day's activities. Ned cut the motor while Robert continued to leaf through the crumpled papers on his lap. He rubbed his forehead and winced. "You okay?" Ned asked.

"I feel like shit."

"You look like shit."

"Thanks. I can always count on you, Ned."

"I can bring you back tomorrow."

"No, I need to do this. Semper fi."

"Everything doesn't have to be a battle."

"This one does. Wish me luck."

"Good luck."

Robert walked up the path and knocked on the door. Ned heard a voice call out and saw his friend disappear. The door was left ajar, and he had a sudden inspiration. Opening and closing his car door as quietly as possible, he tiptoed up the path and peeked inside. Spielberg, Dreyfuss, and Zanuck were sitting at a dining room table, facing him. Carl Gottlieb, the screenwriter, was standing to one side, and there was someone in the kitchen—probably Verna Fields, the film's editor; Ned had heard she did most of the cooking.

Robert was at the table with his back to the door. "Apologies for missing today," Ned heard him say.

"No problem, we shot around you," Spielberg said. "What's up?"

"I've been working on that troublesome speech."

"Great, let's hear it."

"My thinking is to get straight to the point. No history lessons."

"Sounds good. Go ahead."

"It starts with a bang. You know, the Wilder approach. The other Wilder."

Spielberg smiled. "Bob, I know you're a good writer. There's no need for preamble. Let's hear what you've got."

Robert spread the paper in front of him. Then he began speaking in his Quint accent.

Japanese submarine slammed two torpedoes into our side.

We were coming back from the island of Tinian, heading

for Leytee Island. Just delivered the Hiroshima bomb. Vessel went down in ten minutes. Eleven hundred men went in the water.

Robert looked up. "Don't stop," Spielberg said.

Didn't see any sharks that first day. Next morning, though, a twelve-footer come around. Know how you tell the size of a shark when you're in the water? Look from the dorsal to the tail and double the length. What we didn't know was that our bomb mission was so secret, no distress signal had been sent!

Robert picked up a saltshaker and looked at it absent-mindedly. No one spoke.

They didn't list us overdue for three days. The sharks, though, they began circling us that first morning. So we organized ourselves into squares—you know, like you see on a calendar, like Napoleon and his Royal Guard at Waterloo. The idea was to start hollering and screaming and slapping the water. Sometimes it worked—sometimes the shark would go away. Sometimes it didn't work—sometimes the shark wouldn't go away. Sometimes that shark would look you right in the eye. You know the thing about a shark? He's got lifeless eyes, black eyes. Doesn't appear to be alive until he bites you. Then you hear that high-pitched scream, and no matter how much hollering and pounding you do, the ocean turns red, and they tear you to pieces.

Verna came out of the kitchen and sat down. Still, no one said anything. Robert's voice cracked now as he spoke.

By the end of the first day, we'd lost a hundred men. I don't know how many sharks, maybe a thousand. They averaged six an hour. On Thursday morning, I spotted a friend, Herbie Robinson. He was from Cleveland, bosun's mate. Thought he was asleep, reached over to wake him. Well, he just bobbed up and down like a top. Been bitten in half.

Later that day, we spotted a plane. He saw us and circled in low, so low that I could see the pilot's face. He was a young man, younger than Mr. Dreyfuss here. Three hours later, another plane arrived and began picking us up. You want to hear something funny? That was when I was most frightened, waiting my turn.

Robert suddenly winced. He had forgotten about his hangover. He shook his head.

I'll never put on a life jacket again. So, eleven hundred men went in the water, three hundred came out, sharks took the rest. July 30th, 1945.

Robert looked up and raised the saltshaker in a mock toast.

Anyway, we delivered the bomb.

For several moments, no one said anything. One person cleared their throat. Another shifted their chair, making a scraping sound on the floor. Then Spielberg pushed back and leaned against the wall. He had a smile on his face.

"I believe we have our picture," he said.

That night, Robert slept well. His speech could not have gone better, and not just because of Spielberg's response. In his own heart, he knew he had come up with something special. He imagined he had saved *JAWS* from disaster.

He dreamed of his father as he slept. He often dreamed about him, but this one was different. In his other dreams, his father always looked depressed but not tonight. Tonight, his dad was alive and happy. Robert sensed that he had been watching him, that he had been peeking through the door of the cabin to hear his speech. He had seen how good he was, how the others in the room had only stared at him with open mouths.

In his dream, Robert felt an arm on his shoulder and looked up into his father's eyes. "Great job, my boy," his father said. "I always knew you would be successful."

PART IV

WAR & SUICIDE

This will be our finest hour.

— Winston Churchill

Chapter 15

Letters from Home

[Summer/Fall 1939]

"Bloody goddamn hell!"

Dr. Shaw sat in his kitchen overlooking Scapa Flow, a hangover forming. *What have I done?* he thought. *I've blown it all to pieces. My family gone. My children gone. What are people going to say?*

He knew what they would say. Orcadians were not as blunt as the Cornish; they kept unpleasant thoughts to themselves. *But they will think it. What a pathetic creature I have become.*

Victoria Street was its usual bustling self that morning. Shoppers came and went, people gathered on benches and exchanged gossip, sailors spun their tales. But no one called out to the doctor any longer. No one stopped to look through the window of his surgery. No patients knocked on his door.

I need to clear my head, he thought. *Need to relax, get a drink.*

A week later, he composed a letter.

27 June 1939
Seaview House, Orkney

To Doreen Avery Shaw
Treworyan House, Cornwall

My dear Doreen,

My heart is broken. I know you do not think much of me, but I shall make clear why I write.

We are at a crossroads, you and I. Our family awaits our decision, with all the innocence of children. You and I built our family together, but there is more work to be done.

Do you remember what you said to me when first we met? That there would be hard work ahead, obstacles. We both understood life has its peaks and valleys; we spoke of building something special, something that would last, the strongest force in nature—a family.

That is why I address you as "my dear." We must rethink our past and choose a different path forward. Take the road less traveled, as the poet says. The opportunity still lies before us.

I must confess that I miss my family. I miss the children. I miss you. I believe you have misjudged me. Men are, by their nature, prone to excess. I do not deny that I enjoy a stiff drink every now and then, but that is common to my gender. It is our yang, our peculiar fervor. It is what enables the world to move upward. And it is more prevalent in men of stature, like myself. The good doctor, they have always called me, and they will call me that again soon. You know this to be true.

I have discovered who my patients are now calling upon. It is an Englishman—not an Orcadian, nor even a Scotsman! I cannot fathom how these good people would put their trust in such a man. I have met him, he is a most studious fellow, and most dull. He is given to endless discourse on the mundane details of the medical profession. He has not one ounce of humor inside his head. He believes only in technique, ignorant to the art of doctoring.

I can assure you, a doctor who does not have a solid undercarriage—who does not possess a bedside manner that brings a smile—will never succeed.

You, of all people, know that bringing a smile to others is the very essence of my character. I was born to it. It will bring me back to my rightful position. The good people of Orkney understand the skills I possess. They will return.

Doreen, I beg you to do the same. Bring the children back. Come home. This is your home, our home. Remember what we committed to each other. Do not go back on your word.

I await your response with the utmost confidence that you will rethink your actions, admit your mistakes, and remember that your life, our life, is here.

Your loving husband,
Thomas Shaw

He got no response. Over the next few weeks, he became increasingly angry. And alone in his house, he also became introspective. *Why do I drink so much?* he wondered. *I never mean to. But then it's Fred or Johnson or somebody, always somebody, suggesting another round.*

The house seemed so empty. In the children's room upstairs, there were only empty beds. He stopped drinking for a month. It was agony, sitting in the kitchen, staring out the window, watching the fishing boats go by . . . day after day, night after night.

I appreciate a strong woman as much as anyone, he said at one point. *That is why I married her. Always made me laugh. What the bloody hell have I done?*

Then he returned to the pub and hit it hard for a week. Afterward, he composed another letter.

13 August 1939
Seaview House, Orkney

To Doreen Avery Shaw
Treworyan House, Cornwall

Mrs. Shaw,

I have come to understand your decision to leave me. I understand my part in our failure. I even know why my patients lost their faith.

For the past several weeks, I resisted the temptation to drink. I was completely successful. I convinced myself I had gained control.

The result? I deemed it time to reward myself—prematurely, it turned out—and returned to the very establishment from whence my troubles sprang. I thought I could share my good fortune with others and raise my glass in a toast to self-control.

I awoke the next morning in a stupor. I was lying on something hard, my body at a most peculiar angle. Beneath me, I could discern rough-hewn stone, of a rectangular design. As my eyes focused, I could make out green moss between the stone. But upon raising my head, I was surrounded by such a fog that still I could not determine where I was.

And then I heard a sound—it was loud, rushing toward me. It was like the roaring of a waterfall, and I trembled in fear.

But it was nothing more than the Ola going by. I was on our own slipway, my head inches from the water. I raised myself to my knees and discovered my shirt was covered in blood. I must have fallen during the night and lay there throughout.

A feeling of despair overwhelmed me. I stumbled through the garden, into our house, up the stairs. Do you know what I found? Empty beds. The children, their clothes, their books, their belongings . . . gone.

I felt like I had been stabbed through the heart.

I realize now that I am not just an alcoholic. I am a drunk. I have fallen to the lowest rung of our society. I am in the gutter, both literally and metaphorically.

My practice is lost, my family gone, my house empty. How slowly time passes. I imagined myself destined for something else. In school, my aspiration was to become an historian, a man of intellect; do you remember? I had planned to study Cato, Aristotle, Dante.

You have your newspapers; you live in the world as it is. I always preferred to dream, to imagine what the world might become.

I have spent today wondering what would happen if you were to return to my side. Could I be your husband again, father to our children? Could I repair my wrongs? Had you asked me a week ago, I would have answered in the affirmative. Today, I do not believe it so.

I have always considered your tongue sharp, but it is now dull by comparison to the dagger of my own thoughts. The emptiness around me has become a prism, shining directly on my faults. I, alone, am to blame.

Winter is coming, I can feel it in the air. The winds have shifted, the hillside is changing colour. I used to feel a gloom at this time of year, to long for spring. Now I welcome it.

I shall bother you no more. I remain in our house in Orkney. Only time will determine what shall befall me.

Your husband,
Thomas Archibald Shaw

Once again, there was no response. Dr. Shaw had thought of pain as the great teacher, but he began to suspect otherwise. *Pain is very selective,* he decided. *Doreen was always happy, despite her grumpy nature. Yet, no matter how much pain I endure, I cannot be satisfied.*

He did not write again for more than two months. Then he wrote one last letter.

20 October 1939
Irving House, Keinton Mandeville
To Doreen Avery Shaw
Treworyan House, Cornwall

Dear Doreen,
My previous agitation has been dispelled. My enthusiasm for life has returned. Nothing could be clearer to me now.

I once imagined I could have my cake and eat it, but I realize it cannot be. Perhaps for some but not for me. One might believe they can have one drink, perhaps two, and that will be the end. With me, it is not so.

Many weeks have passed since my last drink. It was on the very day of my previous letter. Since then, I have returned to my earlier temperament. Do you remember what I was like when we met? Do you remember how much you enjoyed me then?

I have been ruminating on the twin elements of happiness: pleasure and satisfaction. I always thought pleasure was its own reward, while you have been satisfied with . . . well, with satisfaction. I believe it is what drives us apart. But I appreciate both now.

I beg you to forgive me. I beg you to move back with me. Everything has changed. Britain is at war. A ship was sunk in Scapa Flow recently. There are German U-boats everywhere. There is talk of building causeways across the islands to prevent another such attack.

I have moved to England, taken a house in Somerset. You may be interested to know that one of the previous owners was none other than the great actor, Henry Irving. I can still remember my parents speaking of him: He inspired Bram Stoker's Dracula!

But more to the matter at hand, I have also taken a new position. I work in a hospital nearby and have been well received.

I beg you to reconsider your decision once again. I beg you to move into this lovely house with me, and to bring our children. If I am correct, and have found the secret to a satisfied life, free of spirit, then we shall resume our journey together. And if I am wrong? Then you can leave, knowing in your heart that you did everything in your power to make it right for our family.

Do not presume that I blame you. I am the sole cause of our troubles.

I await your speedy response.

Your loving husband,
Thomas

Dr. Shaw no longer cared that he did not get a reply. He had sold the house in Orkney, had rented a house in Keinton Mandeville, and was now prepared for whatever fate might befall him. He thought of calling Doreen, but he knew Treworyan had only party lines: Everyone listened to everyone else's calls in their part of the world, and he did not want to be the talk of the county.

In early December, he got into his car and turned on the motor. A few moments later, he turned it off. "Not ready," he said aloud.

In mid-December, he repeated the process and drove as far as Somerton. Then he stopped and turned back. "It was not far," he said, "but it is better than the last try."

He spent Christmas alone, sober. The following day, he got in his car again. This time, he kept going. He drove through Somerton, Taunton, and Dartmoor. In Bodwin Moor, he stopped for lunch at the Jamaica Inn, and chuckled at the plaque outside: "Joss Merlyn was murdered on this spot by the good vicar." The inn was already capitalizing on its fame, having been the subject of a recent novel by the Cornish writer Daphne du Maurier.

He ordered fish and chips. When the barman asked what he would have to drink, he gritted his teeth. "Nothing for me today, my good man." He could feel the stares of those around him.

Treworyan was not easy to find. It had been years since he visited, and the narrow lanes and high hedges were confusing. Nothing was marked. At one point, he got out of the car, climbed a hedge, and looked around. "Ah, there it is," he said, spying the two oak trees. "Yes, that is it, and there is the house. Bigger than I remember. Good old Tom. He has done well."

He drove up the lane, stopped in front, and sat in the car. The last few steps would be the hardest. He massaged his hands. He took deep breaths. Then he opened the car door, walked up the path, and knocked. The fog from his breath floated in the dim moonlight. Then the door swung open and he smiled pleasantly.

"Hello, everyone."

Chapter 16

-⟪⟪◆⟫⟫-

The Great War

[December 1939]

Dr. Shaw and Aunt Aileen stared at each other for nearly a minute. For her part, Aileen was trying to decide if this was a good development or a bad one. It all depended on whether her brother-in-law would be taking his family with him or moving in himself. For his part, Dr. Shaw was studying the people gathering behind Aileen. They looked like one big happy family.

Uncle Tom broke the silence. "My goodness, Thomas, what are you doing out there in the cold? Aileen, let the man through." Then: "I think we need some more tea and scones, my dear."

A flurry of activity ensued. Dr. Shaw shook hands with Tom and was ushered in; he hugged his children awkwardly. He turned to his wife, but she took a step back and joined Aileen in the kitchen, where they got busy preparing more tea, more scones, and more clotted cream.

"When Doreen and the children arrived on our doorstep," Uncle Tom said, "we did not know what to think. But, Thomas, I must say, you look well." They sat in the living room by the fire and made themselves comfortable. Soon, Aileen and Doreen returned with trays and handed each of them a cup of tea. The women settled into chairs opposite the men. The children lined up against the far wall, watching intently.

"You have a lovely family," Aileen said. "Such wonderful children." She glanced at Joanna, and her face darkened for a moment.

"Aye," Dr. Shaw said, "I have missed them."

"The children have been an enormous help," Aileen continued. "Robert and Sandy have been hard at work every day. They've become real farmers. Tom sings their praises. And the girls are such dears, especially Elisabeth, always helping around the house."

"I was admiring the farm as I drove up," Dr. Shaw said. "All the fields plowed, livestock in their proper places, no broken fences. All shipshape, Tom, real Bristol fashion. You've done well."

Uncle Tom beamed. "Thank you. I was born on this farm, and I hope my son will one day take over. Who could want more?"

"Aye, who could want more. But do you not miss having people nearby?"

Uncle Tom scratched his head. "I do not believe so. There are too many people in the cities for me. The streets in Truro are so crowded, sometimes I can barely get through. No, I prefer peace and quiet. I'll grant you, there's no pub nearby, but Aileen and I sometimes have a wee glass of wine of a Sunday evening."

Dr. Shaw squirmed a little. "What do you think of Hitler?" he asked. "It is all people are talking about these days."

"Why should I think anything of him?" Uncle Tom responded. "Let the Europeans fight their wars. It has nothing to do with us."

"But the Germans have attacked our allies. We have declared war!"

"Do you think of Poland as our ally, Thomas? I do not. In any case, the Germans will never cross the Channel. They'd be met with pitchforks and bayonets in every town and farm."

Dr. Shaw shook his head. "I tried to sign up, but they wouldn't take me."

Doreen snorted, and everyone turned to her. "Why did they turn you down?" she asked. It was the first time she had spoken to her husband in six months.

"They said it was my back, but I believe they simply think me too old."

"Why fight again, Thomas?" Uncle Tom asked. "You were in the Great War. Why go through it again?"

"There was nothing great about that war, Tom. And Hitler is not going to stop at Poland, nor even France. Furthermore, I do not believe the Channel is wide enough to stop him. Pitchforks and bayonets are no match for armored tanks."

"I do not believe you would fight again," Mrs. Shaw said. Everyone turned to her.

"Run along, children," Aileen said, shooing them away. "We have things to discuss."

Robert led the others out of the room, but instead of going upstairs, he stopped in the hall and sat down. The candles were not yet lit, evening was falling, and they had become nearly invisible. The others sat next to him.

"If you have something to say, Doreen, speak up," Dr. Shaw said. "I have no secrets."

"Very well," she said. Her voice was like ice. "The only thing I heard you say about the war was that it was boring. I, for one, do not believe you are brave enough to fight."

"There is no such thing as bravery in a war," he replied.

"But there is. My father died in the war. *He* knew something of bravery."

"Your father did not fight in a single battle."

"His name is engraved on the monument in Truro, is it not?" Mrs. Shaw replied stiffly. "It commemorates those who died. I can show it to you if you are not familiar."

"Of course I am familiar with it. Everyone from Truro who died in the war is engraved there. It does not mean they fought bravely, or fought at all."

"You may look upon it lightly, but that monument is the highest indication of bravery. Which is more than I can say for you."

Dr. Shaw's face looked like it had been slapped. "Your father fell off a horse while playing polo in India," he said loudly. "I was in the trenches, fighting for my life!"

The room became silent. "I had no idea," Aunt Aileen said.

"You don't have to talk about it," Uncle Tom said.

"Apparently I do." Dr. Shaw took a deep breath. "You have no idea what it was like. When I hear people talk about war, I can only think how lucky they are to know nothing about it. They think of war as some grand adventure . . ."

"You don't have to talk about it," Uncle Tom repeated.

"We were surrounded by rats, sleeping in our own feces, vomiting constantly. It is true what I said about it being boring. There was nothing to do in between battles. We tried to catch up on sleep during the day, because at night we were afraid the Germans might bayonet us as we lay in our bunks."

In the hallway, Joanna noticed Robert and Sandy punching the air with their fists. *They're fending off imaginary Germans*, she thought. Next to her, Liz had a look of horror on her face. It was not the first time she wondered if the differences between boys and girls was learned or innate. Only Michael seemed unmoved. He sat next to them with an impassive look.

"How did you get through it?" Uncle Tom asked.

"Oh, the usual way," Dr. Shaw replied. "French beer, French wine, plenty of both. 'Glad to live through another day,' we would say to each other at night.

"But the boredom was not the worst part, nor even the fear of dying. It was the shelling. One could see people shouting, but you couldn't hear a thing. It was so loud and so quiet all at the same time. I was afraid I would be blown to pieces, but I was even more afraid that dirt would land on top of me, and I would be buried alive."

"You were in the artillery?"

"Aye. I was responsible for the gas cannisters. In the proper sequence, of course."

There was a moment of silence, and Robert peeked around the corner. His mother and his aunt were staring grimly at his father. Uncle Tom was leaning forward in his chair. And then for a moment, he caught his father's eye. Dr. Shaw nodded, about to say something . . .

"What do you mean by sequence?" Uncle Tom asked.

Robert Shaw on the set of *JAWS* with his mother and his sister, Joanna. *Courtesy of Universal Studios Licensing LLC.*

Dr. Shaw returned from World War I a hero but was never the same afterward. Mrs. Shaw raised five unruly children on her own during the Blitz in World War II.

Robert, age three, with sisters Joanna and Elisabeth, along with Great-Grandma Carter, an early suffragette. Although born in England, the Shaws always considered Orkney and Cornwall their true homes. (1930)

The Shaws' Seafield House in Orkney, overlooking Scapa Flow, is where Dr. Shaw taught Robert and Sandy how to box. Wreckage of German navy vessels, scuttled after World War I, could be seen poking above the water.

Robert in a class photo at Stromness Academy, Orkney.
The Shaws were outcasts until Robert formed his own team and challenged the others to a match.
Courtesy of Orkney Library and Archive.

Joanna never smiled for a photograph, but she became a star student
when she and Robert began reading the same books together.
Courtesy of Orkney Library and Archive.

Dr. Shaw, an avid outdoorsman,
often flew to Norway for hunting
and fishing expeditions.
He is seen here at the rustic
Stenness airport in Orkney.
William Hourston, photographer.
Courtesy of Orkney Library and Archive.

Known as the Lighthouse Doctor
because he visited patients in any weather,
Dr. Shaw was depicted in a local newspaper
— complete with medical bag,
stethoscope, and cigarette. (1938)
Courtesy of Orkney Library and Archive.
GB241/D1/200/1.

Near the Jamaica Inn, made famous by Daphne du Maurier's novel, Robert's father drove him into a ditch after a drinking binge. (1940)

Until Robert saw Joanna's home movie with his father's gravestone, he thought he had to keep going to outlive him — then he discovered his father died at forty-one.

TREWORYAN

After their father's death, the Shaws
lived on Treworyan Farm
where they would have become
Cornish farmers if not for their
mother's aspirations.

As World War II began, the Shaws
moved into an oasthouse, previously used
to brew beer, overlooking the Tresillian River.
During air raid blackouts, Robert honed
his early acting skills with dramatic readings
to his siblings in the tower.

Across from the Shaws' house in Cornwall sat a thatched-roof pub, frequented by American soldiers preparing for D-Day. There Robert heard many colorful stories that fueled his later novels.

The Tresillian River at low tide. After Mrs. Shaw purchased a used rowboat for £5, the Shaws became river rats.

After graduating from
Cambridge University,
Joanna went to South Africa
to fight apartheid and confer
with Nelson Mandela.
Pictured here with the faculty
of Adams College in
KwaZulu-Natal province. (1954)
Courtesy of the Campbell
Special Collections/Alan Paton
Centre/Ghandi-Luthuli
Documentation Centre of the
University of KwaZulu-Natal.

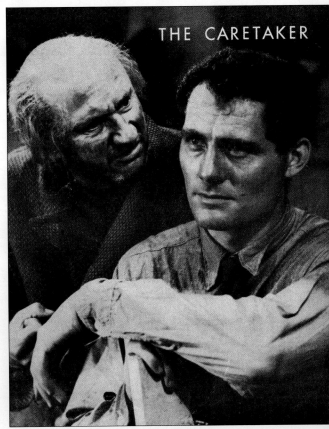

THE CARETAKER

No one in Cornwall thought acting was a real profession
but they changed their minds after seeing Rober
portray a man suffering from electric shock therapy
in *The Caretaker*, with Donald Pleasence

Robert performed Shakespeare
with some of the greatest actors
of his time, including Alec Guinness,
John Gielgud, and Michael Redgrave.
Pictured here (seated) with
Basil Hoskins in *King Lear*. (1953)
Photo by Angus McBean © RSC.

In his second film, *The Dam Busters*,
Robert's speaking lines were cut,
but he could steal the show with
only his eyes. Pictured here
with Richard Todd. (1955)
Still from The Dam Busters *used with
permission of StudioCanal S.A.S.*

Sean Connery co-starred with Robert in a TV movie based on Robert's first novel, *The Hiding Place* (renamed *The Pets*). (1960) *Courtesy of ITV/Shutterstock.com.*

To generate the proper tension while ordering James Bond to "kiss my foot" in *From Russia with Love*, Robert told Sean Connery stories about his wife, whom Robert had dated. (1963)
Courtesy of Eon Productions and Metro-Goldwyn-Mayer Studios.

Both Robert and Joanna loved large families, as seen in this still from their home movie. Robert's second wife, Mary Ure, is on the right. The author is throwing the football.

When Robert was nominated for an Oscar in *A Man for All Seasons*, the nuns at Joanna's college were eager to meet him—but to Robert's surprise, they were more interested in discussing Thomas More than his role as Henry VIII. Pictured here with Paul Scofield. (1966)
A MAN FOR ALL SEASONS © 1966, renewed 1994 Highland Films, Ltd.

Robert helped Paul Newman and Robert Redford turn *The Sting*
into an Academy Award winner. (1973)
Courtesy of Universal Studios Licensing LLC.

Robert was a born storyteller, and entertained Roy Scheider, Steven Spielberg,
and Richard Dreyfuss on the set of *JAWS*.
Courtesy of Universal Studios Licensing LLC.

Robert and Spielberg line up a shot on the set of *JAWS*. Although the young director was not yet famous, Robert already considered him a genius. *Courtesy of Universal Studios Licensing LLC.*

With the success of *JAWS*, Robert achieved everything he wanted professionally. Pictured here on the set of *Black Sunday*. (1977)

Mrs. Shaw (left) never stopped clowning around and outlived Robert by twenty years.
Joanna (below) never stopped fighting for equal rights—and never lost the support of her students.

Robert died of a heart attack at fifty-one near his home in Ireland.
The people who knew him best always remembered that Robert made them laugh.

IN HONOUR OF ROBERT SHAW
WHO LIVED IN TOURMAKEADY
AR DHEIS DÉ 5O RAIBH A ANAM
REQUIESCAT IN PACE

Dr. Shaw turned back to him. "We delivered three types of gas," he said. "Had to be in the proper sequence, or it wouldn't work. The yellow ones went first: They were the chloropicrin, invented by a Scotsman. Was supposed to be a pesticide, but you know how creative the military can be. Those ones didn't kill, but it made them itch like mad. They would tear off their face masks. That was when we fired the second and third rounds: red canisters for chlorine, blue for phosgene. Those can't get through a mask, but with their masks off . . . Do you know why the Germans lost the war?" he asked.

"You bloody well kicked their arses," Uncle Tom answered.

"No, actually, we did not. We pushed them back, it's true. The gas worked, and our infantry fought bravely. But that is not why we won the war. We won it because the German soldiers mutinied. We lost more men, but they stopped fighting. The French had the same problem but not the British. God bless His Majesty. He made sure we had plenty of food and water, and enough drink to get us through it."

An hour later, Dr. Shaw departed. "I must be at work in the morning," he said. Pulling the car into the lane, he waved goodbye. Before he was out of sight, they heard him shout, "There's a home waiting for you in Somerset, Mrs. Shaw. I hope you accept my offer."

That evening, as the grown-ups gathered in the living room, the children sat on the back porch together. While the pigs were getting ready to sleep, pawing the ground and grunting to one another, each kid retreated into their own thoughts. Then Liz interrupted them. "If you had to choose between Daddy and Mummy, who would you choose?"

"What do you mean?" Robert asked.

"If they do not get back together and we have to choose which one to live with, who would you choose?"

Robert and Sandy both said "Mummy" at the same time, but Joanna said, "I would live with Daddy."

They turned to her. "Why?"

"He's not mean," she said. "I like him. He's funny. He lets us do what we want."

"You think Mummy is mean?" Liz asked.

"Of course she's mean," Robert snapped. "That's not the point. The question, Joey, is not who you *like* more. The question is, if you had to say whether Mum or Dad would keep us safe, who would it be? *That* is the question."

Joanna did not like either option, but she had to admit the truth. "I would choose Mummy," she said.

That night, Joanna was unable to fall asleep. She padded down the hallway and stopped by the stairs. In the kitchen, she could hear her mother and aunt talking and sat down to listen.

"I forgot how handsome he is," she heard Aileen say.

"Don't be a fool," her mother replied. "He put on a show for you. That's what he does. He charms people." Then she added, "We never meant to have another baby."

"You don't mean Wendy? But she is such a dear."

They spoke quietly for a while, then her aunt raised her voice: "I heard a story once, a true story, mind you, about a woman who left her husband. He had a drinking problem, like your Thomas. She could have stayed with him and worked it out, but she chose to leave instead and take the children with her. The man was so miserable that he drowned himself." She paused, then added, "Of course, he was a fisherman."

"Well, Thomas is not a fisherman," Doreen said, as if that was the reason the man had killed himself. "Thomas is a doctor. That is why I married him."

There was another pause, then Mrs. Shaw surprised both her sister and her daughter. "But I believe you are right, Aileen. I have no choice but to give the man another try."

"Wonderful," Aileen said.

Joanna made her way back to bed as quietly as she could. She would not have to choose after all. That night, she dreamed happy thoughts— had she known what awaited them in Somerset, however, she would not have slept so well.

Chapter 17

A Pauper's Grave

[January 1940]

Everyone loaded their luggage into Uncle Tom's car and they drove north. Uncle Tom sat in front, with Mrs. Shaw and the baby in the passenger seat and Michael between them. Aunt Aileen sat in the middle row, between Robert and Liz, while Joanna and Sandy wedged themselves into the back, between the boxes and suitcases.

"I'll be sick back here," Joanna complained. "Can I sit in front?"

"Don't be a baby," Aileen answered sharply. "We can't keep bowing to your every desire. This is our car. Michael sits in front."

It was a long drive made longer by Uncle Tom's slow pace and Cornwall's narrow lanes. The car bounced this way and that. They stopped briefly for lunch but were soon on their way again.

"I don't feel good," Joanna repeated.

"Be quiet," Aileen snapped.

A skirmish soon began. Joanna's stomach wanted out, and she began taking deep breaths to try and stop it. She looked out the window, craning her neck around boxes, but the flashes of green only made her feel worse. After a while, the point of no return arrived. Joanna tried one last time to hold it back, but it was not to be. The contents of her lunch rose up and flew into the air. For a brief moment, the arc caught the afternoon sun and sparkled in midair. Then it landed on the back of Aunt Aileen's neck.

Aileen seemed confused at first. She looked up, as if a bird had miraculously pooped through the roof of the car. Then she reached back and felt the gooey mess. A scream filled the air. Uncle Tom slammed on the brakes, and the car skidded to a stop. Everyone piled out as fast as they could—all but Joanna. She remained in the back, horror-stricken.

"What happened?" Uncle Tom asked in bewilderment.

"Joanna vomited on me," Aileen screamed. "She did it on purpose!"

Mrs. Shaw guffawed. "Children don't throw up on purpose, Aileen. You should have let her sit in front."

It took nearly an hour to clean up the mess. Uncle Tom left a pile of rags by the side of the road when he was finished. Even so, it still smelled inside, and the remainder of the trip seemed to take forever. Everyone was relieved when he pulled up to a large stone house and announced their arrival.

Dr. Shaw was waiting for them. "Welcome to your new home," he said, bowing deeply. Then he sniffed the air. "What the devil is that smell?"

Keinton Mandeville was their third home in six months. Once again, the Shaws were introduced to a new set of classmates. Once again, they were deemed outsiders because of their accents, which were now a mixture of Orkney and Cornwall. And once again, their athleticism and intelligence—combined with their refusal to ever be excluded—won the day. As Dr. Shaw had said to his wife when they first moved to Orkney, "They will need to make new friends all through their lives, so they might as well learn now."

It felt like old times for a while. Dr. Shaw went to work at a nearby hospital every morning. He returned at the end of the day, and Mrs. Shaw made dinner for everyone. Afterward, he played with them in their backyard. They were a family again.

"He has learned not to drink," Robert said, and the others agreed.

A week later, Mrs. Shaw invited the neighbors for tea. There was polite discussion, and she was complimented on her cooking. Afterward, one of the men pulled a flask from his pocket and offered it to Dr. Shaw.

He glanced around, saw his wife engaged in conversation, and took a sip. His children noticed, but they also saw him give the flask back without taking any more.

"He has learned how to control it," Robert said, and the others agreed.

The following Sunday, the neighbors came over again, and a game of football began in the backyard. While the children ran around kicking the ball, the women stood on one side and chatted while the men stood on the other side. One of the men pulled a bottle of whiskey from his pocket and handed it around.

Back and forth the kids ran, up and down the yard, scoring goals and celebrating, while the men yelled encouragement. Then, one voice rose above the others. "Put the bloody ball in the goal," Dr. Shaw yelled, and laughed loudly.

After that, he stopped coming home at dinnertime. He began frequenting the local pub instead. It had taken only a few weeks for life to return to what it had been. Nothing had changed.

Mrs. Shaw confronted him angrily again, and one evening she locked him out of the bedroom. He stood outside their door, banging loudly and screaming, "Let me in!"

"No!" she screamed back. "You'll hurt the baby!"

"She's my baby too," he yelled, kicking the door. Downstairs, the kids looked at each other in horror. Then Joanna raced upstairs and grabbed her father's coat. "Stop it, Daddy," she yelled. "Stop it, stop it, stop it!"

To her surprise, he did stop. His entire body seemed to sag. "You love me, don't you, Joey?" he asked.

Robert and Liz were sent to boarding school after that. Mrs. Shaw wanted to get as many children as possible out of the house. Dr. Shaw drove Liz to a school in Devon, then returned to take Robert to a school in Truro. Halfway there, he stopped at a pub.

"You stay here. I'll be right back," he said.

For the next two hours, Robert busied himself with reading. When his father returned, he cranked the motor, backed the car up, and drove right into a ditch. Robert was flung against the dashboard, while Dr. Shaw pounded the steering wheel in fury.

"Bloody useless car," he screamed.

The noise drew the attention of those inside. A woman began attending to Robert, and soon the police arrived. Dr. Shaw was taken to jail, and Robert was driven the rest of the way to Truro, where he was turned over to the schoolmaster, Dr. Magson.

The following day, Dr. Shaw checked himself into a rehab clinic in a wing of Salisbury Hospital. He spent the next week recuperating. Near the end of his stay, Mrs. Shaw took the children to visit him. They found him sitting comfortably in a chair, looking happy and relaxed.

"How lovely to see you," he said.

The nurse told them how charming he was. "Your father is all cured," she said.

The next day, Mrs. Shaw purchased a new sofa to celebrate his cure—a beautiful white sofa. Robert returned to school, while Elisabeth stayed home to help her mother prepare a special meal.

The evening did not go as planned. Dr. Shaw was released earlier than expected, but he did not go directly home. As he passed the pub in Keinton Mandeville, he glanced inside and saw several of his friends laughing gaily. The fire next to them looked so cozy. *Just one*, he said to himself. *I owe it to myself.*

The men were delighted to see him. "Welcome back," they chorused.

"Thanks. I can't stay long," Dr. Shaw said.

"Of course, of course."

Hours later, Dr. Shaw poked his head through the window of the sitting room. Joanna and Sandy were playing cards on the floor because they were not allowed to sit on the sofa. "We must keep it clean for your father," Mrs. Shaw had told them. The two kids looked up to see their father's enormous grin. "Shh," he whispered, putting a finger to his lips. "Don't let your mother know I'm here. I want to surprise her."

Joanna shrugged, and she and Sandy resumed their card game. Dr. Shaw climbed through the window, fell clumsily to the floor, and crawled to the sofa. "What are you playing?" he asked.

"German Whist."

They could smell the liquor on his breath. He pulled himself onto the sofa and lay down. His head rested on one arm of the sofa, his boots on the other. "Just the right size," he said.

Joanna looked up in horror. "Mummy just bought that sofa, and now you've ruined it!"

Her father's grin turned to a frown. He sat up and looked at the mud he had smeared. "It's from the backyard," he muttered. "If I hadn't been trying to avoid the damn woman, none of this would have happened." He glanced at the kitchen. His wife was still cooking, oblivious to what was taking place in the sitting room.

Dr. Shaw stood up suddenly, looked down at his two kids, and said, "You would all be better off without me." He had a grim look on his face. He took a bottle from his pocket and emptied it down his throat. Joanna and Sandy stared at him with blank expressions. They had heard their father say this type of thing many times before, and so they resumed their card game without another thought.

Dr. Shaw then trudged upstairs, leaving a trail of mud behind him. Mrs. Shaw had heard the noise by now and came to investigate. "What on earth?" she demanded. Her eyes flitted from the open window to the grimy sofa and then to the muddy footprints going up the stairs.

"Daddy's home," Joanna said.

Mrs. Shaw was too furious to say anything. She returned to the kitchen, and a banging of pots and pans commenced.

They ate dinner in silence. Their father remained upstairs. After dinner, Mrs. Shaw sent Liz up to check on him. She disappeared for several minutes, then came downstairs with an odd look on her face. "He is dead," she said.

The next time the Shaws saw their father, he was in a coffin.

Following the inquest, Mrs. Shaw went to their local church in Keinton Mandeville to make arrangements for the funeral. The Anglican priest had other ideas. "These are hallowed grounds," he said. "We cannot bury your husband here."

"Why not?"

"He committed suicide."

"Why do you say that?"

"Correct me if I am wrong, Mrs. Shaw, but did not the judge rule that your husband took his own life?"

"He mixed morphine with alcohol," she said. "It was an accident."

"That is not my understanding." Then, thinking to be helpful, the minister added, "I suggest you look into St Peter's Church in Lydford. They have a pauper's grave."

Mrs. Shaw was livid. "My husband was a member of the upper class! His father is buried in Holy Trinity Church in St. Austell!" But her arguments fell on deaf ears. The following day, Dr. Shaw was lowered into a pauper's grave in Lydford.

Robert and Liz were both at school by then, leaving Joanna and Sandy at home. "Do not leave the house until I return," Mrs. Shaw instructed them.

"Yes, Mummy," they said, but as soon as she disappeared, Joanna turned to Sandy. "We must see Daddy buried."

"But Mummy told us to stay home," Sandy protested. Then, seeing the look on his sister's face, he shrugged. "All right, I'll go."

"I'll get our bikes," Joanna said, "and you change into something warmer." Sandy ran upstairs while Joanna pulled the bikes from the shed. Hers had a flat tire, so she went behind the shed where they kept a bicycle pump. By the time she returned, Sandy had come back and, seeing only one bike, thought Joanna had left without him. He took off in mad pursuit.

Joanna came back just in time to see Sandy disappear around the corner, and she also took off in pursuit. With the wind in their faces, her cries of "Wait for me!" did not reach Sandy, while his own plaintive cries of "Wait for me" carried clearly back to her.

They arrived in Lydford out of breath. Peering over the stone wall, they could see a small group of people standing by a grave. "There's Mummy," Sandy said.

"Yes, and that is Mr. Peters," Joanna said, pointing to their schoolmaster.

A priest said a few words, sprinkled some water, and two men lowered the casket into the ground. Later that evening, Joanna confessed to her mother what they had seen. She expected to receive a scolding, but Mrs. Shaw simply nodded.

"I saw our schoolmaster," Joanna said, "and my teacher, Mrs. Granville. And there was Mrs. Richards from next door and an acolyte. Is that right?" Mrs. Shaw nodded. "But I did not recognize the two women standing next to you. Who were they?"

"Barmaids," her mother said.

The Shaws had fallen once again. In Orkney, they had gone from riches to rags and were ostracized by the community. But in Cornwall it was worse: They had become paupers, falling to the very bottom of British society.

This should have broken them, but it did not. Instead, they rallied around each other. They were the Shaws! Without enough evidence to the contrary, they continued to believe they were better than other people.

Even late in life, whenever they got together, it was like they were kids again. With all the fun and hilarity, they felt their ability, their poise, their arrogance, instilled in them by their mother in her need to survive. They knew it made no sense. In their hearts, they knew they were not better than others. But they felt it. And in the days to follow, that feeling would prove invaluable, for there were even darker times ahead.

Chapter 18

-⟨⟨⟨◆⟩⟩⟩-

The Blitz, The Evacuee
& Daphne du Maurier

[1940–1941]

*T*he year 1940 was a challenging one for Great Britain. In April, Germany invaded Denmark, Norway, and Holland. In May, the British army evacuated from Dunkirk. In June, Paris fell. France was supposed to have been impenetrable—the Maginot Line stretched for 280 miles along its border with Germany, but the German army simply went around it. Using the Blitzkrieg, or "lightning war," they avoided France's defenses and attacked from behind. All of Europe came under the control of Adolf Hitler, and everyone thought Britain would soon follow.

Other than these global calamities, however, it was an idyllic year in many ways for the Shaws. They were not surprised by war. Their house in Orkney had overlooked Scapa Flow, where the German navy was scuttled after World War I. Parts of those ships were still visible above the water, so war had always been on their minds.

Mrs. Shaw found a house for them in Tresillian, not far from Treworyan, with a lovely view of the river and ivy crawling up its sides. It was perfect in every way—except for one. "What is that awful smell?" Liz asked.

"It smells like someone has been burning pinecones," Robert said.

"We have work to do," Mrs. Shaw said.

She had rented an oasthouse, all that she could afford. Until recently, it had been used to dry out hops before they were sent to the brewery. Kilns on the first floor had sent heat up into the oast tower, where the hops were spread on the floor. From there, the smoke exited through the roof, which peaked fourteen feet over their heads.

Mrs. Shaw set them all to painting and scrubbing, and they soon did not notice the smell. Slowly, life began to return to normal. On weekends, they went to the ocean together, packing Cornish pasties and riding the bus to Porthtowan, where a natural swimming pool filled up at high tide. They spent the day swimming, then watched daring local boys dive from the cliff into the pool.

"Why don't you do that?" Liz dared Robert.

Robert got up and studied the cliff. He looked into the pool. Doing some quick calculations, he turned back to Liz. "Why don't you?"

The kids hitchhiked home afterward, while their mother and Wendy rode the bus. Having inherited his mother's sense of pride, Robert always told the driver to let them off in front of the biggest house in town. There they stood, waving cheerily goodbye, until the car turned the corner, and they could walk the rest of the way home.

Mrs. Shaw scraped up enough money that summer to purchase four used bicycles, and now they could cycle to the beach on weekends, being careful to avoid the barbed wire that had appeared. During the week, they bicycled the five miles back and forth to Ladock School every day. Mrs. Shaw thought it was better than the one-room classroom in Tresillian and so she claimed they were still living with the Cocks.

But it was when she purchased a used rowboat for £5 that life really picked up for them. The Shaws became river rats, exploring up and down the Tresillian. They were the heroes of Arthur Ransome's *Swallows and Amazons*. Robert was Captain John, Liz was his first mate, Joey was able-bodied seaman Titty, and Sandy was the little boy. The family in the story even had a baby.

More than anything, it was the river that brought them back from the sadness of losing their father. Every day, twice a day, it spilled over its banks and into the marshes below their house. At those times, it was a hundred yards across. In between, it was just a wide mudflat with a thin trickle of water running down the middle.

It was always there, always rising and falling, always the river.

Mrs. Shaw gathered her children around the wireless in their sitting room one day. She fiddled with the dials and they heard a man's voice. "Is that Churchill?" Robert asked.

"Yes," his mother said. "Hush, boy!"

While the prime minister gave a moving speech to his country, the Shaws were more interested in playing with Wendy—until the end. They perked up when Churchill's voice rose dramatically. It felt like he was in the room with them.

> The Battle of France is over, and the Battle of Britain is about to begin. Make no mistake, the fury and might of the enemy will soon be turned upon us. Hitler knows he will have to break us on this Island, or he will lose the war.

> Let us therefore brace ourselves to our duties, and so bear ourselves that, if the British Empire and its Commonwealth should last for a thousand years, men will still say, "This was their finest hour."

Mrs. Shaw cried "Bravo" and Robert and Sandy clapped their hands. "This will be our finest hour" became the rallying cry in Britain. In the months to follow, they watched planes battle in the skies overhead. Robert and his mates were especially fascinated by them. "That one is a Spitfire," Robert said, pointing.

"Yes, and that's a Bf-109," another boy would say. Joanna could not be sure if they really knew or were just making it up. To her, the planes looked like tiny specks in the sky.

Otherwise, life went on as usual. Mrs. Shaw moved Robert into a boarding school in Truro, claiming a residence there. Liz was sent to a boarding school in Devon for similar reasons, while Sandy and Joanna continued to attend Ladock. Their mother kept moving them from one school to another throughout their teenage years, whenever she found something better. At one point she even got Sandy into a prestigious boarding school, through a grant for Children of Dead Doctors.

Robert was a boarder in Truro until the money ran out; then he was forced to live at home and ride his bicycle back and forth. This was an embarrassment for him, because the boarders looked down on day students, and they could tell each other apart by their different caps: One had circles and the other stripes. Being the proud boy, he pinched a boarder's cap and wore it for nearly a year before anyone found out.

The year 1941 was another tough one. Having lost the Battle of Britain, Germany unleashed the Blitz, dropping forty thousand tons of explosives on Great Britain. Most landed in London, but Cornwall got its fair share as well.

In Malpas, the Shaws watched from their boat as enormous anti-aircraft guns rolled onto the Rendlesham estate. At night, when those guns fired, their house shook, and they slept on their mother's bedroom floor. Joanna always staked out a position as far from the door as possible, thinking that if the Germans managed to get in, they would take her siblings and so might be satisfied.

It was during the height of the Blitz that a knock was heard at their front door. From her upstairs window, Mrs. Shaw had been watching a woman make her way up the street, stopping at each house and chatting with the neighbors. Only at the last moment did she realize what the woman must be doing.

"DO NOT OPEN THE DOOR!" she called out. But Joanna had already flung it open. Her jaw dropped in surprise. Standing before her was the most beautiful woman she had ever seen. She was in her mid-thirties and dressed in a very attractive army uniform, with a dark-green jacket and matching skirt, and she had a pair of wings on her shoulder pads. Her trim figure was highlighted by a thick black belt around her waist.

"Wow," Joanna said.

"What is this all about?" Mrs. Shaw demanded, shoving her daughter aside.

"Good morning. Are you Mrs. Shaw?"

"I am. What business is it of yours?"

"My name is Daphne du Maurier." The woman stopped, thinking this would give her some measure of respect, but Mrs. Shaw only frowned. "I am with the Women's Royal Army Corps," she continued. "You have heard about the bombings in London, I presume?"

"Of course."

"Then you must know that thousands of children have been killed. I am responsible for finding homes for those who have survived. The government has asked me to relocate fifteen hundred of them to Cornwall."

"And what of it?"

The others had gathered around her by now, and Robert spoke up.

"You are the writer?" he asked.

"That's right," Miss du Maurier said, pleased to be recognized.

"I've read *Jamaica Inn* and absolutely loved it. How did you get the idea of a vicar, a man of the cloth, leading a gang of cutthroats?"

"We are going to read *Rebecca* next," Joanna said.

"Will you two shut up!" Mrs. Shaw snapped. Turning back to Miss du Maurier, she said, "Do you see what I must put up with?"

"Your children seem remarkably intelligent," she replied.

"Fiddlesticks." Mrs. Shaw shook her head. "I imagine you are intelligent enough to see I cannot possibly take in another child. Look around you. Do you see a man here?" Miss du Maurier glanced around the room. "I am a widow, my husband is dead, and I have been left with five children to feed, with no one to help me."

Miss du Maurier glared at her. "Mrs. Shaw, we are at war!"

"Don't lecture me. I am aware of that."

"Everyone must do their part. Your neighbor has just agreed to take in *three* children, and she is also a widow!"

"Who? Mrs. Roberts?"

"Yes."

Mrs. Shaw sniffed the air in disgust. "And rightly so," she said. "The woman only has one child. She is always complaining that she is lonely. But I do not have that luxury. If you believe four children is the proper number for a widow, then let me remind you that I already have five." She paused. "Of course, if you *truly* believe I should have only four children, then perhaps you would be so kind as to take one of mine and find another home."

She took a step back and surveyed her children, as if trying to decide which one to give up. Robert and Liz chuckled, but Joanna was not entirely certain she was joking.

"It is clear to me," Miss du Maurier said, "that you are quite capable of managing a large group of children. My orders, and they come directly from senior members of His Majesty's Armed Forces, are to place at least one child in every home. I assure you, I will not be leaving here until that is accomplished. So tell me, Mrs. Shaw, will it be one child—or two or three?"

Sensing that she was losing, Mrs. Shaw shifted tactics. "What kind of parent would give up one of their children?" she demanded. "I would never allow one of mine to leave London while I stayed. What an irresponsible, cowardly act!"

Miss du Maurier shook her head. This woman had just been contemplating which child to give up, and now she was criticizing parents who were trying to save their children's lives. In the end, they agreed on one evacuee, and Miss du Maurier handed her a piece of paper.

"This is the name of the child," she said. "The instructions on where to pick him up are on the back." Then, turning, she added, "I trust you will be kinder to the child than you were with me."

"I will treat him like one of my own children," Mrs. Shaw called after her.

A few days later, Robert heard his mother say, "Get your jacket, boy."

"Where are we going?"

"Do as you are told. We have a child to pick up."

They rode the bus to Truro and got off next to St. George's Church. There, they found a long queue of people, all waiting. A short while later, another bus pulled up, and the evacuees descended. Robert had been happy at the prospect of having another younger child to boss around, but his face dropped when he saw the children. They walked in pairs, looking as if they were about to start crying. Many of them clutched a teddy bear under their arm, and they all had a tag on their jacket identifying who they were, along with a string around their neck with a gas mask dangling from it.

The war had come home. Robert could see it in their bewildered gazes, in their looks of despair. When he and his mother reached the front of the line, they were introduced to a young boy about eight years old—four years younger than Robert but wearing the same outfit: gray flannel shorts, knee socks pulled up as far as they could go, and a pea jacket.

"What is your name?" Mrs. Shaw asked.

"Edward Livesey, ma'am," the boy stammered.

"Well, Edward Livesey, this is my son Robert. He will look after you during your stay."

"Yes, ma'am."

On the bus ride home, Robert peppered him with questions.

"What do you like to do?"

"Nuthin.'"

"What's that accent of yours?"

"What accent?"

"*Your* accent. What is your accent?"

"I dunno."

"Cockney, I think," Robert said. "Where do you live?"

"I dunno."

"East London, I imagine. They've gotten the worst of it. You're going to have a hard time in school with that accent, but don't worry, the kids around here are not very bright."

"All right."

Back home, Edward took his belongings, consisting of one small bag, and moved into Robert and Sandy's room, where Mrs. Shaw had set up an extra cot. Poor kid! He was terribly homesick, and the Shaws were not the kindest of families. He kept to himself, saying very little and crying softly when no one was looking. At the end of the week, a teacher found him sobbing in the hall and took him to the headmistress.

"What is the matter?" the woman asked. Edward looked at the floor. "Go on," she urged, "you can tell me."

Edward wiped the snot from his nose. "Elisabeth Shaw has been eating my sweets," he said.

The following day, there was another knock on the door of the oast-house. "What is it this time?" Mrs. Shaw asked, when she found Daphne du Maurier standing there again.

"Do you not know?" the writer shot back.

"Know what?"

"Edward has complained that one of your children is stealing his sweets ration."

Mrs. Shaw's expression was a combination of anger and amusement. "Robert, Liz, Joey, Sandy," she called, "come in here at once." She lined them up, in descending order, while Wendy slept in her basket at the end of the row. Edward came downstairs and stood in a corner, and Mrs. Shaw turned to him. "Someone has been stealing your sweets, I understand?" she said.

Edward nodded.

"Which one?" Mrs. Shaw asked.

"Elisabeth," he said quietly.

Mrs. Shaw guffawed. She turned triumphantly back to Miss du Maurier. "There, you have it. Complete and utter nonsense. If the boy had accused Robert or Joey, I might have believed him. But not Elisabeth. She is the only good one in this family!"

"Which one is Elisabeth?"

Mrs. Shaw pointed to her oldest daughter, and everyone stared. At that time, Elisabeth was the only one in the family who was overweight, while Robert and Joanna were both skinny. Miss du Maurier shook her head sadly. "Mothers are always the last to know," she murmured.

"What did you say?"

Mrs. Shaw was not one to minimize her own faults—she often remarked on how stupid she was or how poor a student she had been—but she would not stand to be criticized about her role as a mother. "How dare you?" she sputtered, her face turning various shades of red. "How *dare* you come into my house and insult me like that. You think that because you write absolute rubbish, your books are simply frightful to read, that you can lecture me on children? You can leave the boy or take him away. Either way, I do not care a fig."

Edward began to sob. Sandy went over to comfort him, but Edward pushed him away.

"Edward," Miss du Maurier said, kneeling next to him. "I have found another home for you. Would like to go see it? There are no naughty children there who will steal your sweets. Shall we see it together?"

Edward nodded. He wiped away the tears and the snot, gathered his belongings, and followed Miss du Maurier out the door. Mrs. Shaw slammed it behind them. Turning to her children, she said, "If I ever catch you reading one of her books again, I shall throw *you* out of the house." Her children stared at her. "Do you understand?" she demanded. They nodded.

The ban was never lifted.

Chapter 19

~≪≪◆≫≫~

Matinee Idol

[1942–1945]

*T*he year 1942 marked the turning point in the war. A month earlier, the Japanese had bombed Pearl Harbor, and people had been dancing in the streets of Tresillian. Joanna asked her mother why anyone would celebrate such a tragedy. "Because America will join the war now," Mrs. Shaw explained. "Good old Roosevelt, he found a way to get it done!"

American soldiers began appearing in Cornwall soon after, preparing for the invasions of Africa and Europe. Robert and Elisabeth went back to boarding school, while Joanna and Sandy formed a close bond at home by themselves. They lived in an imaginary world of their own making. From the orchard above their house, they pretended to shoot at passing soldiers; from the roof of their shed, they spied on people coming and going from the pub; Joanna turned the shed into a one-room schoolhouse, with Sandy as her star pupil.

But when Robert came home the following summer, their innocent games became positively dangerous. He brought a BB gun with him, and instead of spying on people, they actually began shooting at them. They never hit anyone, but they were reported to the Home Guard, who came to their house one day to complain. The Home Guard was a group of men from all walks of life; the only thing they had in common was that each

171

172 ● CHRISTOPHER SHAW MYERS

was too old to be drafted but not too old to squeeze into their ancient uniforms. Their job was to make a last stand should the Germans get past the British army. Some of the men brandished shotguns while others brandished pitchforks. Some wore army caps while others wore buckets on their heads. Mrs. Shaw burst out laughing when she saw them and sent them away.

Truro was bombed that summer. From their oast tower, the Shaws watched the city turn a bright red. Two German Wulf 190s had dropped thousand-pound bombs on the city, killing thirteen people and wounding a hundred more. But what angered Truro's citizens more than anything was when part of Truro's Royal Infirmary was demolished.

Afterward, children began collecting shrapnel along the sides of the road, some of it still warm. They traded them with classmates, the way kids would later trade bubblegum cards. Each piece of shrapnel had a unique shape.

One night, the Shaws were in their oast tower when they heard a faint humming. To the people of Tresillian, it sounded like bees working in the gardens. But as the sound grew louder and bursts of antiaircraft fire began lighting up the sky, they realized it was another squadron of German bombers overhead. One by one, curtains were drawn and lights dimmed. The gas lamps along the street had long since vanished, early casualties of the war. Only the gardens behind each house remained visible, framed in black and white by the moon. Each was meticulously groomed, with flowers and hedges and stone paths: the pride of England.

Soon, all the houses were dark . . . all but one. The Shaws had become so used to the air raids that it no longer bothered them. Robert stood in front of his siblings that night, lit by a candle, a book in his hand. Liz, Joanna, and Sandy sat on the floor in front of him, watching his shadow dance on the ceiling. The thud of bombs began to be felt, rather than heard, and Joanna gazed at the curtains. They were bombing the naval base at the mouth of the River Fal again (Falmouth).

Reading and writing had become their obsession since the start of the war. This is not to compare them to the Brontë sisters, with their brilliant childhood writing on the bleak Yorkshire moors, but it was just the four of them now, reading and writing together in their tower.

They had been raised to think of boys and girls as equals and competed endlessly at both mental and physical games, yet it had nevertheless become apparent that Robert was the best reader. Without realizing it, they had fallen into the habit of choosing a book for him each night. Liz always wanted poetry, Sandy always asked for *Lorna Doone*, and Joanna always chose a Dickens novel.

Tonight, however, it was Robert's turn, and he was a contrarian. He always looked for something they had not read. This often meant finding an American author, since they were not taught in the British school system. He had already been through the American humorists with them, like Mark Twain and James Thurber, and he always had them laughing with his theatrical style and comic timing. Without realizing it, Robert was honing his early acting skills.

"I've found another American," he said. "But this one is serious. No laughing."

"I would prefer a George Herbert poem," Elisabeth said.

"Shut up, Liz."

"Why can't we have Dickens?" Joanna asked.

"This is better."

"That's sacrilege!"

"Joey, be quiet!"

Robert cleared his throat. There would be no further discussion. "*The Bridge of San Luis Rey*, by Thornton Wilder," he said.

> There was something in Lima that was wrapped in yards of violet satin, from which protruded a great dropsical head and two fat pearly hands: it was the archbishop. Between the rolls of flesh were two black eyes speaking discomfort, kindliness, and wit.

The others fell silent, mesmerized by the words.

A curious and eager soul was imprisoned in all this lard, but by dint of never refusing himself a pheasant or a goose or his daily procession of Roman wines, he was his own bitter jailer. Some days he regarded his bulk ruefully, but the distress of remorse was less poignant than the distress of fasting, and he was presently found deliberating over the secret messages that a certain roast sends to the certain salad that will follow. To punish himself, he led an exemplary life in every other way.

"I say," Joanna exclaimed, "that *is* good!"

A banging on the floor halted any further discussion. In the room below, Mrs. Shaw was hitting the ceiling with a broomstick. "Be quiet!" she hissed "There's a war going on!"

The holes in the floor, which had allowed heat from the kilns to dry the hops, had tripped them up once again. Robert put a finger to his lips, and everyone became quiet. The thud of bombs continued to shake the house. Mrs. Shaw stopped her banging. Everyone held their breaths.

Nearly a minute passed before Mrs. Shaw shook her head sadly and went back to her newspaper. "Foolish children," she muttered.

Robert stared at the others for another minute with a grin. Then he resumed his reading. He read in a whisper now, so as not to be heard, but his movements were even more exaggerated. He flung his arms this way and that and adopted what he thought was a South American accent. Soon, the others had tears rolling down their cheeks as they tried to suppress their laughter.

That fall, Robert found a flyer in the hallway of his school:

> *Tryouts for Julius Caesar will be held in the auditorium this Saturday at precisely 11:00 a.m. — Cyril Wilkes*

Robert had always liked the idea of acting, ever since his first time on the stage in Stromness. He disappeared that Saturday without telling anyone why.

"Where is your brother?" Mrs. Shaw asked at one point. The others only shrugged.

Robert returned that evening looking crestfallen. The day had started well: Mr. Wilkes, the drama teacher, brought in lunch and everyone read different parts. Robert was having a jolly time of it, until the end of the day when Mr. Wilkes announced the roles. Instead of winning the lead role of Julius Caesar, Robert had been assigned the role of Marc Antony.

Joanna looked at him in surprise. "Haven't you read the play?" Robert shook his head. "Caesar dies halfway through. Marc Antony *is* the lead role. You know: 'Friends, Romans, countrymen . . .'"

In the weeks that followed, Robert spent hours practicing his lines in the tower, sometimes asking Joanna or Sandy to read with him. "I think Antony should have a stutter," he said at one point. Joanna and Sandy looked at him skeptically.

"Not the kind you're thinking of," he said. "Not at the *end* of a sentence. I'm thinking about the way some people get ahead of themselves because they are really smart. The stutter lets their mouth catch up with their mind."

"I don't think Shakespeare intended Antony to have a stutter," Joanna said.

"Who cares! I don't want people to say, 'That Shaw kid did it the way Shakespeare intended.' I want them to say, 'Do it like that Shaw kid.'"

On the morning of the performance, Robert bicycled into the city while Mrs. Shaw took the younger ones on the bus with her in the afternoon. They stopped for a moment to enjoy the view: Truro High School sat on a bluff overlooking the quarry with a lovely view of the cathedral. They were greeted by Dr. Magson at the door of the auditorium.

"So good to see you, Mrs. Shaw," he said, ignoring her missing finger as they shook—he had already fallen for it several times. "These must be your other children. How do you do?"

"How do you do, Dr. Magson?" Mrs. Shaw said. "Where shall we sit?"

"Ah, I recall you are not fond of small talk," he said with a smile.

"I do not mean to be rude, but I have never seen the point of chitchat."

"But it is so important. We all must make judgments about our fellow human beings, and chitchat helps us do it."

Mrs. Shaw remained on her best behavior with the headmaster. Robert had received a scholarship to the school, thanks to a small lie she had told them about where they lived, and she did not want to jeopardize it. She nodded pleasantly as the headmaster talked, while looking around for seats.

"It is especially important for those who live in large cities like Truro," he continued. "In the country, one does not think about meeting new people, because they are so infrequent. But the rest of us must constantly judge one another. 'Is this someone I can trust? Will this person improve my odds of success? Or will they hold me back?'"

"Yes, yes," Mrs. Shaw said.

"My dear Mrs. Shaw, do you not remember what George Orwell wrote? 'We all wear masks and our faces grow to fit them.' First impressions only see the mask. And when we make a judgment quickly, we then ignore further evidence. No one likes to be proven wrong. That is what makes chitchat so important."

"I bow to your superior knowledge," Mrs. Shaw said. "But we really must find our seats."

As she turned to leave, Dr. Magson had one final thought for her. "Robert has the leading role in this play for a reason," he said. "It was my recommendation to Cyril. I will be honest: Your son is not universally liked, but I believe he has talent. And he does not suffer fools gladly."

"As no one should."

They found their seats, the curtain went up, and the play began. For the next two hours, the Shaws watched the boys of Truro High perform *Julius Caesar*. As in Shakespeare's day, all the parts were played by males. Each of them had a different reaction to what they saw. Mrs. Shaw thought Robert was not very good, but he was better than the other children. Elisabeth thought the other children were good, but Robert was awful. And Joanna and Sandy were simply thrilled to see their brother on stage—they thought everyone was terrific. Robert's soliloquy seemed especially brilliant to them.

F-f-f-friends, Romans, countrymen, lend me your ears;
I-I-I come to bury Caesar, not to praise him.
The evil that men do lives after them;
The good is oft interred with their bones;
S-s-so let it be with Caesar. The noble Brutus
Hath told you Caesar was ambitious . . .

After that, Robert knew what he would do with his life. He would become an actor. This was not unusual for their generation: Kids did not have the luxury of attending college in order to figure it all out. Joanna knew she would become a teacher, as did Liz, and even little Sandy knew that he would become a doctor one day. At Treworyan, he had been the only one who would happily twist the neck off a chicken when Aunt Aileen needed it for dinner.

But Joanna was learning something else about life at the same time: There were far more obstacles in her way than for the boys. Mrs. Shaw enrolled her and Sandy in the local Temperance Society that fall, where they entered a competition about the effects of alcoholism on a family. This was something the two of them knew all too well, and they both won in their categories. For his part, Sandy received a penknife, while Joanna won a pink jewelry box.

"What's this?" she asked.

"A box for your jewelry," the teacher said.

"But I don't have any jewelry."

"One day you will, and then you shall be glad of it."

Joanna tossed the jewelry box in the trash on her way out and was not invited back.

On another occasion, she was in Truro with her mother when they spied a radio crew giving tryouts to children for a chance to be on the air. "Go ahead, Joey," her mother said. "You're a good reader. Recite something for them."

Joanna approached the microphone, pulled it down to her height, and recited *Nature* by George Herbert. She knew it by heart—it was one of Liz's favorites. When she finished, one of the men thanked her, while the other approached Mrs. Shaw. "That was very good," he said. "Your daughter is by far the best we have heard. But I'm afraid this is only open to boys."

Cyril Wilkes became a frequent visitor after the play, stopping by their house each Saturday morning to speak with Robert. The two would disappear for hours, walking along the Tresillian River and talking about theater. He usually stayed for tea afterward, conversing with Mrs. Shaw. Joanna was vaguely aware that he was lonely and thought it must come from working in an all-boys school. She assumed he was flirting with her mother.

Later in life, however, another thought struck her. It was when she read about the scandals in the Catholic church, where priests were having affairs with young acolytes. Then she wondered if it was Robert he had been after.

Robert was a different person after the success of his play. He had always been a top student and star athlete, but now he was also an actor. Joanna noticed the change when she attended school in Truro. They got off the bus together, and the girls walked up Lemon Street while the boys went up Trennick Lane. Everyone eyed each other, and Robert began to pose as he walked, drawing attention to himself. Elisabeth found this embarrassing, but Joanna loved it. All her friends were watching, and they all wanted Robert. It was his looks and his confidence that drew them in. He had become a matinee idol in their small part of the world.

To improve her position, Joanna began making up stories about him, exaggerating Robert's strength and prowess. This helped her become the leader of her class, but she soon discovered a downside to his magnetism. Robert felt his power, drawing girls in and then insulting them. Over time, Joanna discovered that while audiences admired Robert, acquaintances and even close friends did not like him or were afraid of him. The knowledge was vindication for Elisabeth, who had never liked him, but it was very painful to Joanna and Sandy, who adored him.

By early 1944, the slow trickle of American soldiers had become a torrent. They were everywhere: on the streets, in the fields, and especially in the pubs. The Shaws could see the Wheel Inn from their house, and it always had a steady stream of Americans coming and going.

Mrs. Shaw had been taking in officers during the war, renting out Robert's and Liz's rooms when they were at boarding school and moving the children into each other's rooms when they were home. This earned her some much-needed money, and even better, it was another source of cigarettes for her—they had been in short supply since rationing had begun. As a result, she was introduced to an entirely new set of cigarettes: Chesterfields, Lucky Strikes, and Camels. The Americans seemed to have an endless supply.

Dinnertime discussions were often entertaining. One evening, a soldier began talking about the roles of men and women in America and how women knew their rightful place: in the home and the kitchen. "Really?" Mrs. Shaw said. He nodded. Mrs. Shaw glanced at her children and said, "Would someone please get salt and pepper for the table."

Elisabeth began to get up. "Not you," her mother said. There was a pause; then Joanna began to rise. "Not you either." Finally, Sandy stood and got them from the cupboard.

The soldier had an amused look. "I don't mean to be rude, ma'am, but where I come from, boys go to work and the girls take care of the home."

"And where do *you* come from?"

"Georgia," he replied, smiling broadly.

"And where do you go from here?"

"France."

"So, you are proposing to fight the Germans and then come home to a pretty little wife who will cook dinner for you. Is that right?"

The soldier thought for a moment. Then he said, in his Southern drawl, "I tell you what, ma'am. If you would agree to land in France, fight the Germans all the way to Berlin, and maybe get killed along the way, I would be happy to stay home and do the cooking. Do we have a deal?"

Mrs. Shaw thought for a moment. Then she burst out laughing. "When you put it that way, I will do the cooking, thank you."

Mrs. Shaw received a phone call one day and turned to her children. "Robert, Joey, go to the Wheel Inn and pick up my cigarettes. Be quick about it before someone else takes them." The two grabbed their coats and hurried out.

On the way, they were surprised to find that their neighbor, Mr. Phillips, was not on the street corner. Ever since his wife died two years ago, Mr. Phillips stood outside his house every day, dressed only in his bathrobe, inviting passersby to see the memorial he had built for her in a corner of their bedroom. Today, however, they found him inside the pub enjoying a glass of beer, still in his bathrobe.

"Do you have my mum's cigs?" Robert asked the owner, behind the bar. He was given a box of Woodbines with ten precious cigarettes inside. "Thank you."

As they turned to leave, Mr. Phillips said, "I was sitting right here when he came in."

Robert and Joanna turned. There was no one else in the pub. "When who came in?"

"The pilot."

"The one who bailed out of his plane last week?"

It had been the talk of the town. A British pilot had parachuted to safety after his plane had been hit, landing in a farmer's field outside their town. The farmer had confronted him with his pitchfork, but when he realized it was a British pilot, he brought him around to the Wheel.

"He fell right out of his plane," Mr. Phillips said.

"You mean jumped out," Robert replied.

"No, fell out. The young man did not realize, being in the clouds, that he was upside down! As soon as he unhooked his straps, he just fell!"

They glanced at the owner, who just shrugged. It was all true, he indicated. Robert and Joanna had a vague feeling they were forgetting something but wanted to hear the end of the story.

"I bought him a drink," Mr. Phillips said, "maybe two, as I think about it. Then I took him round to my house and showed him my wife's stuff. He was mightily impressed. 'What a wonderful collection of undies,' he said to me. He was a wonderful lad." Mr. Phillips scratched himself. "Mind you, I would not have shown him her undies if he had been a German."

"What would you have done?" Joanna asked.

"I'd have locked him up."

Mr. Phillips turned back to the bar, and Robert turned to Joanna. "Mum's cigarettes!" They were still laughing when they walked through their door.

"What are you two going on about?" Mrs. Shaw demanded. "What took you so long?"

"Crazy Mr. Phillips," Robert said.

"Ah," she said, lighting up. That was explanation enough.

That spring, Joanna and Sandy were playing rounders in the backyard when they heard a shout. "Run!" It was Robert, who had been looking out the window of the oast tower. "There's a German plane coming up the river! Run! Run, I tell you!"

Bedlam broke loose. Mrs. Shaw flew out of the house and pulled Joanna and Sandy inside. Retrieving Wendy, they all crawled into the closet beneath the stairs. Liz, however, went the other way, flying out of the house to grab the bicycles. She shoved them in the shed and said afterward that her only thought was to save their lone means of transportation.

Robert was nowhere to be seen. When Mrs. Shaw poked her head out, she found him coming down the stairs, hands in pockets. "What did you see?" she demanded.

Robert shrugged. "A German plane. A Stuka, I think. Flew by so fast, I can't be sure."

His mother's next few words were somewhat garbled, but it was clear she did not believe him. Robert seemed taken aback, but he did not waver. He was committed. He gave more details, describing the young pilot. "I looked him right in the eyes," he said. "To be honest, it all happened so fast that I wasn't even frightened. Yet my knees were shaking when it was over."

"All right, enough," Mrs. Shaw said. He didn't look frightened to her, but she appreciated a good story as much as anyone.

That week, Robert repeated the story to anyone who would listen, and a local newspaper printed an article about a German plane that flew over Tresillian and bombed their water tower. Several people claimed to have witnessed the attack. The fact that no damage could be seen to the tower did not stop it from becoming part of Tresillian lore.

By the middle of 1944, the war was building to a climax. The American soldiers had been increasing their presence every day, bringing in more supplies, more equipment, and expanding their field exercises in the hills and valleys around Cornwall. Then one day, everything suddenly vanished. The Shaws woke up one morning to find nothing but empty encampments, fields littered with equipment, and pubs with no one in them but the locals.

The assault on Normandy had begun.

Yet life continued. During the day, the Shaws attended school, taking their Latin lessons in the air-raid shelter because their teacher was the Latin scholar. Boys and girls huddled together with various sexual probings, which their teacher ignored because their lives were at stake, they assumed.

In the afternoons, they played together or bicycled to Treworyan to help with the farmwork. Robert continued to get them in trouble when he was home. And of course they continued to read to each other in the evenings, ignoring the air-raid sirens and the planes overhead.

When they looked back on it years later, it all felt like it had been a dream.

It was World War II. It was madness.

The following spring, Mrs. Shaw took the children into Truro to hear a speech by Lady Rendlesham. She was the aristocrat from the Rendlesham estate, where the Shaws had watched antiaircraft guns being installed. The woman was dressed in a simple black dress that was nevertheless elegant. Her face was set in an attitude of resolve.

Lady Rendlesham spoke of her two sons, brave soldiers both, who were fighting for the preservation of the Empire. Her older son had been captured in Germany, where he was put in shackles and subjected to solitary confinement. She wiped a tear from her eyes as she said she had not heard from him since. Her younger son had also been captured, but he had been a prisoner in Italy, where his guards served him tea in the morning. "Cream and sugar, sir?" they would ask.

Lady Rendlesham's message was clear: Hitler was an evil man who wished to destroy the British Empire, but he would fail. "The British Empire has been the greatest force for good that the world has ever seen," she told them. "In places like India, Egypt, Burma, and Zambia, we have replaced corrupt governments and brought prosperity to the people."

The lady spoke at length about right and wrong, good and evil, and especially about all the wonderful things Great Britain had accomplished in the world. She finished her speech by quoting Princess Elizabeth, who had recently addressed the children of the nation: "When peace comes, it will be for the children of today to make the world of tomorrow a better and happier place."

The war ended soon after. Germany fell, then Japan. Everyone in Britain celebrated. No one thought about the awful consequences of the atom bombs, or the hundreds of thousands of Japanese civilians who had been killed, or what it heralded for their future. They only saw an end to messengers knocking on doors and telling another family they had lost a loved one. The Shaws celebrated along with everyone else, bicycling into Truro and joining the longest conga line they had ever seen.

But despite Lady Rendlesham's predictions, the war did mark the end of the British Empire. India, Burma, and Ireland soon declared independence, and others followed. And that was not the only change. The British class system was also transformed. The Shaws had seen it for themselves, although they did not realize it at the time. They had seen it in the queue for rations, where rich and poor alike mingled without any thought to one's status. They had seen it in the eyes of the London evacuees and in the people who had taken them into their homes without considering what rank those children held. They had seen it in the antics of the Home Guard, in the posters and slogans that urged people to come together, and in the way everyone embraced a common enemy and cause.

And the war brought an end to the Shaws' idyllic life in Cornwall as well. Robert moved to London and became a teacher; Liz enrolled in Oxford; Sandy went to boarding school; and even little Wendy was sent away to school. This left Joanna at home by herself with a mother she had always scorned. And yet, without her other children to divide and conquer, Mrs. Shaw seemed to change. She and Joey both enjoyed long walks, and the two of them spent hours hiking along the Cornish cliffs together or on the pathways that ran through the local farms and fields. They talked and talked and talked on those hikes—about their lives, their ambitions, and their desires—and this brought about the biggest change of all, as momentous in its own way as any of the global events and disasters. Joanna discovered she liked her mother.

PART V

JAWS &
MRS. SHAW

Every man has his secret sorrows
which the world knows not.

— Henry Wadsworth Longfellow

Chapter 20

An Offer She Can't Refuse

[Late summer 1974]

Robert was out of breath as he trudged up the hill. It was steep, and he was in full Quint costume, which included several layers of padding. Behind him, the sun sparkled on the ocean, and the dock was a hive of activity: Cameramen were busy adjusting cameras, lighting men were busy adjusting lights, and miscellaneous other crew were busy performing miscellaneous other tasks. Boats came and went, ferrying people and equipment here and there.

Several members of the crew passed Robert on their way to work. "Good morning, Mr. Shaw," they said. Robert only grunted in response. At the top of the hill, he stepped into a phone booth, but before dialing, he turned and yelled down to them, "Call me Quint, dammit!"

The other end of the phone was in a small kitchen in Philadelphia, where Joanna had her own problems. In one arm she cradled a baby while her other arm was busy pouring bowls of cereal. In between, she shuffled through student papers and stuffed them in a briefcase that was propped on the counter. Three teenage boys were at the table, reading cereal boxes or staring into space. Next to them, another baby was in a highchair.

Joanna's other children were . . . well . . . they were somewhere. Like working mothers all over the world, she was overworked, underpaid, and more than a little stressed. "Where's your father?" she asked the boys.

"He left."

"Of course!"

In a corner of the kitchen, Mrs. Shaw was observing everything with a critical eye. "If you had raised your children correctly," she said, "they would be making their own breakfast. I always said you should have given them a proper British upbringing."

"We're not in England, Mother. These are American kids."

"That's the problem!"

"At least my boys put the toilet seat down when they're finished. That's more than I can say for yours." Joanna was saved from further criticism when the phone rang. She was too busy to pick up, and everyone else ignored it. Nearly a minute passed. Robert waited patiently.

Finally, Joanna grabbed the receiver. "Who is it?" she demanded.

"Joey, is that you?"

"Oh, Robert! We were just talking about you."

"What about?"

"If you must know, we were having a very interesting discussion about how you never put the toilet seat down when you're done."

Robert paused. "Never a dull moment in the Myers house, eh?"

They both laughed. "Where are you?" Joanna asked.

"Martha's Vineyard. We're shooting a movie about a shark that attacks a small town."

"Sounds like a masterpiece," she said, her voice dripping with sarcasm.

"The book's awful, but the movie has potential. The trouble is, I've got so much time on my hands that I'm drinking too much. Come and keep me company."

Joanna paused. "It's lovely up here," Robert added.

"My summer classes do finish today," she mused. "I suppose Walt could look after the kids, and I could sure use a break."

"Jolly good! I'll have a plane waiting for you in the morning."

Then Joanna remembered her mother. Cupping her hand over the phone, she whispered, "Wait, Mother is staying with me."

"Oh no," Robert groaned. "Leave her behind!"

"I can't do that."

"Yes, you can. Have her look after the kids."

"And what do you think would happen?"

"Someone would be killed," Robert was forced to admit.

"Exactly," Joanna said. "And we both know it wouldn't be Mother."

Robert sighed. He pulled a flask from his pocket and stared at it. "Okay," he said, "I guess she'll have to come. Now I'll *really* have to cut down on the drink!"

Joanna hung up and stared at her mother. Mrs. Shaw returned her gaze. Had she been a different sort of mother, Joanna would certainly have asked her to stay behind. She and Robert would have had a lovely time. But given the circumstances, she had no choice.

It turned out to be a memorable week.

Chapter 21

⫷⟨⟨⟨◆⟩⟩⟩⟫

An Awkward Lunch

[The following day]

Joanna and Mrs. Shaw made their way through Philadelphia's crowded airport, dragging suitcases behind them. After several wrong turns, they found the section for chartered flights and found a small plane waiting. "Are you Mr. Shaw's party?" the pilot asked.

"That's right," Joanna said.

"Mr. Shaw only mentioned one person."

Mrs. Shaw raised an eyebrow. It was clear which person had not been mentioned, but she professed otherwise. "It seems Robert was not expecting you," she said to Joanna.

The pilot surveyed their bags. "It's okay. It's going to be tight, but we can still make it. The smaller of you will have to ride in the back, though. That would be you, er, Mrs. . . .." He looked at Mrs. Shaw and smiled.

Mrs. Shaw pretended to be incensed. Drawing herself up, she said, "My name is Mrs. Shaw, and I can assure you I am not climbing into the back of your plane!"

"Don't worry," the pilot insisted. "You'll be fine back there. But I do have to balance the weight."

Mrs. Shaw turned away dismissively. "Joey, get in the back of the plane."

Joanna looked from her mother to the pilot, then back again.

Thirty minutes later, they were aloft. In the front seat, the pilot fiddled with his instruments, gripping the wheel nervously. Next to him, Mrs. Shaw sat bolt upright, observing the lovely scenery below. In the back, Joanna was scrunched between suitcases, bouncing all over the place and wondering why, at the age of forty-four, she still did everything her mother told her to do.

Robert and his colleague, Richard Dreyfuss, stood in a corner of the tiny airport on Martha's Vineyard. The runway seemed to emerge from the lush greenery around them. Overhead, seagulls wheeled and cried out. The smell of saltwater filled the air.

"Tell me again," Dreyfuss said, "how you played that Churchill character."

"Lord Randolph?"

"After all the Shakespeare you did, how do you play someone with syphilis?"

Robert grinned. "I became something of an expert on the subject."

Dreyfuss chuckled. "Gives method acting a whole new meaning."

"That was Churchill's father," Robert said. "Brilliant politician in his day but prickly. You either loved him or hated him. There was very little in between."

"And syphilis brought him down?"

"Yes, very embarrassing for Winston. It gets passed from parent to child, you know."

They heard the plane before they saw it. Then it appeared beneath the clouds, waggling its wings and descending toward them.

"Who's visiting?" Dreyfuss asked.

"My sister. You'll like her. Strong woman."

"Strong woman?"

"Yes, you know the type, Richard. They're the ones who frighten you."

Robert grinned and Dreyfuss smiled, unoffended. Suddenly, Robert became serious. "And there's another passenger . . ."

"Oh?"

"My mother."

"Ah, the plot thickens!"

"She takes a little getting used to. I would say she is a bit like Lord Randolph—nice underneath but prickly in public."

Dreyfuss considered this. "Let me see if I understand. Your mother is like Lord Randolph?" Robert nodded. "And syphilis gets passed from parent to child?"

Robert laughed. "That's right. Very good, old boy, you *do* have a sense of humor! I always suspected it."

The two men were still smiling as the plane came to a stop. Two women got out and marched toward them. Before Robert could say anything, Mrs. Shaw slapped him in the stomach.

"You've put on weight, boy."

Joanna started to laugh, because it was so typical of Mother, but she stopped when she saw the look on Robert's face. She decided it was because Dreyfuss was there. Robert had said similar things many times before, even using the word "boy" with the same inflection. He had developed the trait in school, when he wanted to impress others yet could not resist bullying them. The victim always had mixed feelings: They wanted to escape, but at the same time they wanted to please the bully. This was different, though; Dreyfuss did not look like someone who could be bullied. He was looking from mother to son with obvious amusement.

"It is good to see you, Mother," Robert said stiffly.

"What have you been doing with yourself?"

"Making a lovely little picture on this island."

"You know what I mean. Why have you gotten so fat?"

"Ah, that. Simply enjoying life, I suppose. Let me introduce you to my colleague, Richard Dreyfuss."

"Hello, it is great to meet you," Dreyfuss said, offering his hand. Mrs. Shaw extended her gloved hand, and they began to shake, but he pulled away quickly, like so many before him.

"Is something wrong?"

"No, no. Robert was just telling me about you," Dreyfuss said. Then, under his breath, he added, "Though not everything."

"What's that? Please speak up."

"Robert has had nothing but good things to say about you," he said, recovering. "I have learned so much from him in such a short time."

"Not that short a time," Robert murmured, thinking of Paddy's.

"Oh, Lord, you sound like another actor I once met," Mrs. Shaw said. "What was his name, Robert? The one who stuck his nose through my window in Spain?"

"Leonard Whiting, I believe."

"Perhaps." Mrs. Shaw put her nose in the air. "He did some perfectly wretched movie and thought he was a high and mighty lord."

Robert cupped his hand over his mouth and whispered to the others, "The wretched movie was Zeffirelli's *Romeo and Juliet*."

"At least you introduced yourself politely," Mrs. Shaw said, looking at Dreyfuss.

There was an awkward silence. Then Robert took Joanna by the arm. "So much for introductions, let's get some lunch. Richard, welcome to the Shaw family!"

They settled into a table overlooking the marina. Boats of varying shapes and sizes lined the pier, while families came and went, preparing for a day on the water. A waiter began taking their orders. "Your usual drink, Mr. Shaw?"

"Nothing for me today, Phil," Robert said.

Joanna turned to Dreyfuss. "Is this your first film? You seem very young."

"Thank you, I think. Is that a compliment about my youthful energy yet mature persona?"

Joanna smiled. "Sure, let's go with that."

"Good, I like that," Dreyfuss said with a grin. "I've mostly done television, but I made two movies recently, so here I am!"

Mrs. Shaw interrupted. "Let me tell you about youthful energy." She turned to Dreyfuss. "Are you the oldest child?"

"No. Why?"

"Robert was the eldest, that was the reason for his energy. He and his friends would get into so much trouble, we had to send him to boarding school."

Everyone stared. Mrs. Shaw put her hand over her mouth in mock surprise. "Have I said something wrong?"

"Yes," Joanna said. "Robert had energy. All kids do." She turned back to Dreyfuss, but before she could say anything . . .

"They would shame each other, you know," Mrs. Shaw said.

Robert shifted in his seat, caught the waiter's eye, and raised two fingers. The waiter nodded.

"And you would punish them?" Joanna asked.

"Joey, please don't encourage her," Robert said.

"Oh no, not me," Mrs. Shaw said. "That was your father's job. When he was alive."

Robert and Joanna glanced at each other but did not say anything. Dreyfuss's eyes flitted from one Shaw to the other.

"There was one time," Mrs. Shaw continued, "the gardener was planting bushes in front of the house, but as fast he put them in, Robert pulled them up. The man reported him to us."

Dreyfuss turned to Robert. "The *gardener* turned you in?" Robert shrugged. The waiter put a drink in front of him, and he took a grateful sip.

"Yes, the gardener," Mrs. Shaw said. "Of course, his father had to send him to his room. I told him he was being silly, but the man was drinking in those days, always drinking. He insisted on doing everything his way. 'I shall teach him a lesson,' he said. But when we went up to his room—and mind you, it was only a short while later—do you know what we found? The bedding had been tied to the window and his lordship had made his escape!"

Mrs. Shaw laughed in delight but stopped when she saw no one else was laughing. "But don't you see? It would have been cheaper to buy new plants than new bedding."

Now, everyone did laugh. Robert tried to shift the conversation. "Joey, Richard has some interesting political views. I think you'd be interested."

Joey glanced at her brother and realized he had a lot of respect for the young actor. She turned to Dreyfuss. "I find it absolutely incredible," she said, "the corruption in American politics. With the scandal of Richard Nixon, and before him the scandal of Spiro Agnew, Ford now seems like such a pathetic figure."

"Yes, but that's a good thing," Dreyfuss said. His enthusiasm for the subject was obvious. "We're lucky to now have a weak figure as president. Otherwise, we might have slid into a dictatorship. The real lesson is that our checks and balances work. Even with a figure like Nixon, we move on."

Before he could say anything further, Mrs. Shaw interrupted again. "I do not mean to go on and on about Robert, but I do remember how the maid could not even put sugar on the table. Every time she did, it vanished as soon as she turned her back!" She shook her head sadly. "Oh no, you couldn't leave anything lying around."

Mrs. Shaw turned to Dreyfuss. "And you also have youthful energy, I understand?"

Dreyfuss stared back, at a rare loss for words.

The dishes were being cleared and coffee served when a man spotted them from across the patio. Dreyfuss waved him over. "Roy, you have to hear this. Robert's mother thinks acting is"—he turned to Mrs. Shaw—"what did you call it?"

"Rubbish!"

"Yes, rubbish," Dreyfuss finished.

"Why, Mrs. Shaw," Scheider said politely as he sat down, "acting is the noblest of professions."

"Is that so?"

"Sure." He continued to smile but began to squirm under her stern gaze.

"Very well, let us discuss acting, then, since you brought it up. I understand you are making a movie about a shark." Scheider nodded. "And you have a mechanical shark that you pretend is real?" Scheider nodded. Mrs. Shaw folded her arms. "Does it work?"

Scheider considered this. He thought back to all the times they had tried to start the shark, only to hear the gears grind to a halt.

"Well, no," he admitted. "To be honest, the shark doesn't work, uh, pretty much, uh, ever."

"I see," Mrs. Shaw said. "Let us try something else, then. Mr. Dreyfuss tells me it is quite expensive to film a movie on the ocean. I imagine, if that is the case, you must make very good use of your time out there?"

Scheider thought back to all the hours they had spent sitting around, waiting for the weather to clear . . . or sailboats to move out of the way . . . or the equipment to cooperate. One memory was especially painful. He had been practicing a line, one that he had come up with himself: "You're going to need a bigger boat." He repeated it over and over until he was sure he had it right, but just as Spielberg yelled "Action!" another voice yelled, "Sailboats in the way! Shut it down." Scheider was left with his mouth half open.

His cheerfulness began to ebb. "I guess we don't make very good use of our time, actually," he said.

"I see." Mrs. Shaw straightened herself. "But then, if the mechanical shark doesn't work and you are forever sitting on your bottoms and twiddling your thumbs, I imagine that on those rare occasions, those *very* rare occasions when everything is working, the acting itself must be very exciting. Is that correct?"

Scheider thought back to how often he had to perform a simple task, like drumming his fingers on the side of the boat, because that was all the director needed.

He sighed. "I guess you've got me there too."

Mrs. Shaw turned triumphantly to Robert. "Noble profession indeed! I always said you should have been a doctor, like your father."

Scheider looked at Dreyfuss and shrugged. "Roy," Dreyfuss implored, "you can't let her get away with that."

"Ricky, she just hit on everything wrong with this film within two minutes."

Dreyfuss desperately wanted the film to be a success, but even he had to admit they were in trouble. "Gottlieb even fell in the water the other day," he said.

"Hey, I did too," Robert pointed out.

"Let's face it, this is a shit show," Scheider said. He turned to Mrs. Shaw. "Pardon my French, but I'm going to need a psychiatrist when this is over."

"You'd have to be mad to see a psychiatrist," she said. "They only make things worse."

As Scheider pondered this, Robert stood up. "I don't know which is the greater compliment," he said, "to have the energy of youth or the wisdom of age. Mother, the girls are at the bungalow and would love to see you. Roy, thank you for stopping by. Richard, be a good soul and help my mother with her luggage. I've got something to show Joey."

Robert grabbed Joanna by the arm and ushered her across the patio before anyone could object. Scheider was left trying to make sense of what had happened, while Mrs. Shaw and Dreyfuss eyed each other suspiciously.

"Where on earth are you dragging me off to?" Joanna managed to ask when they had crossed the road and were on the beach.

"The editing room," Robert said.

"Out here?"

"Yes, I think you'll find it interesting. It's where movies actually get made."

They were interrupted by a "Yoo-hoo!" Turning, they saw their mother waving to them. "Christ, I can't get away from her," Robert said. "She seems to be in better shape than me."

"She did say you've put on weight."

"Remind me again why you brought her?"

"I had no choice, remember?"

"I'm not asking for pity, but do you ever bring her into your classroom?"

Joanna laughed. "Are you kidding?"

Mrs. Shaw was soon beside them, breathing heavily but otherwise looking fit as a fiddle. "Interesting fellow," she said, "the one with the beard."

"Richard Dreyfuss," Robert said.

"Is that his name? I believe he compensates for his smallness by being pushy and opinionated."

"I didn't think so at all," Joanna said. "I found him very intelligent."

"Well, whatever you think of him, he was good enough to take our luggage." Then she added, "Very opinionated, though, wouldn't you agree?"

"Perhaps," Robert said, "but aren't we all?"

"Not me!" Mrs. Shaw said.

They looked at each other for a moment, then burst out laughing.

The editing room was just a small hut by the side of the water, its windows covered by curtains. Inside, they found Verna Fields splicing reels of tape, hanging them on the wall, and labeling each one. Robert greeted her with a peck on the cheek. "Verna, my dear," he said, "have you turned the dribs and drabs of yesterday into your latest masterpiece?"

"I've got some wonderful footage of you on the gunwale," Verna said. "Your eyes say it all."

"Must have been the liquor you saw. Let me introduce you to my mother and sister."

They greeted each other with pleasantries. Verna noted the odd handshake from Robert's mother but did not say anything. Instead, she commented on Robert's extraordinary acting.

"Extraordinary?" Mrs. Shaw said. It was more of a demand than a question, and Verna tried to think what she had said to provoke her.

"Do you have children?" Mrs. Shaw asked.

Verna nodded.

"Then surely you must understand the difference between ordinary and extraordinary. Robert could not stop showing off. There is nothing extraordinary about that."

Verna smiled, unsure what to say.

"There was one time," Mrs. Shaw continued, "he was playing with his sister—not this one, a different one. Liz would tease him. 'Give us a kiss,' she would say. But she was missing some teeth, so it came out 'Kith me, kith me.' Robert was *furious*! 'I am *not* going to kiss you, you naughty girl.' And do you know what he did? He stuck his head through the banister, like this."

Mrs. Shaw bent low to the ground, cupped her hands around her face so that only her eyes and mouth were showing, and puckered her lips.

Then, imitating a little boy, she said, "Kith me, kith me." She was still laughing when the door opened, and a man entered. A beam of light fell on Mrs. Shaw's face, and the man looked down in surprise. "Am I interrupting?" he asked.

Robert started to say something but took a step back instead. Joanna suppressed a giggle. Mrs. Shaw straightened herself and extended her hand in greeting. "How do you do?" she said. "I am Mrs. Shaw."

But the man had already moved on. "Verna, do you have those clips from yesterday? I'm working on tomorrow's script, need to run it by Steve tonight."

"Yes, I've been playing with the timing of the shark's appearance as it breaches the boat."

"Good, good, let's see what you've got."

The two moved to the other side of the hut and began examining reels of tape. Mrs. Shaw was left standing by herself, her hand (minus one finger) still extended.

Later that day, the three Shaws arrived at Robert's bungalow, where they were greeted by two of his young daughters. Joanna gave them a hug. "So good to see you," she said. "You're getting big."

"Where are our bags?" Mrs. Shaw demanded.

The girls looked at each other. They were being evicted.

"Ignore them, Joey," Robert said. "There's a king-size bed in my room, plenty of space for the three of us."

"You can't be princesses all your life," Mrs. Shaw said.

Joanna tried to smooth things over. "Your father and I are just used to it, that's all," she told the girls. "At least you have a private bathroom. We had to share an outhouse with two toilets when we were your age."

The girls' eyes opened wide. They could not understand why there would be two toilets in one room, but to Joanna it seemed completely normal. "It was all we had," she said. "We kept each other company. We chatted while we pooped."

The fact was that Joanna shared Robert's nonchalance about the sleeping arrangements. They had grown up in a British middle class that was not squeamish about such things. In America, she was constantly surprised by Americans' puritan ways. Not only could her boys not swim naked in the ocean, but they could not even *change* on the beach. Yet, it had not taken long for her to fall into the same way of thinking. A few years later, when Sandy visited America and began stripping down on the beach to put on his bathing suit, Joanna scolded him. "Cover yourself with a towel," she ordered. Sandy obliged, but when a gust of wind blew his towel away, he skipped merrily down the beach after it—completely naked and completely unaware of the commotion he was causing.

Robert's girls were not American, but Joanna knew they were of a different generation, and they were rich. "I understand," she said, trying to be sympathetic. "Today, everyone sits on the toilet by themselves and reads the newspaper. We didn't have that luxury."

That night, Robert snored loudly and slept soundly. His daughters . . . not so much.

Chapter 22

Coffee & Vodka

[The following day]

The following morning, Joanna was woken by a noise. Next to her, Mrs. Shaw snored softly. The clock read 5:00 a.m. At first she thought it was a burglar. A few years ago, she had woken with a similar feeling, only to discover a homeless man in their house. The man thought the house was deserted and fled in a panic when Joanna confronted him.

Then Joanna heard a familiar noise. Throwing on a bathrobe, she made her way to the kitchen and found Robert rummaging in the refrigerator. "What on earth are you doing at this hour?" she asked, yawning.

"You know, the life of an actor," Robert said, without looking up. "It's not all fun and games." Then, in frustration, he said, "I can never find anything in this bloody icebox!"

Joanna laughed. "Sit down," she ordered, and began making breakfast. "Do you remember the day I cooked you breakfast in Stratford? I think it was about this same time of morning. Took you forever to answer the door."

"Of course. I was doing shows at *night* back then. I had just gone to bed!"

"You should have seen the look on your face."

"Was it anything like the look on yours," Robert said, "the day you tried to leap across Ladock Falls and landed on your bottom?"

"I wouldn't have tried if you hadn't been pushing me."

"You were a willing collaborator."

"What else could I do? I worshipped you."

"Worshipped?"

"Don't let it go to your head, mister," Joanna said with a laugh. "That's what little sisters do." She began to turn away, but then she saw Robert pull a flask from his pocket and pour it in his coffee.

"What is that?" she demanded. "Alcohol?!"

"No, vodka," Robert said. "Don't confuse the two."

Joanna's body sagged. "That's what Dad used to say."

"I can't act anymore without it," Robert mumbled. Joanna didn't respond. "I'm trying to feed my family," Robert said more loudly.

"What on earth are you talking about? You make loads of money."

"You have no idea," Robert began to shout. He stopped. His family was asleep. "You have no idea what my bills are like," he hissed.

"Maybe not," Joanna said, "but I know one thing. It is five in the morning and you're already drinking. Robert, that is not good! You should go back to writing if this is what acting does to you. You enjoy writing, don't you?"

"Of course," Robert said, "but it doesn't pay. That is the problem. But I will say this: If the stars ever align, I would like to write one great thing before I die. Just one bloody great thing."

Robert's death was not where Joanna meant to steer the conversation, but before she could say anything further, a horn sounded on the beach. Looking out the window, she saw a boat pulled up below the bungalow. Robert hurried to finish his breakfast.

"That's my ride," he said. "Time for my hour upon the stage."

"To strut and fret and be heard no more?"

"That's right," he said, grinning. "You know your Shakespeare. Be a dear and do something with the girls this morning. They've been complaining all week. Meet me at the pier at ten; we'll have a lovely day of it."

Joanna gave him a mock salute. "Aye-aye, Captain."

While Robert was in makeup, Joanna got everyone up and fed. She piled them into Robert's large Cadillac and maneuvered into traffic. She was not a small woman, but even so, she had to sit up as far as she could just to see over the dashboard. They made their way onto a small ferry, and everyone got out to enjoy the scenery. The girls leaned on the railing, looking bored, while diesel fumes gushed over their heads.

Joanna joined the girls and asked how they had slept; she laughed when she heard about Robert's snoring. "Wait until you're married," she said.

A family of ducks scurried away from the ferry, and the sights and sounds of the small inlet slid past. Joanna told the girls she wanted to find the bridge where Ted Kennedy drove off. Seeing the curious look on their faces, she explained how Kennedy had left a party one night with a woman, had driven off a bridge, and then left the woman to die without reporting the incident until the next morning.

"Kennedy was able to get away with it," she said, "because he comes from royalty." Seeing their curious expressions again, she continued. "Americans think of the Kennedys as coming from Camelot. England may have its kings and queens, but Americans have their tycoons. Either way, you have royalty."

Soon they were on the road again, making their way south on Chappaquiddick Island. Old farmhouses and rolling hills flew by. A song came on the radio, Abba's "Waterloo," and the girls began singing loudly. Even Joanna found herself humming the melody.

Then she slammed on the brakes. The car swerved back and forth—time seemed to stand still—and they came to a stop on a low-slung bridge. Everyone got out and peered over the edge. The water was only a few inches below them, with no railing separating them from its murky depth.

"Joey, you nearly killed us!" Mrs. Shaw exclaimed, uncharacteristically frightened.

They all gazed into the water, imagining what it would have been like to plunge in. Meanwhile, across the island, a mechanical shark was being towed out to sea.

Joanna got them to the dock without further incident, and the four ladies made their way along its crowded surface, zigzagging between people and equipment. Halfway up, they heard a cassette playing a song by The Mamas and the Papas. At the far end, Robert was waiting for them on a boat with the name *Whitefoot* on its stern. Sitting high above the pier, he looked like a king surveying his realm.

"Over here, ladies," he called. "Welcome aboard my ship. Every bit as sturdy as *Orca II*."

A man was standing on the dock below Robert wearing shorts and sneakers, his T-shirt barely covering his belly. With his curly hair and bushy red beard, Joanna thought he looked like a jolly fellow.

"If this boat is as sturdy as *Orca II*," the man said, referring to the prop boat that would be sunk in the movie's final scene, "your ladies are in a fair bit of trouble, Mr. Shaw."

His name was George, a "gofer" on the set who did whatever was needed by the crew. Today, his job was to take care of the Shaw family. George helped the girls on board, then turned to help the two ladies.

"Come on board, Ouma," one of the girls called.

"Ouma?" George asked.

"That's right," Mrs. Shaw said. "It's Dutch Afrikaans for "Grandmother." I was raised in Swaziland."

"Oho, it gets better and better. What is Swaziland like?"

"It is the most beautiful place in the world." Mrs. Shaw thought for a moment, then added, "Save for one."

"I know," George said, looking around. "This island is great, isn't it."

"I was referring to Cornwall."

"Oh." George paused. "Should I call you Ouma?"

"Are you my grandchild?"

"No."

"Then please address me as Mrs. Shaw, thank you."

"Yes, ma'am. Mrs. Shaw it is," George said, smiling. He was one of those people who always seemed to have a smile on his face. "Now please give me your hand, Mrs. Shaw," he said with affected politeness, "and I shall help you on board."

"I do not need any help climbing onto a docked boat."

George's smile widened. "But I have to keep you safe, Mrs. Shaw."

"My goodness, what do you tell people? That you take care of old women?"

George laughed. "I have to admit, it sounds silly when you say it like that. But I have my orders." He pointed a thumb over his shoulder.

"I can assure you I am not giving you my hand," Mrs. Shaw said.

"Then I can assure you I will sling you over my shoulder and carry you on board."

"The nerve! You are a very silly young man!"

"That may be, but then you must be a very silly old woman."

George continued to smile as Mrs. Shaw glared at him. Then she burst out laughing. "Very well. I suppose no one wants to see my bottom slung over your shoulder." She gave him her hand.

With everyone on board, the captain guided them away from the dock. As they slid past East Chop, the sights and sounds of the harbor were replaced by those of the ocean. The boat followed the ocean swells as waves splashed against its side. Seagulls wheeled overhead, calling to each other and looking for food.

Safely out to sea, George glanced over his shoulder and caught Robert's eye. Robert nodded and gave him a thumbs-up, making sure his mother did not see. Twenty minutes later, the captain cut the motor and anchored the boat. A flotilla of motor craft was anchored fifty yards away, clustering around the *Orca*. A small motorboat appeared and ferried George to the film barge.

The Shaws were left to themselves with nothing to do but wait for Robert's turn on camera. "What did you ladies do this morning?" he asked.

"Visited Chappaquiddick," Joanna said.

"Nearly drove off a bridge," one of the girls added.

"Joey wanted to give us the full Kennedy experience, apparently," the other said.

Robert laughed. "I put you in charge."

"I can see how Ted Kennedy did it," Joanna said, shrugging. "I don't mean to excuse him, but it's just a bump in the road."

"Well, that deserves a toast." Robert pulled a bottle of orange juice from beneath his seat, along with two plastic cups. He poured juice into each cup and topped them off from his flask. "Here's to surviving your Kennedy experience," he said, handing one to Joanna. She hesitated.

"Come on," Robert said. "How often are we on the ocean together? It has been a long time."

Joanna thought for a moment, then shrugged. She took a cup and raised it. "Salut."

"Salut."

Robert turned to the girls. "What do you have to say about this island paradise?"

"It's nice," they answered.

"Wonderful!"

"Robert, they live in Jamaica," Joanna pointed out. "All you've done is move them from one paradise to another. And away from their friends."

"You're wrong; they love it here!"

"They've been bored all week."

"Not true." Robert turned to the girls. "Have you girls been bored?"

"No, Dad."

"There, you see," he said.

Joanna nearly choked on her drink. "Yes, I do see. I see how clueless you are!"

"That is an understatement," Mrs. Shaw said.

"I don't mean to say you're not a good father," Joanna continued.

"And that is an overstatement," Mrs. Shaw said.

"All fathers are clueless when it comes to children."

Robert laughed. "Give me an example."

"All right," Joanna said. "Do you know how mothers cross the street?" Robert shook his head. "They keep their children in front of them all the way across, watching everything closely."

"Sounds reasonable. And fathers?"

"Fathers walk ahead of their children, oblivious to what is trailing behind them."

Mrs. Shaw snorted. "I have to side with Joey on this," she said. "You aren't right very often, but on this point I agree."

"Thank you, Mother," Joanna said sarcastically.

"And do you know what happens next?" Mrs. Shaw took up the story. "Halfway across, with your children still in the middle of the road, you spot your good friend on the other side. Of course, you have to wave to him because you are absolutely delighted at discovering him there."

Joanna giggled. "Let's call him Andrew."

Mrs. Shaw considered this. "Andrew? Why yes, I believe it was Andrew. Robert's good friend." Mrs. Shaw adopted a male voice and waved her hand back and forth. "Yoo-hoo, Andrew! What are you doing tonight? Will I see you at the pub?"

"Meanwhile," Joanna said, "while you and Andrew are having the time of your lives, your children are still in the road, examining all those fancy cars around them."

Robert grinned. "But you don't understand. We fathers give them their freedom. You ladies take it away at every opportunity."

"We're only talking about crossing the street, you know," Joanna said.

"Well, perhaps you're right on this one small point." Robert stared wistfully out to sea. "But in my defense, I hadn't seen Andrew in ages."

"Who's Andrew?" one of the girls asked.

"I don't know. You'll have to ask your grandmother."

"Your father was even worse," Mrs. Shaw said. "When you two were little, he let you wander off anywhere you jolly well pleased."

"I rather enjoyed the freedom," Joanna said.

"Aha!" Robert said. "You've proved my point!"

"But he was hopeless at discipline," Mrs. Shaw said. "If it hadn't been for me, you two would have gotten into trouble at every step."

"Mother, you don't know half the things we did as children," Robert said. Mrs. Shaw looked at him skeptically. "I probably shouldn't say this in front of the girls," he continued, "but I brought a BB gun home from school one summer. We used to fire it from the top of the shed. Had loads of fun!"

"Fun?" Mrs. Shaw said. "Was it fun poking holes in Mrs. Richard's laundry?"

Robert stopped. "You knew about that?"

"Of course. She came to me, very puzzled, and said the moths were eating her laundry. I told her they were eating mine as well, and I blamed it on the Americans."

The girls giggled.

"Then how about the time I hit that American soldier with our water gun," Robert said.

"You didn't hit him," Joanna pointed out. "That was Sandy. You were the one giving orders, but somehow you always managed to avoid the dirty work."

"That's right," Robert said, "I was in charge; that's how it works. Anyway, we were aiming at the man in the passenger seat, but we hit the driver instead. Back then, I didn't realize the Americans had their steering wheel on the wrong side. We had to run for miles to get away."

"No," Mrs. Shaw said, "he stopped chasing as soon as you began running."

Robert and Joanna looked at her in surprise. "You saw that too?"

"Watched it all from the upstairs window."

"Why didn't you stop us?"

"I had to let you children make your own mistakes."

"You mean you had to let Robert and me make our own mistakes," Joanna said. "You were always harder on us than the others."

"I most certainly was not," Mrs. Shaw replied. "You children were all equal in my eyes."

Robert and Joanna looked at her in disbelief, until Mrs. Shaw added, "Equally insufferable!"

"Ah," Robert said, "the world returns to its natural order."

The morning moved along slowly. The girls chatted or looked out to sea, while Robert and Joanna drank and talked and laughed. Mrs. Shaw interjected her opinions here and there. Lunch was brought to them at one point. In the afternoon, a small motorboat approached.

With the sun in their eyes, it was impossible to see who was driving until the boat had pulled up next to their barge. A young man was behind the wheel, dressed in shorts and a T-shirt, his dark hair flowing from beneath his baseball cap.

"Hey, Shaw," the man called, "are you sober enough to do your scene today?"

Robert stiffened. "Of course I am. The question is, will you ever be ready?"

"Yes, in ten minutes. Who are these people with you?"

Robert introduced his family, and the young man pulled a camera out of his bag. "Good to meet you," he said cheerfully. "You look great up there. Let me snap a picture." He took several shots and put the camera away. Turning the boat, he yelled over his shoulder, "Ten minutes, Shaw. Stay sober!"

The Shaws sat quietly until he was out of earshot. Then Mrs. Shaw exclaimed, "What cheek!"

"Who was that snotty-nosed kid?" Joanna asked in disbelief.

Robert scratched his cheek. "That snotty-nosed kid is a genius."

"What? Why do you say that?"

"He's young, I'll give you that. That's Steven Spielberg, the director."

"I think Joey has it right," Mrs. Shaw said. "A snotty-nosed kid, that one."

"Why do you like him?" Joanna asked.

Robert thought for a moment. "For starters," he said, "he doesn't have an ego, or not much of one. In this business, that is extraordinary all by itself. But what I really like about him is that he listens to everyone. He gets the most out of everyone. He's not afraid to take suggestions, and he's constantly innovating."

Joanna looked around her. The ocean seemed to stretch on forever. "What possible innovation could be happening out here?" she asked.

"Joey, do you know where we are right now?" Robert asked.

Joanna was going to say, "On a boat off Martha's Vineyard," but she stopped. Robert had a serious expression on his face. "Where are we?" she asked.

"On thirty feet of water," he said. "No one ever made a movie like this before."

An hour later, another motorboat returned, this time with George at the wheel. "We're ready for you, Mr. Shaw," he sang out.

Robert shoved a pile of empty cups into a corner of the boat and stood up. He swayed unsteadily and nearly slipped as he grabbed the ladder. George saved him from falling. Joanna leaped up to help, but she also stumbled and nearly fell overboard. Mrs. Shaw rolled her eyes.

Safely on the motorboat, Robert stood and faced his family. As the boat pulled away, he began to sing:

> Farewell and adieu, my dear Cornish ladies,
> Farewell and adieu, these ladies of mine,
> For I've received orders, to sail round from Boston,
> But fear nevermore, I shall see you in time.

From their seats on the *Whitefoot*, Joanna and the family watched as Robert climbed unsteadily onto the *Orca* and made his way along the bowsprit. He was given a harpoon and began jabbing it at an imaginary shark. He did this over and over, while Dreyfuss knelt behind him, pretending to adjust straps on a set of yellow barrels. With every take, Robert stumbled or swayed or did something else to ruin the shot.

"Come on, Bob," Spielberg implored. "Can't you do it without stumbling? Stand up straight. I know you can do it. Keep the cameras rolling; let's try it again."

But no matter how many times they tried, Robert could not get it right. The director finally gave up in frustration. "Ricky, you're up," he said. "Bob, stay where you are, I want you in foreground."

While Spielberg gave additional directions to his crew, Robert leaned over to Dreyfuss. "Mind your mannerisms, Hooper. Don't let them see the Dreyfuss in you."

The director yelled "Action," the cameras began to roll, but Dreyfuss just looked up, a blank expression on his face. He had forgotten his line.

"Cut!"

Late that afternoon, they made their way back to shore. It took over an hour to return, as Spielberg kept stopping to capture some new angle on film. When they finally arrived and the *Whitefoot* had been secured, they found Richard Dreyfuss waiting for them on the dock.

"What was going on out there, Robert?" he said angrily. "You can't keep doing this; they're going to shut down the picture!"

"You just mind your mannerisms," Robert said.

Dreyfuss shook his head. "You're still drunk."

"Yes, I am," Robert said. "Which reminds me, I left something on the boat. Hold this."

He handed his flask to Dreyfuss and began to climb back onto the *Whitefoot*. Dreyfuss took one look at the flask, then turned and flung it in the ocean. It landed with a splash and disappeared. A gasp could be heard from several members of the film crew who were standing nearby.

Robert turned and realized at once what had happened. "Why, you ass," he snarled. "What do you think you're doing?"

"Helping you."

If looks could kill, Dreyfuss would have died on the spot. As it was, he took a step back. But he did not lose his nerve. "The great actor gets to do whatever he wants, is that how it works?" Dreyfuss asked defiantly.

"I need that to act!"

"Bullshit!"

Robert appeared ready to explode. Then without warning, he regained his composure. "That was a present from Paul Newman," he said. "He gave it to me when we wrapped up shooting on *The Sting*."

"Okay, I did not know that. Sounds like it was special."

"Yes, it *was* special," Robert said. "*Was* being the operative word." He thought for a moment. "All right, Mr. Hooper, we will do it your way. I'll see you in the morning." Robert turned to leave but then stopped. With a voice dripping in sarcasm, he said, "I do believe we'll have fun out there tomorrow. Yes, sir, Mr. Hooper, I do believe we'll have some fun."

Robert continued down the dock, and the Shaws followed behind. One by one, they passed Dreyfuss with sheepish expressions . . . all but Mrs. Shaw, who held her nose in the air and gave him a withering look.

When they were gone, George walked over. "Nice move, Mr. Dreyfuss."

"Think so? I don't know."

"No one else was going to do it. Took guts."

"Maybe. Anyway, it's done."

"Tomorrow should be interesting. Looking forward to it?"

Dreyfuss stroked his beard thoughtfully. Then he brightened. "You want to know something? I *am* looking forward to it."

Chapter 23

I Know You!

[The following day]

The next day began much like the day prior. Joanna woke early, heard Robert rummaging in the refrigerator, and made him breakfast. She watched him pour vodka into his coffee, then the two of them stood on the beach, waiting for his ride and complaining about their mother.

When everyone else was up and fed, Joanna took them shopping in Edgartown. They went in and out of various souvenir shops, and Joanna asked the girls to model some T-shirts. As they preened and pranced like models, even Mrs. Shaw was laughing. Then Joanna purchased a few things for her kids and drove them to the pier.

As they made their way through the labyrinth of people and equipment, Verna Fields spotted Joanna and waved her over. "Thought you'd like to meet the female lead in this picture," she said. "It's not just a bunch of tough guys on a boat. Joanna, this is Lorraine Gary."

They exchanged pleasantries, and Lorraine introduced her husband, Sid Sheinberg. Hearing that Sid worked for the studio, Joanna ventured to say, "I hear the bills are piling up."

"Yes, they are."

Then, not being familiar with Hollywood etiquette, she blurted out, "What do you think of the director? He seems like such an immature young kid."

Lorraine smiled and turned to her husband. It was not clear whether Sheinberg's expression was one of amusement or annoyance. "It was my decision to hire the director," he said.

"Oh."

Joanna was at a loss for further words, but she was saved when Robert yelled across the dock. "Joey, what are you doing with those people? Stop lollygagging and get over here. We're ready to go." He had just received a present from an anonymous crew member, a shiny new flask, and was eager to get out to sea and fill it from a bottle he had.

Once again, time passed slowly on the water. Joanna had a crossword puzzle and began throwing clues at Robert, thinking it would slow down their drinking. It worked for a while, but as the hours dragged on, they grew bored, and Robert filled two cups with orange juice and vodka.

Later in the morning, a megaphone could be heard from across the water, "Ten more minutes, everyone. Waiting for the sailboats to clear."

"Ten minutes!?" one of the girls screamed. "It's always ten minutes!"

Robert smiled. "What did you ladies do this morning?"

"Went shopping in town," Joanna said.

"That's right," Mrs. Shaw said. "Always buying things, aren't you?"

"What are you talking about? I got a few souvenirs for my kids."

"Yes, you pretend to be so poor, but then you're always spending money, aren't you."

Joanna shook her head. "Why are you always criticizing us?!"

"Would you prefer I were a hypocrite?"

"Actually, yes, now that you mention it. I could use a little hypocrisy from you."

"Poppycock!" Mrs. Shaw said. "Why?"

"You make me feel stupid, that's why. But that's not the worst part. The worst part is that I find myself doing the same thing to my own children. At least I see what I'm doing and stop."

"I am helping you be a better person," Mrs. Shaw said. "I tell you the truth."

"Truth? What truth? Who are *you* to give us *your* truth?"

Mrs. Shaw drew herself up. "I am your MOTHER, that is who!"

The girls looked up in surprise. Mrs. Shaw turned her gaze out to sea. "If I hadn't been tough," she said quietly, "we wouldn't be here today."

In the silence that followed, Joanna thought back to her childhood. Cornwall had been so lovely in the spring, with its narrow lanes and high hedges, and again in the fall, when the chestnuts had fallen. She and Robert had spent many idyllic days on those lanes, chatting about books or other things. But it all changed. Those narrow lanes became positively dangerous, with their high hedges, when their father's car came careening toward them.

Robert was thinking the same thing. He put a hand on his mother's shoulder and said, "We know why you do it. It doesn't make it any easier."

A few hours later, Robert was picked up and deposited on the *Orca*. He found Dreyfuss waiting for him, and they shot several scenes in quick succession. When the director called for a break, Robert turned to his colleague. "Richard, that was sloppy. Your mannerisms keep popping in."

"Thanks for the feedback. I'm just glad you're not drunk today."

"Oh, but I am. You can't tell the difference."

"Who are you kidding?" Dreyfuss said.

Robert stiffened. "How did you get so fat? It is perfectly disgusting."

"Didn't I hear your mom say that about you?" Dreyfuss shot back. "I could swear I heard her say the exact same thing."

"Look, boy, I was in fantastic shape when I was your age. I could do fifty push-ups without thinking."

Dreyfuss flexed his muscles. "Don't judge a book by its cover."

"Bah. I'll bet you can't do ten."

"I'll bet I can!"

"Let's see it then," Robert said. "I'll give you two hundred dollars if you can do ten."

"You're on!"

From their vantage on the *Whitefoot*, the Shaw family watched Dreyfuss waggle his head back and forth. They saw him stretch his back muscles, spit into his hands, and rub them together. Then he dropped to the deck. All they could see now was his head bobbing up and down above the gunwale. All they could hear was Robert counting: "One, two, three . . ."

The girls looked at Joanna. "Is this part of the script?"

Joanna shook her head. "I have no idea."

That evening, Robert and Joanna got everyone settled and went out for dinner. Afterward, they made their way through a throng of tourists in Edgartown. "What was going on out there today?" Joanna asked.

"Where?"

"Thought I saw Richard doing push-ups."

"Oh." Robert chuckled. "He's just trying to lose a few pounds."

Joanna looked at him skeptically, then she spotted a movie theater. "Look what's playing," she said. "I haven't seen *The Sting* yet."

"What? I thought you saw all my movies as soon as they came out?"

"I used to. Before seven children."

"But this one's been out for six months. Won the Academy Award!"

"Will you see it with me?"

Robert offered his arm. "It would be my pleasure."

As the movie unfolded, it seemed that Robert was nowhere to be found. Joanna had never worked out how long it took for him to appear on screen—when it is your brother you are waiting for, it can seem like a very long wait. But in the end it was worth it; once again, Robert had stolen the show. The crowd booed as he was hustled out of the bookie joint.

"At least they're responding to you," she laughed.

They exited the theater in the dark, and Joanna fumbled in her purse for a cigarette.

"Thought you quit?" Robert said.

"I cheat every now and then. When the kids aren't around."

"Then pull one out for me. I'll join you."

"Dammit, I forgot a light."

"That's okay." Robert turned to a man exiting the theater behind them. "I say, old chap, do you have a light?"

The man pulled out a lighter and lit Robert's cigarette, illuminating his face. He took a step back in surprise. "Why, I know you!" he said.

Robert took the lighter and held it to the man's face.

"Why, I know you too!" he exclaimed with phony delight. "We *have* met. Poolside, perhaps, at the Colonial Inn?"

"Oh no," the man said. "I can't afford that. Perhaps at the gym in town?"

"No, no," Robert said. "I don't go in for exercise. Do you travel much? I have a vineyard in Sonoma."

"Never been, never been," the man said, thinking hard. Then he noticed Joanna giggling. He took the lighter and put it back to Robert's face.

"Of course! You were in the movie! Robert Shaw!"

Robert laughed. "Didn't mean to pull your leg, old man. Just having some fun."

"Not at all, you were terrific. I wish I could do what you do."

"Don't do it unless you have to. Anyway, thanks for the light. Have a good evening."

They continued up the street, drawing smoke into their lungs and savoring the feeling. "I always knew you'd be famous," Joanna said.

"Don't be silly—that was just another supporting role. If you want to know the truth, I've always been jealous of you."

"Now you're insulting me."

"Not at all. Teaching literature, working with articulates every day. I would enjoy that."

"Robert, I'm stuck in a small college so I can be near my kids. That's what mothers do. It's not a career, it's a dead-end."

"Why don't you run the English department?"

"I can't. You need a PhD in this country. They don't recognize my Cambridge degree over here."

Robert stopped and looked at her. "That's all you need? A PhD?"

"What do you mean *all*? That's a lot!"

"Then I will pay for it."

"What? You can't do that. It costs a fortune."

"Consider it your birthday present."

Joanna's mouth opened and closed wordlessly. Robert laughed.

Finally, she managed to stammer, "I don't know how I would do it. I would have to teach every day *and* manage my family *and* work full-time on a PhD. I would have to do all of that at the same time!"

Robert turned to her. "Look, Joey, all I'm offering is to *pay* for your PhD. *You* need to figure out the rest."

Chapter 24

—≪≪◆≫≫—

In a Glass Booth

[The following day]

*T*he dock was its usual cocktail of activity that morning. As the Shaw ladies made their way through the chaos, the director spotted Mrs. Shaw and called out. "Hi, you're Bob's mother, aren't you?" He offered his hand. "We didn't get a chance to meet. I'm Steve."

"How do you do?" Mrs. Shaw said. She extended her left hand, and they shook. It was obvious there was something wrong, but Spielberg did not say anything. He looked at her questioningly.

"I lost my finger when I was a young woman," she explained.

"What happened?"

"It became infected."

"Bad infection, I take it?"

"Very bad. The doctors wanted to take my entire arm off. I wouldn't let them."

Spielberg looked at her arm and nodded. "Good call," he said.

Just then, a crew member interrupted. The director was needed elsewhere.

"I have to go," he apologized. "It was very nice to meet you."

Mrs. Shaw watched him leave. "Likewise," she murmured.

After another lengthy wait, Robert was taken to the *Orca*, but a light rain halted filming almost immediately. Scheider moved to the film barge, where he had his newspaper, while Robert and Dreyfuss made themselves comfortable in the cabin. A megaphone blared, "Ten minutes, people, waiting for the rain to clear."

Dreyfuss laughed and cupped his hands over his mouth. Imitating the megaphone, he said, "Hold everything; the shark is not working. Okay, it's working now. We're ready to go. Everyone take your places. Wait, wait, the shark is not working. I repeat, the shark is not working!"

"Enjoying yourself?" Robert asked.

"Yep." Then Dreyfuss noticed the papers in Robert's hands. "What's that?"

"This?" Robert answered nonchalantly. "It's just my play."

"*The Man in the Glass Booth*? I hear they're making it into a movie. Congratulations."

"Hold the applause," Robert grunted. "I'm having my name removed from the credits."

"Why?"

"They took out all the controversy. Made it boring."

Dreyfuss nodded. "I know what you mean. I learned from an early age how not to be boring."

"Oh really?" Robert asked.

"Yes, really. It's a simple formula. Just be honest."

Robert's face brightened. "That's right."

"It's the Adolf Eichmann story, isn't it?"

"In reverse. Eichmann lied about everything; my protagonist tells the truth, the whole truth, and nothing but the truth."

"What made you write a play about the Holocaust?"

"It began as a novel, but Joey convinced me to convert it into a play. The original idea came when the pope forgave the Jews. I always thought it should be the other way round."

"Can't disagree. Whose script is that, yours or the studio's?"

"Mine."

"*With* the controversy."

Robert nodded. Dreyfuss leaned back. "Let's hear it, then," he said. "We seem to have all the time in the world these days."

Robert was not the type of person who needed encouragement. He stood up at once, thumbed through the script, and began reading. With each character, his accent and mannerism changed. First he was Arthur Goldman, the millionaire Jewish financier who managed his fortune from a Manhattan penthouse overlooking Central Park. Then he was Charlie, Goldman's faithful servant, wishing his boss a happy birthday and injecting an air of normalcy into the play.

"Doesn't sound controversial," Dreyfuss said. Robert smiled and continued reading. It soon became clear that Goldman was either very eccentric or completely mad. He spoke of hiring naked female servants to replace his wife, of "knocking up" Miss America if he were to meet her, of sinister agents who were watching him and wanted to kidnap him.

Dreyfuss nodded. "Okay. I'm beginning to see the controversy."

Robert continued reading, and the two men became absorbed in his performance. It turned out there *were* secret agents spying on him—Goldman was not mad. He is kidnapped and transported to Israel, where he is accused of being a Nazi, Adolf Dorf, who murdered thousands of Jews. Dorf is put on trial and placed in a glass cage for his protection; there, he spouts horrific truths about the concentration camps.

Robert morphed into something different with each new character. He moved effortlessly between the defendant, the prosecutor, the judge, and various witnesses. One witness claimed that Dorf murdered his family. Instead of denying this, Goldman/Dorf boasts of how he forced prisoners to kick each other, how he made them beg to use the latrine, and how he had them "do it" with their wives and children in front of everyone.

With each new description of the horrors, Robert's energy level rose another notch. Dreyfuss could only watch in stunned silence.

Then Robert stopped suddenly. He had heard a scraping noise above Dreyfuss's head. The two men looked up to find the entire film crew standing on the gunwale, peering through the glass windows. Spielberg was with them.

"Don't stop," the director said.

Robert nodded. He looked back at his script and resumed. With his voice rising to a crescendo, he took on Dorf's role again and spoke of his love of Hitler—the man who had come from humble beginnings, who had been uneducated, and yet who rescued Germany from the depths of despair.

Robert slammed his fist on the table, causing several crew members to jump in surprise. He practically screamed the controversial ending to Dorf's speech:

> At the end, we loved him. With the killers of the world at our throats, we loved him! People of Israel, people of Israel. If he had chosen you, would you not also have followed him?

Robert stopped. No one said anything for a while. Like Dreyfuss, the crew was mesmerized, their mouths still agape. Finally, George spoke up. "Holy shit!"

"Exactly," Robert said. With the tension broken, everyone laughed.

"Robert, help me understand this," Dreyfuss said. "A Holocaust victim pretends to be a Nazi so he can tell the truth about the concentration camps. That is interesting. But the last part, do you really think Israel would have followed someone like Hitler?"

"Richard, I am just the writer." Dreyfuss was not satisfied, but Robert turned to Spielberg. "Don't ever let them stop you from being honest, Steven."

Spielberg shook his head. "No one's going to stop me."

Another awkward silence followed, once again broken by George. "I'll drink to that!"

Everyone laughed again. "I might even join you this time," Spielberg said. "We're done for the day. Let's pack up."

From their perch on the *Whitefoot*, the Shaw ladies were once again scratching their heads. They had seen the crew move from the film barge to the *Orca*; had seen them surround the cabin and peer through the windows; had seen them jump back in surprise at times. But they could not see what they were watching, nor hear what was being said.

"Is *this* part of the script?" one of the girls asked.

"I have no idea," Joanna said.

Chapter 25

⚜

A Gruesome Death

[The following day]

Joanna was making breakfast in the kitchen when Robert shuffled in. The clock read 9:00 a.m. It was the first time she had slept in since arriving on Martha's Vineyard, and it felt good. The girls sat at the table, while Mrs. Shaw was in the other room reading the local newspaper, her glasses dangling in front of her and an ashtray slowly filling with ashes. Robert sat down heavily and rubbed his forehead.

"Must have been quite a party last night," Joanna said.

"Uh-huh."

She handed him a cup of coffee. Robert reached for the milk, but his hand was shaking. Joanna moved it away and poured the milk for him.

"Thanks. I'm never drinking again."

"I'll hold you to that," Mrs. Shaw called out.

Robert shook his head. "Doesn't miss a thing, does she?"

One of the girls asked if he was hungover, catching Robert by surprise. "Now where did you learn that?" he asked. Like so many fathers, Robert was often surprised at how fast his children were growing up. A short discussion followed in which Robert shared his frustrations about acting.

"Let me tell you something about the movie business," he told the girls. Everyone looked up expectantly, but all he said was, "Don't get involved."

"I thought you liked it." Joanna said.

"It's okay for a man," he said. His voice trailed off, and it seemed he would not continue. Then he said, "A man gets by if he's got talent, but it's different for a woman. In this business, men look at women the way they look at a horse. Up and down. My advice is to find something where women are treated the same as men."

"There isn't a profession in the world where that's true," Joanna said.

Robert grunted. "Some are better than others."

He stood and walked into the living room. Sitting opposite his mother, he took a sip of his coffee, savoring the smell. "It always feels good in the beginning, doesn't it?" he said.

"What's that?"

"A cup of coffee, falling in love, your first drink of the day. They always feel good in the beginning . . ."

Mrs. Shaw stared at him.

"I'm getting too old for this game," Robert sighed.

"I've already lost a husband. Am I going to lose a son?" she asked.

"I'm not going anywhere."

"Are you sure? Robert, why are you not happy? There's no reason for it."

"That's a funny question, coming from you."

"I'm happy." Mrs. Shaw scrunched her face into a frown. "This is my happy face."

Robert laughed. "Is that the trick? To be a grouch?"

"I am *not* a grouch! You put on makeup, I put on this face. I heard you with your daughters just now. Are you too old for them?"

"Of course not! They mean absolutely everything to me."

"Then treat everything like it's your children."

Joanna had been listening from the kitchen, but this was too much. She stood and planted herself in the doorway, arms folded. "I wish you would follow that advice," she said angrily. The girls peeked out from behind her.

"I *do* follow that advice!" Mrs. Shaw said.

"I never saw it."

"Then open your eyes."

Joanna threw her arms up. "What is wrong with you? Why are you so hard on us?"

Mrs. Shaw thought for a moment. "Your father was useless, that's why. If I hadn't been tough, we wouldn't be here today." She turned to Robert. "You wouldn't be famous, for what that is worth." Robert shrugged. "And you," she said, turning to Joanna, "you would still be in a one-room schoolhouse in Cornwall."

"I think I would have liked that, actually," Joanna mumbled.

"I didn't see it coming," Mrs. Shaw said. "He was so charming. Everyone loved him, and he loved everyone. Do you know how to tell if someone is a drunk?"

"How?" Robert asked.

"Everyone loves them, and they love everybody."

"Ah."

"Before I knew it, I had five children on my hands and one drunken husband. It was all right at first. He had a good practice; we had good friends. Threw wonderful parties, such wonderful parties. Do you remember them?"

Robert and Joanna nodded.

"Do you remember who was the loudest?" Mrs. Shaw asked.

"Daddy," Joanna whispered.

"I suffered a thousand humiliations. I could never speak to you about it—you were both so young." She turned to Robert. "He drove you into a ditch one day."

"I remember. Taking me back to school."

"Found a pub along the way, though, didn't he? He was always doing that. I began to fear for your safety. Do you remember the night he killed himself?" Robert glanced at his daughters, and Mrs. Shaw waved a finger at him. "Go ahead, tell them," she urged.

Robert shifted in his seat. "I was at boarding school when it happened," he said. "Your aunt was there."

The girls turned to Joanna. She looked at Robert, and he nodded.

"It happened just before the war began," Joanna said. "Ouma finally had enough of him, I suppose. She took matters into her own hands and moved us all to Cornwall. It couldn't have been easy, I imagine. Managing five children, one of them a baby."

"Nothing is easy," Mrs. Shaw said.

"Anyway, he followed us to Cornwall," Joanna continued. "Knocked on our door one day. We were in Treworyan, and he appeared at the door quite unexpectedly. Begged Ouma to forgive him. He swore he had changed, so we moved back in with him."

"At first, he didn't drink." Robert picked up the story. "We said to each other that he's cured. We really thought that was the case."

"But then he did begin to drink again," Joanna said. "It was only on social occasions, so we thought he had learned how to cope with it. But that didn't last either. He was soon drinking as much as ever. Everything started up all over again. The anger, the shouting, the coming home drunk. It lasted a month or two, I suppose. At some point he went to a rehab clinic. Ouma took us to see him, and the nurses told us he was all cured."

"He charmed them, like he charmed everyone," Mrs. Shaw said.

"A few days later, we were waiting for his cured self to arrive home. Sandy and I were playing cards on the floor. Your grandmother had purchased a white sofa in his honor, a beautiful white sofa, and we weren't allowed to sit on it."

"You were always making a mess," Mrs. Shaw said.

Joanna ignored her mother. "So we were on the floor, and the window opened and his head poked through. There was an odd expression on his face, as I recall. A smile, I think, as if it was all just a big joke."

"He was drunk," Mrs. Shaw said. "That was how long his cure lasted."

"He put a finger to his lips," Joanna continued, "and motioned for Sandy and me to be quiet. Then he fell through the window and crawled to the sofa."

"The white sofa?" one of the girls asked.

"The previously white sofa. He was caked in mud—must have gone round back and slipped. Trying to avoid your grandmother, I imagine."

Mrs. Shaw remained silent.

"I looked up and said, 'Don't sit there, Daddy, Mummy just bought that and now it's ruined.' I don't believe he even knew he had made a mess, until then. That's when he stood up and said, 'You'd all be better off without me.'"

"Oh no!"

"He said that sort of thing many times," Robert said. "We didn't think anything of it. Ouma used to tell him to go ahead and do it, just not in front of the children."

Mrs. Shaw remained silent.

"Then he took something from his pocket," Joanna continued. "I can still see it—it was a small brown bottle. He pulled it out, threw his head back, and drank it down in one gulp."

Robert's flask from the night before was on the side table. He looked at it without thinking, then saw that Joanna was also staring at it and looked away quickly.

"He went upstairs after that," Joanna said, "and never came down. That was it, the end of him. I never saw him again."

No one said anything for a few moments. Mrs. Shaw took a puff on her cigarette and blew smoke into the room. Then, stubbing it out, she turned to Robert and Joanna. "Thank you for that lovely sermon, but you have not told the entire story. The fact is that your father, Thomas Archibald Shaw, mixed morphine with alcohol that night. That was what he had in that 'little brown bottle.' Morphine. He knew what he was doing."

"But you always said it was an accident," Joanna said. "Do you mean he took it on purpose?"

"Of course he did," her mother answered. "He drank to give himself Dutch courage, took morphine to dull the pain, and mixed the two so he could avoid any responsibility in life. I imagine he avoided a more gruesome death, but it was not very civil of him. Until that day, I had never known poverty. I had never known what it was like to raise five children by myself. And with a war going on!"

She looked at Robert and Joanna. "We made it through, though, didn't we?"

They pursed their lips and nodded.

"I had to be tough," she continued. "I knew you would hate me for it, but I had to be tough. It was the only way we could survive. The world was beating everyone else down, but nobody was going to beat us. I made sure of that."

There was no remorse in her words, no apology, no regret. Her face only hinted at how grim it must have been. Joanna let out a long sigh and turned back to the kitchen. "Come on, girls. Let's finish breakfast."

Left alone with his mother, Robert became pensive. "Treat everything like it's my children?" he asked.

"Did I say that?"

"I suppose if you don't need the money, you can get away with that sort of thing."

"What are you going on about?"

"You know exactly what I mean. I can't afford to sit around. I *have* to work."

"You call what you do work?"

"Oh, please, Mother!"

"Your father had a real job. You should have gone into medicine."

"DAD IS DEAD!" Robert shouted. Then, with a glance at the kitchen, he added quietly, "And this is what I do."

"Well, you don't have to go on about it," Mrs. Shaw.

"I shouldn't have to."

"Perhaps."

"He was a good man, though, wasn't he? The Lighthouse Doctor, they called him. Kept a medical bag on every island in case he had to swim ashore."

"He was NOT a good man," Mrs. Shaw said. "We could have had a wonderful life if he had behaved himself."

Robert chuckled. He had heard his mother start many a sentence like that. Sometimes it was, "If your father had behaved himself, you would have all gone to boarding school and we would have only seen you on holidays." Sometimes she would say, "If your father had behaved himself, you would have had your own boats and learnt to be yachtsmen." And sometimes she would turn to Liz and Joanna and wag her good finger at them. "If only your father had behaved himself, we would have hired a governess for you girls."

"You think this is funny?" Mrs. Shaw asked. "Do you know what your problem is, Robert?" He shook his head. "You are exactly like your father. There, I've said it. Exactly like your father. When you see something nice across the street, you go and get it. But then it's never good enough, is it?"

Robert shrugged. "I can't afford to settle."

"You can't afford to keep doing this."

"You have no idea what I can afford. It costs me a fortune to keep my children happy."

"Your children do not need your *money* to make them happy!"

"What, then?"

Mrs. Shaw shook her head. "Isn't it obvious?"

Robert thought for a moment. "Perhaps." He grabbed the flask from the side table and poured it in his coffee.

"We're done then, are we?" Mrs. Shaw asked.

"I believe so."

She shook her head. "Why do you do this?"

Robert looked up with the hint of a smile. "Isn't it obvious?"

[The following day]

Robert emerged from the makeup tent that morning and made his way along the dock. The sun was out, and he felt great. Passing a small group of men preparing their equipment, he heard "California Dreamin'" on a cassette. He stopped and listened.

"You the Mamas and the Papas fan?" Robert called out.

One of the men looked up and nodded.

"Did you hear about Mama Cass?"

The man shook his head. Robert made a motion of cutting his throat. "Dead!" he said.

The man's eyes opened wide. He turned to one of his companions, who nodded that it was true. Robert continued down the dock, humming "All the leaves are brown" to himself.

Back on the ocean, back on the *Whitefoot*, the Shaws were once again waiting for Robert's turn on camera. To one side they could see the beautiful bluffs and beaches of Martha's Vineyard. On the other side, the ocean seemed to stretch on forever, undulating and intoxicating. It truly was an island paradise—and Joanna was thoroughly bored with it all. This was the worst part of making a movie: all the sitting around and waiting. And what made it even worse was that you never knew when someone would show up for Robert. It might be a few minutes, or it might not happen at all that day.

The family stared into space. They watched the seagulls flying about. They observed the film crew making their preparations. They shared small stories with each other. After a while, Robert pulled a cup from underneath the bench, poured orange juice into it, and reached for his flask. Suddenly, he realized his mother was staring at him. Slowly, he slid the flask back into his pocket.

"Another day in paradise," Joanna observed.

"Another day at the office," Robert replied.

"Another day of boredom," Mrs. Shaw said.

"When are we going home?" one of the girls asked.

Several hours later (or "ten minutes" in Hollywood-speak), a motorboat pulled up. George was at the helm, and he assisted Robert on board. No one stumbled this time. As they pulled away, Robert turned his back on his family and pulled the flask from his pocket. He took a long swig, then another. Looking up, he found George watching him with a grin.

"Not a word of this to my mother," Robert said. "Understand?"

George nodded, still grinning. Robert took another swig and held his hand to his face. Steady as a rock!

Orca II was tilted at a steep angle for Quint's death scene. The crew maneuvered the shark into position, Robert took his place on the cabin floor, and the director yelled "Action!" As the shark began chomping, Robert released his grip and slid down the deck into its open mouth, kicking and screaming. When he bit down on a capsule, fake blood spurted from his mouth, and he was dragged into the ocean.

On *Garage Sale*, George shook his head in admiration. "What an actor! Awesome stuff!"

"Yea, he's good," someone next to him said.

"And he does it drunk or sober," George said. "Doesn't matter. When the cameras roll, he is just on, man!"

"Yep. Don't know where he gets it."

George turned to his friend with a grin. "You obviously haven't met his mother," he said. "She's scarier than the shark!"

Spielberg yelled "Cut!" The film crew high-fived each other, and divers began pulling Robert out of the shark's mouth.

From the *Whitefoot*, the Shaw family watched with a mixture of surprise and horror. They had seen their son/brother/father die on screen before, but never in front of the camera, and never like this. It was unexpectedly gruesome. For Joanna, it was an especially sad moment, one she would remember for a long time, the way Americans remember where they were during Pearl Harbor or the Kennedy assassination. She had seen Robert drink before, she had been drunk with him before, but she had never seen him begin drinking before breakfast and then continue throughout the day. While she watched Robert being devoured by the shark, all she could think about were the demons eating away at her brother from the inside.

Beneath the waves, scuba divers also watched the death scene unfold. The boat and the shark were silhouetted against the sky above them, shaking violently, but the only sounds they could hear were their own air bubbles racing to the surface.

That evening, Robert joined his colleagues for a small celebration. Not wanting to be stuck at home, Joanna made her way to the editing hut, where she found Verna watching a movie by herself. A small projector clicked away in the dark, while images flashed on the wall opposite.

"Mind if I join you?" Joanna asked.

"Not at all," Verna said. "I'd love the company."

Joanna sat down and realized Verna was watching one of Robert's old films: *The Caretaker*. It was the very scene that had so amazed Joanna when she first saw it on Broadway: Aston's speech about electric shock therapy.

"You know the odd thing about *JAWS*?" she said.

"What?" Verna asked.

"Everyone seems so normal. I've been on a lot of movie sets, and I've always had to gush." Adopting a fake royal accent, Joanna said, "You were so marvelous, darling, such a magnificent performance. I worship the very ground you walk on."

Verna chuckled.

"But the only time my gushing was ever genuine," Joanna said, "was when I watched Robert do that scene."

"He did something earlier this summer that was just as good."

"The speech about the sailors eaten by sharks?" Joanna asked. Verna nodded. "Yes, Robert told me he wrote that himself. Completely hung-over, I might add. He said it all just spilled out on paper one morning." Joanna paused. "But it doesn't matter now, does it?"

"What do you mean?"

"I hear they're shutting down the production."

"No one is shutting us down."

"I heard they are."

Verna stopped the projector and turned on a small light. "Do you remember when I introduced you to Lorraine Gary the other day?" she asked. Joanna nodded. "And do you remember her husband?"

"Yes, he said he works for the studio. What about it?"

"That was Sid Sheinberg. He's the *head* of the studio."

"Oh." Joanna considered this. "And his wife is in the film?"

Verna smiled. "You catch on fast. That immature kid, as you called him, is no dummy. Lorraine's a great actress, but she's also insurance. As for the other problems, we'll get through them."

"Will the movie be any good, then?"

"That I can't say. I've liked everything I ever worked on, but the audience doesn't always agree. The shark will bring people in, I'm sure of that. We're going to scare the living daylights out of them. But if this movie ages well, it will be because of that speech your brother wrote."

"Robert always preferred writing to acting. I wish he'd stick to that."

"But he's so good at both."

"He wants to be the best at everything."

"Yes, it's what makes him so brilliant." Verna paused. "And so troubled."

"You think he's troubled?"

"Have you ever known an alcoholic who wasn't?"

Joanna stared at her for a minute. Then she stood up. "I'll let you do your work."

Later that night, with the girls in bed and their mother reading her newspaper, Robert and Joanna took a stroll on the beach. They walked barefoot, arm in arm, while the waves lapped at their feet and the moon shimmied off the water. "That was a fitting end to the week," Joanna observed.

"How so?"

"Seeing you die like that. Eaten alive. It was horrible!"

"Wasn't much better on my end," Robert grunted.

"Your screams were so real," Joanna said, shuddering involuntarily. "Wonderful acting."

"I am not one to be humble," Robert said. "Did you know that?"

"Yes," Joanna laughed.

"I'll be the first one to tell you when I've done a good job. But I give everyone their due, you know that as well. Today, however, I was not acting."

"What do you mean?"

"Joey, I was absolutely terrified out there today!"

Joanna considered this. It didn't surprise her. Her mind went back to the time in Treworyan when Robert had a stomachache for a week and had to use the outhouse every night. He always woke her and took her with him. Together, they groped their way through the dark, scared by the hooting owls and whatever else lurked in the undergrowth. The memory was still fresh in her mind, and she absolutely *loved* it.

Robert interrupted her thoughts. "Do you know what I had to protect me out there?"

"What?"

"Two scuba divers. Their job was to pull me out of the water if I started drowning!"

"That does sound scary," Joanna had to admit.

"And the irony is that just the other day, I told Steven to always be honest." Robert shook his head mournfully. "But this might be taking honesty too far, being dragged into the ocean by a bloody mechanical beast that never worked."

Joanna shrugged. "It looked great to me."

"Really?" Robert brightened. "Perhaps it was for the best, then." He became serious just as quickly. "What did you think of Mother's speech? The one about Father. Or Daddy, as you called him."

"Ever read Sylvia Plath's poem, 'Daddy'?" Robert shook his head. "When your father dies before you are a teenager," Joanna said, "he will always be 'Daddy' to you."

"Ah, and that is us. Speaking of which, do you remember showing me your home movies last summer?"

"From our trip to England, sure."

"I had a rather morbid shock that night," Robert said. "There you were, prancing around the churchyard with your kids, and up popped Dad's grave."

"We were in Lydford. What about it?"

"But you see, until that night, I thought Dad died when he was forty-eight."

"What? No, he was forty-one when he died."

"Yes, I know that now. But until that night, sitting on your couch, I thought he was forty-*eight*. Don't you see? I had been thinking I must keep going, in order to outlive him. Until that night, I didn't know that I had already outlived him."

Joanna shook her head. She could not think of anything to say.

"I still dream about him, you know," Robert continued.

"What about?"

"It's always the same. We're walking in a field, just the two of us, and I look up at him. He was so big, wasn't he? Or were we just small back then? In any case, I look up at him, and I can see the sadness in his eyes. So, I say to him, this is what I always say to him in my dreams: 'Don't worry, Dad. Everything will be all right.'"

"Simple enough. What happens then?"

"Then I wake up."

Joanna frowned. "Robert, are you depressed?"

"No, of course not!"

"Are you in denial?"

He smiled. "Maybe. But aren't we all?"

"Do you think Mother drove him to drink?"

"Absolutely not. You can't blame anyone but yourself."

"I'm glad to hear that. So, what is your excuse?"

"Ah, I should have seen that coming. I suppose I'm administering my own therapy."

"Like Dad."

"Not like Dad at all," Robert said. He said it loudly, with conviction, but Joanna wasn't sure he believed it himself. "But enough about me," Robert continued. "What about you? Are you going to run the English department?"

"I've been thinking about that. If your offer is still on the table, I'll take you up on it."

"Wonderful!!"

"And something else."

"What?"

"I've decided to stop drinking."

Robert turned in surprise.

"Good for you," he said.

"But what about you?" Joanna asked. She hooked her arm in his and they continued down the beach. "I'm flying home with Mother tomorrow," Joanna said. "I'm going to quit drinking and get my PhD. What will you do?"

"Tomorrow?"

"Yes."

Robert turned and faced the ocean. His face registered a mixture of frustration, determination, and its usual undercurrent of amusement. "I will tell you precisely what I shall do tomorrow," he said. "I shall wake up at 5:00 a.m. and get dressed, as I have done every morning. Then I will shuffle down the hallway to that miserable icebox, where I will scrounge around for some meager nourishment. Most likely, I will have searched in vain. Then I will get picked up and taken to the dock, where I will spend hours and hours in makeup sitting next to Richard and Roy and listening to them blather on about their petty grievances while I am transformed into another person."

He paused.

"And then?"

Robert shrugged and pointed into the blackness. "Then I will go back out there again and be the best damn Quint I can be."

[The following day]

The sun was low on the horizon when Joanna and Mrs. Shaw arrived at the airport. They found the same pilot waiting for them. "Oh, it's you," he said, unable to hide his disappointment. He looked at their bags. "I still have that weight problem, you know."

Mrs. Shaw turned to Joanna.

"Don't look at me, Mother. It's your call."

Mrs. Shaw turned back to the pilot. For several moments, the two of them stared at each other like two sumo wrestlers squaring off, shifting back and forth, searching for an opening, trying to spot a weakness in their opponent. Then Mrs. Shaw shrugged unexpectedly. "I suppose I had better get in the back," she said. Grabbing the handle of the plane, she pulled herself into the rear seat.

Back at the bungalow, Robert fumbled through the refrigerator. He looked on the top shelf, on the bottom shelf, in the pullout trays. As predicted, he found nothing to eat. He sat down with a sigh and poured a cup of coffee. Emptying his flask into the cup, he sat at the table for a long time, watching the steam drift upward.

Chapter 26

—⋘◆⋙—

Show Me the
Way to Go Home

[One year later]

Back in Paddy's Bar, Robert was pouring pints of Guinness for the locals again. He was in a good mood. Several Irishmen sat at the bar, while his friend, Jack, snored quietly in a corner.

"Your movie was a hit, I take it?" one of the men asked.

"I'll bet you haven't even seen it," Robert said, grinning.

"No, but the lads in town are all talking about it."

"Can you do that scene we've heard about?" someone asked.

"Which one?"

"The big scene, the one in the ship's cabin at night."

Robert beamed. He was proud of the *Indianapolis* scene. The reviews for *JAWS* had been glowing, and many of them had pointed to his speech as the highlight. Ever since, he had been getting big movie offers.

"I wrote that speech," Robert said. "And yes, I'll perform it for you this evening—but it'll cost you."

"Still thinking about money?"

"Of course. Which reminds me." Robert turned to Paddy. "I can afford to buy the bar now, what's your price?"

"It's still not for sale," Paddy said.

"Why not?"

"Mr. Shaw, you don't understand. It's not about the money." Paddy put his hand on his heart. "It's about what's in here."

"Following your dream, are you?"

"The key to a happy life!"

"Then you'd better keep it." Robert turned back to the Irishmen. "You want to hear my big scene, do you?"

"Aye!"

Robert leaned across the bar and pushed his cap back. He adopted a more serious look on his face. Then he began speaking in his best Quint accent.

> Japanese submarine slammed two torpedoes into our side, Chief. We were coming back from the island of Tinian to Leyte . . .

"Not that one," one of the men interrupted.

"What?" Robert stopped.

"The song. We want to hear the *song*. All the lads are singing it. The one they sing in the ship's cabin at night."

"You mean . . ." Robert began to sing, his voice a high falsetto. "Show me the way to go home?"

"Yes!! That one!"

Robert laughed. This was why he kept coming back to western Ireland.

He began to sing:

> Show me the way to go home,
> I'm tired and I want to go to bed.
> I've been traveling on this road for an hour or two,
> and it's gone right to my head.

Soon, everyone in Paddy's was singing along with him. Even Jack woke up and joined in. With each verse, their voices grew louder. With each verse, fists pounded on the bar.

> Wherever we may roam,
> on land or sea or foam,
> you will always hear me singing a song,
> show me the way to go home . . .

PART VI

LEAVE THEM LAUGHING

Last night, I dreamt I went to Manderley again.

— Daphne du Maurier

Chapter 27

JAWS

[1975]

It is one thing to watch a movie being made and quite another to see it in its final form. One can never tell what is in the director's mind until you see it on a big screen. Two weeks before the release of *JAWS*, Robert called Joanna to say he had two tickets to a private screening in Philadelphia. Local theater managers were seeing the movie in order to decide whether to show it in their cinemas that summer. He asked Joanna if she wanted to attend, and of course she did.

Walt was working that day, so Joanna picked up Christopher and drove downtown. Chris was eighteen years old, in his final month of high school, and had just been accepted to Trinity College, in Hartford, Connecticut. Joanna peppered him with questions on the way.

"Why did you pick Trinity?" she asked.

"It's a good school."

"But you're a great student and a squash athlete."

"Trinity has one of the top squash programs in the country."

"But you had better options."

"Mom, they've given me a full scholarship. What is your problem?"

"My problem is that no one has heard of Trinity."

It did not matter what she said, Chris had made up his mind. Joanna found the theater, and they went upstairs to the screening room, where a dozen men were already gathered, dressed in suits and ties. A table of food and beverages was against one wall. A large screen was in front of the room, with several rows of chairs facing it. Joanna and Chris took their seats, and the movie began almost immediately.

The opening scene caught them completely by surprise. There were no reviews out yet, no trailers, no gossip from other moviegoers. They gripped their chairs in horror as a young woman was attacked while swimming at night. After the attack, Joanna heard Chris say, "I didn't think it was possible to pull a stomach muscle."

In the next scene, when the body is discovered on the beach, the police chief asks a young man some questions about the attack, the first being: "Who are you?" The young man gives his name and then, to establish credibility, says, "I am a student at Trinity College in Hartford, Connecticut."

Now Joanna could hear Chris chuckling in the dark. "Everyone will have heard of Trinity now," he whispered. The movie continued, and both of them began to worry because Robert was nowhere in sight. But—and a big BUT it was—from the moment he entered the film, it came to life.

Ultimately, *JAWS* was a scary movie, something people tend to forget after seeing it so many times. That weekend, Walt and Joanna drove their family to Ocean City, New Jersey. Walt and the other children who had not yet seen the movie skipped merrily into the ocean. But Joanna and Chris stopped by the water's edge and scanned the horizon. Up and down the beach, they saw families playing together, children building sandcastles, young couples frolicking in the waves. It was exactly like the scene in the movie. Everyone was oblivious to the danger.

"I don't think I'll ever enjoy the ocean again," Chris said. Joanna had to agree.

That fall, Joanna was in a faculty meeting when the subject of *JAWS* came up. Her colleagues generally scoffed at such movies—they were intellectuals who preferred foreign films to popular movies—yet there was unbridled enthusiasm in the room. Joanna asked why everyone liked it so much.

"For me," the biology professor said, "it was because we never saw the shark during the first half of the movie. All the action was seen through the *eyes* of the shark, rather than the victims. We are land-based animals; when we venture into the ocean, we can't see what is beneath us. So, the fear that was generated in the film was not from what we *could* see but from what we could *not* see."

"For me," the music professor said, "it was those two notes, those two magical notes. Da-dum. The shark! And they were not the usual French horns. I think it was a tuba. When those two sinister notes sped up, I could almost feel the shark moving through the water. It was the music that made the film so brilliant."

"I agree," the psychology professor said, "and I would add that when the shark finally made his appearance, the music stopped completely. That was even more frightening."

"For me," the drama professor said, "it was Quint's speech about the sailors who were eaten by sharks. I found it very moving. It was like a Shakespearean soliloquy, like 'To be or not to be.' Quint had not made any sense until then. He broke the radio instead of calling for help. He burned out the engines, and he kept doing things that appeared insane. But then it all became clear. I understood him. And equally important, he seemed to understand himself. That was when he asked Hooper if he could kill the shark. That was when he found the desire to live. Of course, it came too late, as it did for Hamlet."

"For me," the Latin professor said, "it was the lead characters. They represented the three aspects of Plato's soul: Quint was the aggressor, Hooper the intellectual, and Brody the statesman. Those qualities were amplified in each character, of course, but that only served to show what can happen if we allow our personalities to get out of balance."

"For me," the history professor said, "the movie felt like a documentary. We saw the ferry bringing in tourists at the start; we heard people talking over each other in meetings. It was regular people going about their regular lives. Which made the second half of the movie all the more dramatic, because it did not feel like they were actors. It felt like they were real people, three men in a real life-or-death struggle."

"For me," the sociology professor said, "I found the movie funny. I laughed when Hooper crushed the Styrofoam cup after Quint crushed his beer; I laughed when the police chief looked at his appendix scar after the other two were comparing shark bites; I laughed when a license plate came out of the shark's stomach, and they wondered if it had swallowed a car. I laughed more in that movie than I do in most comedies."

The group paused. Someone turned to Joanna. "But you haven't told us what you think."

Until that moment, Joanna thought of *JAWS* as just another scary movie. The reaction of her colleagues made her think further. Then she remembered what someone else had said to her about the movie. "For me," she said, "it was the director who made it great. He's a genius."

"The director? Who's the director?"

Joanna thought for a moment. "I don't recall his name."

In the years to follow, Steven Spielberg would prove that *JAWS* was not a fluke. Ultimately, he would be viewed as one of the great directors of his time, the Alfred Hitchcock of his generation. But in the fall of 1975, to Joanna Shaw, he was still just a snotty-nosed kid.

Chapter 28

Robert Shaw

[1927–1978]

By the time he was in his mid-thirties, Robert had written two novels, starred in a hit Broadway play, and was on his way to becoming an international film star. He had accomplished all of that without compromising himself or caving in to the wishes of older actors. And more important, after falling to the bottom of the Shaw family, he was once again the golden child—despite his mother's disdain for both acting and writing.

In 1959, Robert published his first novel, *The Hiding Place*. It was well received by critics and surprised everyone in the Shaw family. Somewhere along the way, Robert had learned how to write. The first chapter begins:

> It was Monday, the first day of a heat wave, and the sun was just beginning to shine down on the shabbiest suburb in Bonn . . . . Frick got out of bed, put on slippers, and limped over to the window. The dawn was so beautiful that he blinked his eyes in astonishment.

From there, Hans Frick puts on his army uniform, makes breakfast, and takes a tray of food to the basement. It is a soundproof wine cellar, where he has two men chained to a post: British pilots, shot down over Germany and held captive by Frick. Frick chats with them, tells them of another German victory, and deflects their anger at being captive with a story of two other pilots who were also shot down recently and then killed by an angry mob. His message is clear: These men are lucky to be alive.

Like all good writers, Robert was drawing from personal experience, using the sight of Germany's scuttled ships in Orkney to create a rich visual opening and using his next-door neighbor in Cornwall, Mr. Phillips, as a model for Frick. Everything leads us to believe World War II is still raging overhead. But as the chapter closes, Frick goes back upstairs, changes out of his Nazi uniform, and puts on a suit and tie. He does all the normal things that someone would do: He feeds the cats, tends to his garden, and locks his door before bicycling to work.

It is June 12, 1952. The war has been over for seven years.

The two men in Frick's basement are being held captive, not because they are prisoners of war, but because Frick is a lonely old man. *The Hiding Place* is a study in the psychology of long-term captivity, delving into its effect on each character. The first pilot spends his time writing about his Orkney childhood; he adjusts to his captivity and makes the most of it. The second pilot spends his time brooding about his wife and cursing his captivity; he is slowly being destroyed by it. And Frick is the lonely zookeeper who loves his pets; he convinces them to accept their situation. Long before the "Stockholm Syndrome" was a term, Robert wrote a novel about what it meant to both captive and captor.

There is plenty of humor in the story as well: When the two pilots escape, they believe they are still at war with Germany, so they sneak through the countryside, rummaging in trash cans and stealing clothes. Eventually, they find a boat and row to Switzerland and "freedom."

The Hiding Place spawned three films, two on television and one in theaters. The first, on Playhouse 90, starred James Mason as Frick and Trevor Howard and Richard Basehart as the pilots. The second, broadcast on ITV, starred Sean Connery and Robert as the two pilots. The third was a film retitled *Situation Hopeless—But Not Serious*, starring Alec Guinness as Frick and Robert Redford and Mike Connors as the two pilots. The television adaptations were faithful to the novel, but the movie turned the story into a farce: Redford and Connors swing like apes in their cage, begging for food. When they escape, they run into a film crew shooting a movie about World War II, further adding to their confusion.

The movie was a flop, but the acting was superb. Guinness gave Frick multiple layers of nuance, using subtle eye movements to convey how much he needed these two men in his life. Redford demonstrated the early promise of a great career, and Mike Connors was, well, he was *Mannix*.

Two years later, Robert published his second novel, *The Sun Doctor*. This also relied on character development to drive the story, rather than action sequences. A doctor, an Albert Schweitzer–type of figure, travels to Africa to help a village eradicate an odd disease: The people are unable to sweat. Sweat being necessary to regulate body temperature, he does everything he can to help them, but the village elders, who also suffer from the disease, do everything in their power to thwart him. They want to stay in their positions of power, and so they convince the villagers that *sweating* is the real problem.

The story is autobiographical in many places. Robert was clearly exorcising some demons. The doctor is from Orkney; his father was in a gas attack during the war; and like Dr. Shaw, the father was an alcoholic who killed himself (although in this case, his death was an accident). The father in the story even used the same language as Robert's own father: "You'd all be better off without me."

The Sun Doctor won the Hawthornden Prize that year, given annually to a work of "imaginative literature." Previous winners included Robert Graves (*I, Claudius*), Evelyn Waugh (*Edmund Campion*), and Graham Greene (*The Power and the Glory*). Robert had joined an elite group of writers, but the reaction within the Shaw family was decidedly mixed. Elisabeth did not like it, of course, and of course Joanna and Sandy both loved it. It was Mrs. Shaw, however, who reacted most strongly: She was furious. She berated Robert for his depiction of the mother, who was blamed for the father's problems:

Your mother wouldn't drink with him. So when he needed to drink, and had to, he'd get to feeling guilty since she wasn't there, and then he would drink some more to forget her. I don't say she drove him to it, and what went on between them alone we'll never know, but to my mind she went about things the wrong way.

In 1963, Robert appeared in the James Bond sequel *From Russia with Love*. The idea for the movie began on March 17, 1961, when President Kennedy said the novel was his favorite of Ian Fleming's books. *Dr. No* was already in production by then, but when that movie was a hit, the filmmakers chose Kennedy's favorite for the sequel.

Robert had already costarred with Connery in the TV version of *The Hiding Place*, and now his friend was able to pay him back, helping Robert secure the role of Red Grant, the Russian assassin. Robert was playing a homicidal maniac, a man who did not simply want to kill James Bond—he wanted to make him suffer. With his gun pointed at Bond during their fight scene, Robert hisses, "The first one won't kill you, nor the second, nor even the third . . . not until you crawl over here and you *kiss my foot*!"

Of course, Bond used Red Grant's own malice to defeat him; it was the assassin's fatal flaw. The movie was an enormous hit, and as movie scholars like to point out, a movie only produces a sequel if it is a hit, and a sequel only produces another sequel if it is also a hit. In the case of *From Russia with Love*, a franchise was born. Over the next four decades, a new James Bond sequel was released every two years.

Robert visited Joanna shortly after the film came out and took her boys to see it. When they returned, the kids could not stop talking about what they saw—all except Tim. He was uncharacteristically quiet. Tim was Joanna's third child and the one most like Robert (brash and aggressive). He was upset that Robert lost the fight on the train.

"You would have beaten him in real life, wouldn't you?" Tim asked his uncle. Robert assured him he would have.

That evening, Robert and Joanna went out to dinner, and he shared some gossip with her about the movie. Lotte Lenya, who portrayed the head of Russian intelligence, had cried after she punched Robert in the stomach. "They were just rubber knuckles," he said with a chuckle, "but I told her to hit me as hard as she could, and she did. If you look closely, you can see the tears in her eyes as she runs away." Barbara Jeffords, Robert's friend from their Stratford days, played the voice of Bond's love interest. "An Italian actress played the Russian spy," Robert said, "but they needed an English actress, Shakespearean trained, to get the Russian accent right."

Even more surprising, Robert told Joanna how he had gotten Sean Connery angry during their fight scene. "I shared some rather juicy information with him about Diane," Robert said. Diane Cilento was Sean's wife, and she had been Robert's girlfriend before Sean knew her. But Robert would not divulge what he had told Connery. "As an Englishman and a gentleman," he told her, "I can only say that Sean was *very* surprised."

At the time, Joanna was not sure whether to believe him, but over the years she saw Robert do the same thing to other actors, getting under their skin in order to create tension in a scene. Most notably, she witnessed it on the set of *JAWS*, where Robert goaded Richard Dreyfuss, and the young actor turned in one of the great performances of his career.

As Robert's success grew, he began visiting America more often, often stopping by Philadelphia to visit Joanna and her family. With his growing stature, Joanna's friends and neighbors all wanted to meet Robert, and so she organized a small party at her house. Everyone was eagerly waiting to meet the villain of the latest James Bond movie, but when Robert walked into the house and saw everyone staring at him, he blinked in surprise. Then he said loudly: "You will have to forgive me if I fart. I have a medical condition, and my doctor tells me I must not hold it in." The adults in the room looked uncomfortable, but Joanna's four boys burst out laughing. To them, Robert was just their crazy uncle.

More often, however, Robert's travels took him directly to New York City for a play, a movie premiere, or some other event. Joanna began visiting him there, often taking her oldest child, Christopher, with her. On one of those visits, Robert and his second wife, Mary Ure, were busy during the day, so Joanna took Chris to see their latest movie, *The Luck of Ginger Coffey*.

Robert and Mary play a husband and wife in the film, Irish immigrants struggling to make ends meet in Canada. Ginger Coffey wants to be a writer, but he can only get low-paying jobs. Vera Coffey is so frustrated that she leaves him, and their marriage breaks apart.

Of all Robert's movies, this was Joanna's favorite. She always thought that would have been Robert's life, had he not made it as an actor. Christopher, however, hated it. He was seven years old and was worried about his own parents' marriage; the movie only heightened his concern. When they got back to the hotel room, they found Robert and Mary on one sofa, and Harold Pinter and his wife on another. Chris marched past everyone and confronted Mary angrily. "You should have let Robert be a journalist," he told her. "He would have made it in the end."

Mary was very much like herself in the film, always nervous and worrying, but she was very good with children. Kneeling down, she put her arm around Christopher and said, "Looking back on it, I believe you are right. I will make sure I do that next time."

The following year, Robert played a Nazi tank commander, Colonel Hessler, in *Battle of the Bulge*. He was the only non-German to play the part of a German in the film, and he bonded with his colleagues to learn the proper accent. The German actors later joked that Robert's accent was better than theirs. Robert had a supporting role, but once again he stole the spotlight from the film's star, Henry Fonda. In those days, Americans were always the heroes in World War II movies and the Germans always the villains, but Robert somehow turned Hessler into a noble, though tragic, figure.

In 1966, Robert received an Oscar nomination for playing Henry VIII in *A Man for All Seasons*. His entrance is one of the iconic scenes in movie history. Henry is on his royal barge, making his way up the River Thames, when he leaps off into the low-tide mud, splattering his royal garments. His entourage gasps in horror, fearing someone will lose their head. It is only when Robert bursts out laughing that they laugh along nervously. The stage is set: Henry is a very dangerous man.

Robert only has fifteen minutes of camera time, but his performance hangs over the rest of the film—like the axe hanging over Thomas More's head. *The New York Times* wrote: "Shaw's portrayal of the tempestuous and unbalanced Henry VIII was like the sweep of a hurricane: first roaring, then ominously calm, then wild with fury and wrath—a frightening portrait of the heretical king."

Robert had taken another major step forward, and Joanna was once again using it to her advantage. In Truro, when Robert had been a local matinee idol, she had improved her standing with her classmates by telling stories about him. Now his fame helped her secure more teaching assignments at the college and get better reviews from her students, and she became the spokesperson for the college, appearing on television whenever they needed someone to represent them.

That spring, Joanna invited Robert to visit her college; the nuns all wanted to meet the actor who had opposed their hero, Thomas More. She began with her boss, the head of the English department, Sister Anna James. After polite introductions, the sister asked, "Why was the movie titled *A Man for All Seasons*?"

Robert was prepared to discuss many things about the film. He could explain why Henry had married Catherine, a Spanish princess (because Henry's older brother had married her but had died before becoming king, and England wanted to keep the peace with Spain). He could explain why the pope allowed the marriage, despite the Bible's view that marrying the widow of your brother is incest (because there had been no children). Robert was even prepared to explain why the pope refused to annul the marriage afterward (because Spain had invaded Italy by then, had a knife to the pope's throat and wanted to keep their Spanish Queen on England's throne).

Robert was prepared to answer all these questions and more, but he had not thought about the movie's title. He paused. "Why do *you* think it was called that?" he asked.

Unlike Robert, Sister Anna James had put a lot of thought into the question. "I believe it was a reflection of his steadfast nature."

"Whose nature? Henry's or Sir Thomas More's?"

"*Saint* Thomas More."

"He was *Sir* at the time," Robert pointed out.

"He may not have been a saint with a capital *S*," Sister Anna James said, "but he was always a saint with a lowercase *s*." Robert smiled in acknowledgment. "From the beginning of the film until the end," Sister Anna James continued.

"When More loses his head," Robert interjected.

"Yes, through the entire film, through every season of his life, Saint Thomas More remained true to himself. No matter the consequences, he stayed true to God. He never once became angry, never once became bitter, never once raised his voice. He had a remarkable intellect and used every nuance of the law to try and save himself. Even at the end, when he knew his fate, he never swerved from his devotion to God's law above man's."

"My God, Sister," Robert exclaimed, "that is well said!"

Joanna had to run off to a class, and she left Sister Anna James to shepherd Robert around the school. When she returned, she learned two things in quick succession. The first was that Robert had been asked by one of the nuns to be the keynote speaker at the college's upcoming commencement ceremony. The second was that the president of the college had already rescinded the offer.

Afterward, the president explained why. "Joanna, your brother is charming, but he is unpredictable. I would like you to give the commencement speech."

"If you are referring to his role in the movie," she said, "he was just playing a part."

"No, I spent time with him," the president said. "He is just as volatile and unpredictable as Henry. I cannot take a chance on what he might say in front of my students and faculty. You are the safer choice."

Joanna was not sure whether to be pleased or offended, but she gave the commencement speech and said all the proper things. Later in life, however, when she looked back on her speech, she could not remember a single word she had said. That was when she decided the college missed a wonderful opportunity—whatever Robert might have said that day, he would have given a speech the college would have never forgotten.

That summer, Joanna attended a party in New York to celebrate the movie's six Academy Awards. At the last minute, she discovered it was a black-tie affair, and she had not brought an evening dress with her. She searched all afternoon to find one, finally stumbling on a bargain-basement store where she purchased a dress for $8.00.

Back in the hotel, she apologized profusely to Robert, thinking she was letting him down, but he only laughed. "You think you've got it bad. I just bumped into Sean Connery, and I've borrowed his tuxedo."

"What's wrong with that?"

"The man never uses deodorant."

When Joanna received an invitation from Robert's close friend, Alan Bates, to opening night of his Broadway play, *Butley*, she took Walt with her, leaving Christopher, now fourteen, to look after the other children. She and Walt enjoyed the play very much. How could they not? It seemed like a reflection of their own lives: college professors struggling with money and marriage. Afterward, they made their way through the labyrinth of dirty, narrow corridors to Alan's dressing room. Joanna was reminded how shabby everything is in a theater, when you get behind the curtain, yet every actor she knew preferred the stage to making films.

They found Alan's grubby little dressing room and discovered him changing the diaper of one of his twin boys while his male partner was across the room, changing the other diaper. She and Walt could see they were intruding and beat a hasty retreat.

By the early 1970s, Robert was churning out major films. He was in a cast of stars in *Battle of Britain*, which did well in England but not so well in other parts of the world. He played Winston Churchill's father, Lord Randolph, in *Young Winston*. Randolph was a powerful politician who died of syphilis, and once again Robert stole the show. His tortured speech before Parliament, while he was suffering from both a physical and a mental breakdown, was memorably disturbing.

Robert wrote another play, *Cato Street*, starring Vanessa Redgrave. He starred in another Harold Pinter play, *Old Times*. Then he took the lead role in a musical, *Gantry*. The play was based on the Sinclair Lewis novel and had been a popular movie starring Burt Lancaster. Robert was excited to be in a musical and thought himself a good singer. Joanna took Christopher with her to opening night, February 14, 1970, and they both looked forward to hearing Robert sing. They had often heard him sing in their living room and in hotel rooms and knew he had a good voice.

The play opened, and Robert interacted with the other actors. Then he broke into a song, at which point the audience broke into laughter. The play was not supposed to be a comedy, but the laughter continued throughout. Joanna thought it was because people could not see past the tough-guy persona that Robert had adopted in so many film roles. Whatever the reason, when she and Christopher went backstage to Robert's dressing room, they found him in a foul mood. The producers had already canceled the show, even before the reviews had come out. There would be no grubby little café that night, and no further performances.

Despite a few setbacks, Robert was now making more hits than failures. Most of his prior movies had been English productions, and the few American movies he had made were with less-known directors, usually filmed in Spain to keep costs down. But when Robert hired a new and more aggressive agent, the result was a role in a major Hollywood production, *The Sting*, starring Paul Newman and Robert Redford.

Newman also played a role in getting Robert the part. His character was named Mr. Shaw, which made him think of Robert for the role of Doyle Lonnegan, the Chicago gangster they would "sting." Once again, Robert played the villain, and once again, the movie was an enormous hit, sweeping the Oscars.

But while Robert's professional life was soaring, his personal life was not. He was drinking too much, and Mary was drinking even more. Joanna and Christopher discovered this for themselves in the fall of 1974, when Mary was rehearsing for a play in Philadelphia, *Love for Love*.

Chris was assigned to be Mary's chauffeur that week and drove her back and forth from her hotel to the theater every day. Even at seventeen years old, he could see that something was wrong with his aunt. She talked to him about Sylvia Plath and about a book she had just read, *The Savage God*, which explained why Plath committed suicide.

Mary was fired from the play before it opened and was replaced by Glenn Close. Close later said Mary handled it very well, even sending her a congratulatory note and best wishes. Afterward, Robert called Joanna to get her point of view. He was thinking of suing the producers. But Joanna had been to Mary's dress rehearsal with a colleague, and she told Robert that Mary's voice was off, and her colleague thought there was something wrong with her. "Okay," Robert said, "that's what I thought. I'll drop the lawsuit."

A few months later, Mary was dead. It happened two months before the release of *JAWS*, two months before the crowning success in Robert's acting career. She mixed alcohol with sleeping pills and never woke up. It was clearly an accident—she had just come from a party celebrating the success of a new play in London—but the parallel to Robert's father was troubling. Needless to say, it was a horrible time for Robert and his family made worse by the tabloids, which took full advantage of the story.

A few weeks later, with the release of *JAWS* approaching, Robert went on several talk shows to promote the movie. One of them was *The Mike Douglas Show*, which was filmed in Philadelphia. He organized tickets for Joanna and her family, and they sat in the front row, thrilled to see him on stage and clapping wildly whenever the "Applaud" sign flashed overhead.

Mike Douglas opened the show with a song, as he always did. Then Robert entered and sat down, and Douglas asked his first question, "Robert, how is your wife, the lovely actress Mary Ure?"

Robert frowned. "She's dead," he answered.

Douglas apologized for his mistake and quickly moved on to other topics, but from her seat in the audience, Joanna could see the pain on her brother's face.

After the show, Robert treated the Myers family to lunch. The kids all piled into the back of a large taxi cab with him, and they made their way to Bookbinders, a fancy restaurant along the Delaware River. Soon, however, they became stuck at a light in Philadelphia's crowded Center City traffic. With pedestrians milling about on all sides, Robert suggested that Jennifer, who was ten years old, open the window and sing a song for everyone outside the car.

Jen looked at him in shock. "Go on," Robert encouraged her. He pulled a $20 bill from his pocket and waved it in the air. "I'll give you twenty dollars to sing for these lovely people."

"No way!" Jennifer stammered.

"I'll do it," Tim offered.

"I'll do it too," Joanna called out from the front seat, "for twenty dollars."

"No, this is only for Jennifer," Robert said. "Be quick about it; all you have to do is roll down the window and sing a song."

Jen shook her head, unsure whether to laugh or cry. "I can't do that," she said.

"Yes, you can," Robert said. "All you have to do is get started. But you have to hurry!"

They went back and forth like this until the light turned green; then the car lurched forward and they were on their way again, leaving the Myers family wiping tears of laughter from their cheeks.

With the making of *JAWS* fresh on his mind, Robert regaled them at Bookbinders with stories of what happened during filming. He and Joanna could barely talk, they were laughing so hard, as they recounted how their mother had terrorized the other actors and crew members. Then Robert shared some personal stories, recounting how he had nearly drowned when his boat sank, how the mechanical shark had never worked properly, and how he had accidentally swallowed fake blood during his death scene.

It was an afternoon filled with laughter, but that evening, when Joanna watched the *The Mike Douglas Show* on television, her earlier sadness came flooding back. She assumed the awkward part about Mary would be cut from the show, but it was all in there. For the second time that day, she was forced to watch the host ask Robert about his wife, and for the second time that day, she was forced to see the look of sorrow on his face. As Robert always said, when you are famous, they will take your worst day and make it seem normal.

Robert had his share of ups and downs in life. He had professional successes and failures, personal successes and failures. He lost his father as a boy. He lost his wife. He was at the Munich Olympics when terrorists murdered eleven Israeli athletes—he heard the machine-gun fire and saw the dead bodies. Yet through it all, he never changed as a person. Spending time with Robert was like reading poetry: not only did he speak like a poet—brilliant, well read, a deep thinker—but his face also read like poetry: expressive and guileless.

One could always tell what Robert was thinking without hearing a single word. He never held anything back. This could be a pleasant experience, or an unpleasant one. If Robert thought something you did was good, he said so. If he thought something was bad, he said that as well. And in both cases, he would not only say what he thought about it, but he would tell you *why* he thought that, *what* you must do now, and *how* he would have done it differently.

Robert was like this with his family, with his friends and colleagues, and even with people he had just met. During one Dick Cavett interview, he appeared with another guest, George Gilder, who had written a book titled *Sexual Suicide*. The book challenged the thinking behind the feminist movement, and Gilder defended his position intelligently. He was a graduate of Harvard University, a speechwriter for Richard Nixon, and the author of several books.

Traditionally, guests play a well-defined role on these talk shows: They promote their own book or movie, and then they keep quiet while other guests do the same. Robert, however, was not the traditional talk-show guest. He had read Gilder's book, not out of interest in his anti-feminist views but because he knew Gilder was going to be on the show. He had picked up a copy the night before and read it in his hotel room.

As Gilder became increasingly condescending to the feminists in the audience, Robert interrupted him. "I quite agree with much of your general observations," he said, "but I do not think you should write this kind of a book unless you learn—and this may sound terribly rude—but unless you learn how to write. I can't understand three quarters of your jargon."

Gilder was taken aback and asked Robert for an example. Robert picked up the book, opened it randomly, and said, "Let me pick one page, let me turn anywhere . . . okay, page 117:

> The only surprising fact about our ghetto tragedy is the way we doggedly refuse to understand it—and the way we endlessly perpetuate it. It should be clear to any sentient observer with a smattering of anthropological and psychological insight that the worst parts of the ghetto present a rather typical pattern of female dominance, with women in charge of the family and male gangs away on the hunt.

As he read, Robert's disdain was obvious. "I had to stop and think what 'sentient' means," he said at one point. When he read about 'male gangs,' he turned to Cavett and the other male guests and said, "Presumably he means us."

Robert then held the book up and asked the audience, "Now what have I said? What have I said? That's what makes me so annoyed."

With the success of *JAWS*, Robert achieved everything he had hoped for: more money, starring roles, and greater fame. He made several more films over the next three years. Some were good, some were bad, none were great.

When Joanna visited him on the sets of *Black Sunday* and *The Deep*, she discovered his drinking had become even worse. More than once, she found him falling down drunk. Ned Lynch was with her on those sets, and the two could only shake their heads in disbelief. Like Joanna, Ned had known Robert for a long time, had seen him through good times and bad, but he had never seen him like this.

Mary's death did not help, but everyone is responsible for their own health. "There is no such thing as an enabler," he once said to Joanna. When he was asked if Mary was an alcoholic because she had at least one drink every day, Robert said, "My God, if that is your definition, then we are all alcoholics."

After Mary's death, Robert married his longtime secretary. Jay was a remarkably level-headed woman, and Joanna thought that if anyone could rescue him, it would be Jay. But it was not meant to be. In August of 1978, Joanna received a phone call from Sandy. "I have some rather awful news," he said. "I'm afraid Robert has died."

For the first and only time in her life, Joanna wept. As a little girl, she had lost her father. Now she had lost her best friend. Robert had been like a father to her as a teenager, helping the family overcome poverty, a world war, and the stigma of their own father, who was buried in a pauper's grave.

And Robert was the most generous person she had ever known. He would do anything for his family or friends. Even as a struggling young actor, Robert always told everyone about a new role, if he heard it first. "May the best person win," was his motto. He brought out the best in people. He put Joanna on a new career path with his offer to pay for her PhD. It was his energy and hubris that carried them along with him, but it was also his energy and hubris that hastened his death.

Mrs. Shaw was staying with Liz at the time, and Joanna called them with the news. They decided to travel to the funeral together. It was an emotional journey. Mother's first child had died, and although everyone had a different relationship with Robert, he had been a very important part of all their lives.

The public funeral was held at St. Martin's Church, in London, where Harold Pinter gave a wonderful eulogy. There were many celebrities present, and Sandy had to shove Mother into the back of the church to avoid a scene. Afterward, Michael asked to join the private family service at Robert's home in Ireland: Drimbawn House. Everyone agreed that Michael was part of the intimate family, and they decided to meet at Heathrow Airport.

Everyone was exhausted and sad by the time they reached the airport. Michael, however, rushed forward to embrace Mrs. Shaw with his usual warmth, coupled with his inability to ever perceive her coldness toward him. She had a suitcase with wheels attached to it, an old-fashioned contraption with lots of hooks and straps. Sensing a disaster about to unfold, Joanna stepped forward to stop Michael from tripping over the contraption. The two met in the middle, became entangled in the straps, and sprawled to the floor together. To those in the gate area, it appeared they were copulating as they struggled to free themselves.

At that very moment, a flight attendant for Aer Lingus stepped behind the counter and announced in a strong Irish accent: "Will the bereaved family please step forward?"

Michael and Joanna froze in place, too embarrassed and overcome with laughter to respond. The man repeated himself, louder this time: "Will the bereaved family please come forward!"

Still, there was no response. The people at the gate looked down at the couple on the floor, but the agent could not see them from his position. He was becoming increasingly agitated, repeating his request louder and louder. Finally, Joanna managed to pull her hand free and wave it feebly from beneath Michael's burly body.

"We are the bereaved family," she said.

The agent peered over the counter in surprise, but he recovered quickly. "Please follow me," he said, and waved his hand toward the gate. In varying degrees of embarrassment, Joanna and Michael untangled themselves, gathered their luggage, and boarded the plane with the rest of the family.

By the time they reached Drimbawn, Jay and Sandy had returned from Northern Ireland, where they secretly cremated Robert's body, cremation being illegal in the Republic of Ireland. The family then held a ceremony and scattered Robert's ashes on the golf course he had built around his estate.

Two years later, Joanna was back in England when she got another call from Sandy. He said he had something important to tell her but would not say what. She assumed he was getting a divorce, but when she arrived at his house, Sandy showed her a tin can that had come by special delivery. On the outside was a piece of tape, with the words "Robert Shaw's ashes" scrawled across it.

Joanna called her mother and Jay, and they all drove down to Malpas, where the Tresillian River flowed into the Truro River. As the tide went out, they scattered Robert's ashes for a second time.

Joanna never found out which strewing was of the right ashes. She later told the story to a worker at a crematorium, and he just laughed. "We sweep up ashes every day," he said, "and put them in tins. When someone comes to claim their family ashes, we hand them any old tin."

Susannah York once described Robert as "enormously alive," perhaps the nicest compliment anyone can receive. Robert was certainly a larger-than-life figure. Yet, that does not capture his true legacy, not to those who knew him. On her way home from the funeral, Joanna stopped by his flat in London and found the rest of the family gathered there. They sat and looked at one another awkwardly for a while. Everyone was somber. Then someone told a funny story about Robert, and they began to laugh. As others shared their stories, they laughed some more. What each of them remembered about Robert, first and foremost, was how much fun they had with him.

They have been laughing ever since. Whether they were cross or pleased with Robert, they laugh and laugh and laugh. Elisabeth chortles, Sandy chuckles, Wendy bellows, Mother weeps tears of amusement, Jay breaks into hysterics, and even Robert's self-styled butler, as Ned Lynch likes to call himself, guffaws.

The odd thing about Robert was that he did not laugh very much. He made others laugh.

Chapter 29

-⋘◆⋙-

The Ghost of
Drimbawn

[Spring 1988]

Joanna Shaw did not believe in ghosts, even though she was raised in a Church of England community and attended church regularly. She was not sure if God existed, but neither did she doubt it. When it came to ghosts, however, she simply did not subscribe to that way of thinking. Nevertheless, as best she could recall, this is what happened to her in Robert's home ten years after his death.

Joanna had not been to Drimbawn House since the family memorial in 1978. She had earned her PhD by this time and was head of the English department, which enabled her to organize college trips to Britain each spring. She took her students to see the homes and pubs where writers like Shakespeare and Dickens wrote their greatest works. The students paid their own way, plus a little extra to cover Joanna's expenses, and in return, she got to see her family once a year.

That spring, she decided to include Trinity College on her trip, in Dublin. Trinity was where some of the greatest Irish literature had been written, including works by Samuel Beckett, Jonathan Swift, and Oscar Wilde. It was also where her closest friend, Lester Conner, was working with the Irish poet, Seamus Heaney.

When the other students had gone home, Joanna decided to pop over to Drimbawn. She had written to Jay asking if they could visit, but Jay did not get the letter until the day they arrived. Joanna showed up unexpectedly with Lester; her oldest daughter, Jennifer; and two of Jen's college friends. Always gracious, Jay took it all in stride—she got help from a woman in Tourmakeady and together they made up beds, shopped for food, straightened up, and everyone moved in.

Poor Jay. What she had to put up with from Robert's family. But she had bedrooms for everyone and put Joanna in the largest, an enormous room with a comfortable bed. It even had its own bathroom across the hall. Everyone was tired, so off early to bed they all went, each to their separate rooms.

Joanna fell asleep almost immediately, but she was woken in the middle of the night with a feeling that someone was in the room with her. She thought it must be Jen, but when she called out, no one answered. She had a sudden feeling of dread and cowered under the blankets. Abruptly, they were yanked off her. She leaped out of bed in a fright and dashed across the hall, where she locked herself in the bathroom.

Joanna was terrified, but after a while she pulled herself together. *How can I be so stupid?* she thought. Yet, she could not bring herself to leave the bathroom. As she was wondering what to do, she spied a book on the windowsill: David Niven's autobiography, *The Moon's a Balloon* (the title is from an E. E. Cummings poem that Joanna always liked). She spent the rest of the night reading his story. It was so entertaining that she forgot completely about the ghost and was forever grateful to Niven for distracting her that night.

When dawn finally arrived, Joanna's back was aching from the hard lavatory floor. Still, she could not bring herself to go back to that room and went instead to Jen's room and crawled in bed with her.

Later that morning, Jay went to Joanna's room with a cup of tea. Not finding her there, she began knocking on everyone's door until she came to Jen's. Then she and Joanna went downstairs to make breakfast. Joanna was still in her nightdress, unable to go back to her room and change.

While they sipped tea, Jay casually asked if there had been any drama during the night, and Joanna said she must have had a nightmare.

"What kind of a nightmare?" Jay asked with great concern.

At first, Joanna pretended not to remember, but Jay persisted. It was more like an interrogation than a sympathetic ear. "Did you feel that you were struggling with an evil spirit?" Jay asked. "Did you sense a presence in the room?"

"Well, that is a bit strong," Joanna said. "But yes, something like that did happen."

She related the events of the night, and to her surprise, Jay told her that when Robert died, and she did not want to sleep in the master bedroom by herself, she had moved into that bedroom and had a similar experience: namely, that she had struggled against a woman with long white hair who was dressed in a flannel nightgown. The housekeeper found her the next morning on the floor, scratched and fevered.

Jay went on to say that a few years earlier, someone by the name of Robin Leach—a host, apparently, on some television show about the rich and famous—had come to interview her, and she had put him in that same room. The following morning, she found him downstairs, sitting bolt upright in a chair, as white as a sheet. Leach demanded to be driven to the airport, but he refused to say why.

Joanna slept in a different bedroom for the remainder of her stay and was not bothered again by the ghost. But she did have a vivid dream about Robert the following night. In her dream, she was in her bed in Philadelphia when Robert woke her up. "You must take my children for the day, Joey," he said. "I've got important things I must get done."

Joanna was annoyed at first. She had children of her own to look after and a job of her own to get to. She began to scold Robert, but then she woke up and remembered, with an overwhelming feeling of sadness, that he would never do that sort of thing to her again.

Chapter 30

Joanna Shaw

[1930–present]

After graduating from Cambridge University, fighting apartheid in South Africa, and starting a teaching career in America, Joanna Shaw had become a stay-at-home mom. By her mid-thirties she had five children. She had been almost continuously pregnant since the day she and Robert and Liz had strolled up Broadway, arguing about her situation. It was not the life she imagined, nor the life she wanted—but she was happy. She and Walt were raising a family; they were in it together. They were both certain they had the most beautiful and smartest kids in the world.

Joanna knew other mothers felt exactly the same way about their own children, but it did not change how she felt. She developed three rules for child raising:

Rule 1: Survival. Joanna had been a daring kid, but when it came to her own children, she straddled that unsteady line between keeping them safe and giving them the confidence to take risks. When they vacationed by the ocean, she stood knee-deep in the water, keeping herself between the boys and the wide-open sea. She remembered her childhood in Cornwall, when every summer brought news of a drowning. "Another tourist gone," her neighbors would say with unkind disdain.

Rule 2: Athleticism. Joanna wanted her kids to be good enough at sports to hold their own so they would never be embarrassed at a party. She taught them how to hit a tennis ball, ski down a hill, and swim the length of an Olympic pool. As for team sports, she figured their schools would take care of that, and in any case, those had a limited lifespan.

Rule 3: Intellect. Joanna wanted her kids to be academically success-ful: smart enough to get decent jobs but not so smart that they became targets of vindictive opponents. She did not want a Kennedy type of fam-ily (and indeed, she had nothing to worry about).

Joanna took care of the first two rules, and Walt took care of the third. He took a job at a private school in Philadelphia, the William Penn Charter School, founded in 1689 by William Penn. One of the perks was that children of faculty members could attend for free; the school did not know Walt had five children and would soon have two more.

Everything in her life had fallen into place, it seemed, but then Joanna woke up one morning and realized something was missing. With her kids in school, she spent her days with the other women in the neighborhood. The talk was always the same. They discussed what product was best for cleaning windows, how to scrub the kitchen floors, or how many potatoes one had peeled by eight o'clock in the morning.

Joanna began to grow bored. She did none of those things. Instead, she sat in the squalor of her house and read to her children when they got home. If there had been enough money to get help with the house, have lunch with friends, or go to museums, it might have been different. But not being able to afford any of those, she decided she must go back to work.

Knowing that her babysitting would be limited, she got out a map and drew a three-mile circle around their house so she could get home quickly to the children. At the edge of the circle was an all-women's Cath-olic school, Mayapple Hill College. Piling Walt and the boys into the car, Joanna went in search of the president's office.

She was confident. Teachers were in high demand, and she had her accent, her attitude, and her Oxbridge degree. The interview, however, was odd. The president was a gracious, dignified elderly nun. Joanna sat across from her while Sister Mary Xavier examined her resume. "I see you worked for a Congregational mission in South Africa," she observed.

"Yes." There was a pause. "But I am not a Congregationalist," Joanna said.

"Hmm." Sister Mary Xavier read further. "I see your children attend a Quaker school."

"Yes." There was another pause. "But I am not a Quaker."

"I see." The Sister looked up. "Mrs. Myers, have you ever worked with nuns before?"

Joanna thought for a moment. "To be truthful, you are the first one I ever met."

"Hmm."

When she related this to Walt, he thought the nun was trying to find out if Joanna was at least a Christian. That had not occurred to her. Meanwhile, Walt had his own problems that day. Another nun offered to show him the chapel, but when they got inside, the four boys went wild, running up and down the aisles and playing cowboys and Indians. One of them hid under the altar and began shooting the nun in the back with an imaginary gun. "Ping-ping-ping," he chirped. Walt was looking daggers at him, letting him know how much trouble he would be in, while still smiling at the nun and trying to distract her.

Despite the awkward interview, Joanna was offered a job in the English department and began teaching that fall. Walt was surprised she wanted to go back to work; he claimed to be envious of her staying home. Yet later in life, when he lost his job and Joanna suggested he take over the housework, Walt said, "What kind of life is that for a man?"

As Ruth Bader Ginsburg said, "Our generation of educated women expected to finally become professionals, but our generation of men expected us to still cook, clean, and comfort them."

Walt did not abandon Joanna to raise the children, just as Robert did not abandon Jennifer, Mary, or Jay, yet the children always remained the primary responsibility of the women. The husbands would help if they were asked—but they had to be asked. In those days, fathers never worried about a child being sick; that was the mother's responsibility. Fathers never rushed home to pick up a child from daycare; that was the mother's responsibility. Fathers thought they had the right—and mothers did as well, in those days—to stop for a drink on their way home from work.

In a faculty meeting one day, a male professor suggested that everyone should socialize more often after work. The men in the room all applauded, but the mothers only laughed. They knew they could not give up a valuable hour of class preparation—there would be no time for it when they got home.

Mayapple Hill College was a strange new world for Joanna. There were religious statues everywhere, compulsory theology and philosophy courses, and students who put a funny squiggle at the top of every paper and always mentioned God or America. After a few weeks, Joanna made an announcement to her class: "From now on," she said, "I will throw out any paper that has a squiggle at the top or which brings in God or country."

But it was Joanna's first Halloween that demonstrated how very different this culture was from anything she had known. There was a fancy luncheon that day with an orange tablecloth and black paper plates in the shape of bats. The conversation turned to trick-or-treat and how much fun it had been to dress up and go from house to house asking for candy.

One of the sisters turned to Joanna and asked if children did that in Britain. "No," she said, "but it sounds similar to what we did on November fifth—Guy Fawkes Day."

"What did you do?"

"We cut faces out of turnips and went from house to house, carrying candles and saying, 'A penny to burn the . . .'"

As Joanna came to the last word, she remembered where she was and stopped. Everyone stared at her. She desperately tried to remember who was king at the time, or the Archbishop of Canterbury, or some other important figure, but her mind had gone blank. Her mouth opened and closed wordlessly. Finally, she came out with the fatal word: *"Pope."*

The room became silent. The nuns stared in disbelief. One appeared about to faint, fanning herself vigorously. Finally, the president turned it into a joke. "Well, Joanna, we will have to donate your salary to the missions this year." It turned out not to be such a joke, as she would later discover.

When she first arrived at the college, Joanna thought of the nuns as idealists, but what she came to discover was why young women, in the prime of their lives, sign up for servitude. They were not as holy as they seemed, and with only a few exceptions, were a bundle of neuroses.

Like the rest of us, they made their choices for a variety of reasons, and most had nothing to do with a religious calling. Many of them joined because they had a crush on an older nun in high school. For the poorer girls, the convent was a means to have their own bed. Their allure was for a world that was different from that of their mothers, an escape from a life in which they would always be pregnant, have too many children, and work from sunrise until late at night. And for the brighter girls, it was a chance to get a free education—the nuns who taught them all had degrees. And like the rest of the world, there was a class system within the convent. Daughters of elite families went right into positions of leadership, while daughters from poor families worked in the kitchens.

Joanna loved teaching, but over time she became bored. The quality of students had slipped since her arrival, along with the faculty. She wanted to be in charge, but a PhD was required. That all changed during the filming of *JAWS*, when Robert offered to pay for it, and she began the process a few years later.

Getting into a program turned out to be the easy part. The University of Pennsylvania accepted her at once when they saw her scores on the literary exam. How could she miss? She had been teaching literature at an institution where no one had a specialization; she taught a variety of new subjects every semester.

To her horror and sorrow, Robert died before she began her first term. She and Walt barely made enough to get by, and Joanna knew that neither the University of Pennsylvania nor Mayapple Hill would let her do both at the same time . . . so she told neither one.

It was not easy. Joanna's youngest daughter said that her principal memory of growing up was seeing her mother typing at the kitchen table when she went to bed and then finding her still typing there in the morning. Walt took it in stride, and Joanna could not have done it without him. It began the transition into the third phase of their marriage, where they went from fighting constantly to enjoying each other's company again.

Joanna became head of the English department after that, yet the bias against women still ran deep. It took her a long time to understand the reverence for men within the Catholic church; the assumption was that women were simply in this world to serve as "helpmates." Joanna was astounded that a group of men could form an institution in which so many intelligent women were regarded as second-class citizens.

And those women loved the pope. They applauded when Pope Francis welcomed divorced and gay men into the fold, even though women were still not allowed to become priests. In John Stuart Mill's *On the Subjection of Women*, the tyrants only won when they convinced the victims they really were inferior. *Oh well*, Joanna thought, *I like Pope Francis too*.

There were many irritations at the college based on gender: sabbaticals for the men, teaching awards for the men, better schedules, leadership roles . . . But the salaries were kept so secret that the gap in pay was not evident. Joanna should have realized that no family man could exist on what they were paid. Naively, she thought they were all in it together, doing their mission work. She thought they must have some private means. Why else would they be there?

Then Joanna received a visit from a young woman whom she barely recognized. It was Caroline Morgan, the child she had tutored in South Africa, the girl she had taught to be boring in order to pass the so-called intelligence tests. Caroline had moved from South Africa to England, thinking women were better treated there, but she discovered the men working for her in London were earning more money than she was and so she came to America. Joanna was not so sure it was any different.

A short time later, Joanna read a story in the local newspaper. An investigative reporter had dug into the salaries at Mayapple Hill College and published every professor's earnings. Needless to say, Joanna read the article with great interest. Scanning through the names, she looked for her own name and found it near the bottom of the list. Like Caroline, the men working for Joanna were making more than her—a *lot* more.

She began by speaking with the president of the college, thinking the article would finally create some action. The president listened to her politely. She read the article. Then she looked up and said, "But, Joanna, you have a husband. Men are the primary earners in a family."

Enough was enough. Joanna had been complaining about the disparity in pay all her life. She decided to do what her Great-Grandma Carter had done when she protested for the right to vote. Joanna would make a stand. *Suffragettes unite!*

She began by asking her son, Tim, for help. Tim was a lawyer now, having put his brash and aggressive personality to good use. He filed the necessary paperwork and a deadline was set; the college could either work out a settlement, or Joanna could sue.

Over the next two years, offers were made and resolutions put forward, but there was never an agreement. Tim had to make endless requests for information. Each month brought a new set of processes and procedures. The college argued that male teachers were paid more because of extra duties, but Joanna knew this was false. There are no secrets in a small college; everyone knows exactly what everyone else is doing.

The school kept on saying they would settle right up to the deadline. Only then did they agree to terms. They said they would sign the documents the following morning, on the day of the deadline. But early that morning, Tim received a phone call from the college's lawyer. Something had come up; they would have to wait one more day for signatures. The lawyer assured Tim they would settle matters *after* the deadline had expired. Tim knew he was lying. He leaped in his car and drove to the courthouse in record time, going through stop signs and red lights all the way. Five minutes before the deadline, Joanna's case against the school was entered into the court records.

It was a noble effort on Tim's part, but it was Joanna who was in the spotlight. When she picked up the Philadelphia newspaper the next morning, she found herself on the front page.

FEMALE PROF AT MAYAPPLE HILL COLLEGE SUES OVER PAY
Joanna Myers Says Male Teachers Get Higher Salaries

Joanna knew there would be some publicity, but she never dreamed it would be a front-page story. For God's sake, the pope was coming to town. O. J. Simpson had just been acquitted. Yet there she was, with her picture in the newspaper. In thirty minutes, she had to go to work.

Joanna had never felt so alone. Walt was out of town, her two youngest children were in Florida, and the other children were scattered around the country. Even Tim was not available; he had a court case that day. Alone in her living room, Joanna felt herself lifted in the air. Looking down, she could see herself on the sofa, could see the newspaper on the table, could see the look of horror on her face.

Pulling herself together, she drove to school. Ironically, she would be teaching a course on gender in literature that morning: teaching her students how women have been mistreated throughout history. She dreaded facing them, knowing they would have all heard the news. Fortunately, one of her colleagues had seen the story, and when Joanna arrived, she was greeted with a warm hug and words of encouragement. It was that small act of friendship that got her through a tough day.

Despite all the heartache that followed, there was one bright side: the knowledge of one's true friends. Joanna was astonished that some unexpected people stood by her. At the same time, she was dismayed to find that other people, whom she thought were close friends, publicly disowned her.

The lawsuit sparked energetic debate among students, nuns, and faculty, but one group never had a doubt—the college administration fought the case for years. Tim managed everything: more filings, more procedures, more paperwork, more delays. It reminded Joanna of the 100-year-old lawsuit in *Bleak House*, and for the same reason; the longer it dragged on, the more it wore her down. Joanna had gained and lost friends. Every day brought some new tension. Life had lost its joy.

Four years after learning of the discrepancy in pay, Joanna told Tim she was ready to drop the case. She hated letting the school get away with discrimination, but it was preferable to always smiling through gritted teeth.

Tim argued with her. He wanted to fight on. But his mother insisted, and so he began preparing the necessary paperwork. Tim, however, was not done fighting. He would go on to prosecute some of the biggest cases in Philadelphia's history, but even then, in his early thirties, he was bold and creative. He decided to make one last attempt at winning the case.

Tim had been to his mother's college many times. He knew it inside and out, and so he knew there was an old-fashioned switchboard in a corner of the basement, where an operator sat before a pegboard, wearing a headset and plugging in calls to the appropriate trunk line as they came in. It reminded Tim of a *Laugh-In* sketch he had seen in which Lily Tomlin plays a telephone operator who listens in on calls: "Is this the party to whom I am speaking?"

Instead of going to his mother's office that day, Tim went to a pay phone and called her. When the operator picked up, he asked for Professor Myers. "I have some important information about the lawsuit," he said. When Joanna picked up, Tim began speaking quickly. "Mom, I've decided to go public about the nuns. I know you don't want me to do that, but the college has given us no choice. I am going to file the paperwork early tomorrow morning. Have to run now, will explain everything later. Bye."

Tim hung up abruptly, leaving Joanna staring at the phone, wondering what had sparked the call. She had told Tim everything about the college as part of the discovery process, including some things that were still frowned upon in those days. But she and Tim both agreed they would never use the information. It had nothing to do with gender discrimination, and in any case, it was their own business.

She tried phoning Tim that evening, but he did not pick up. The next day, her phone rang early in the morning. "I just got a call from the diocesan lawyer," Tim told her. "They've agreed to all our terms."

Tim's plan had worked. He would later say he had not been bluffing: He would have gone public to win the case, had it come to that. There was a catch, however. The college insisted that Joanna resign. She was being ex-communicated. She called up a few friends to get their thoughts, and every one urged her to fight on. They saw it as a loss. Joanna did not see it that way. She was happy to put four years of anguish behind her. She was ready to move on.

Joanna signed the papers the following morning. As she descended the courthouse steps in downtown Philadelphia with the papers in her hand, a friend from Rutgers University spotted her. "Joanna," he called out, "I am so glad to bump into you. We're looking for someone to teach in our English department this September. Any chance you might be available?"

Then he stopped and looked around. "By the way, what on earth are you doing at the courthouse this morning?"

Chapter 31

-⫷⫸-

Mrs. Shaw

[1904–1998]

When Doreen Avery Shaw was in her fifties, she showed up unexpectedly in South Africa while Joanna was teaching at Adams. Joanna had written to her expressing some homesickness. Instead of writing back, Mrs. Shaw shut down her house, pulled Wendy out of school, and sailed halfway around the world.

When Joanna met them in Durban, she learned that her mother had applied for a job teaching kindergarten, but she still needed an interview to secure the position. They went in search of the school together. Joanna did not know how to find it, so they followed the train line. It was a typically hot day, and the flies were oppressive, but Mrs. Shaw did not seem bothered by them. She spent the entire time talking about her age and how she had lied about it on the application. Now she was nervous that they would not accept her when they met her in person.

Joanna was astounded. Her mother had pulled Wendy out of a prestigious school, given up her home, and traveled halfway around the world based on a deception. She shook her head in amazement. Whatever she thought of her, Joanna had to admit her mother had guts.

Mrs. Shaw did secure the position, and this began the next phase of her life. She rented an apartment on the outskirts of Durban overlooking the Indian Ocean. Joanna spent many an afternoon with Wendy that spring, fishing from the dock and watching porpoises leap in the waves.

But that was also the year when the Bantu Education Act was passed and when inspectors began arriving at Adams. Joanna was deported when the term ended, and she eventually landed in America. A year later, Wendy also left her mother—she was eighteen years old, had gotten her teaching certificate, and wanted to begin her career back in England. Mrs. Shaw was completely abandoned now by her children, but like parents throughout the ages, this became a turning point in her life. With no responsibilities, she took a better teaching position in Mozambique, where she met a Portuguese man, Mr. Nevis, who was recuperating from a heart attack. Doreen used her nursing skills to nurture him back to health, and they fell in love.

Mr. Nevis had a wife back in Portugal, where divorce was not legal, so he decided to stay in Mozambique and live with Doreen. They had been together for several years when Robert decided a family delegation was in order. He arranged and paid for Liz and Joey to visit their mother, along with their two daughters. The four of them flew into Durban, rented a car, and drove to Mozambique. The country was as beautiful as Joanna remembered, and she delighted in pointing out all the places of interest to her sister.

In Namaacha, they pulled up in front of their mother's house and watched her come out the door with Mr. Nevis, hand in hand. "Oh my God," Liz exclaimed, "our mother is someone's mistress!"

Joanna was delighted. "Yes, there is hope for us all!"

Mr. Nevis was everything they could have hoped for, charming and gracious. He seemed completely devoted to their mother and even enjoyed her pranks. She made him laugh.

For the next fifteen years, they lived together in Mozambique. When he died, Joanna could feel the sadness in her mother's voice. For the first time, she had seen the stiff upper lip crack.

When Doreen was in her seventies, Robert took a look at her one day and said to Joanna, "I guess everyone loses it in the end." He was referring to her looks, and, indeed, only those who die young, like Robert himself, are remembered as good-looking.

One does not notice the aging process; it happens so slowly. We all gaze in the mirror each day, moving a strand of hair here and there. But Joanna was sure the process was different for women than for men. For most of their lives, she thought, women have to count on their looks to get by. They don't have to be beautiful, just reasonably pleasant, and they work at it in a way that men do not . . . because they don't have to.

But time catches up with everyone. The feeling of youth persists for as long as we have our wits, but at some point we catch sight of ourselves in the mirror and the shock is immediate. "Oh God, look what the cat has dragged in!"

As she grew older, Joanna found that she had two groups of female friends: Those who, like Joanna, remained untouched by the knife and began looking so very witch-like as a result, and the others, who sought out the plastic surgeon but ended up looking like Victorian China dolls, all expression of personality lost.

Yet, each group persevered. At one point, when Joanna was in her sixties, she dyed her hair, trying to preserve her dark tresses. She developed an allergy to the dye, however, and her face swelled up like the Hulk. Looking in the mirror, she found herself hideous—even her own children shied away. When she went outside, people actually recoiled from her. She knew then how sentimental and untrue the saying, "It is the inside of a person that counts." She knew then what it was like to be ugly.

Let us be honest, she said to herself. *It is the outside that matters, and you become what you are because of the way people treat you in life.*

When Doreen was in her eighties, she joined Joanna and Christopher for a two-week driving tour through Cornwall. As they passed the Merry Maidens, Joanna insisted they stop. The Maidens were prehistoric stones, similar to Stonehenge but much smaller. She and Robert had played on those stones many times as children, and all the happy memories came flooding back.

The previous night's rain had left puddles of water everywhere. To reach the Maidens, one had to cross a narrow path alongside one of the largest puddles. People stepped gingerly around it in single file. Chris went first, taking his three-year-old son on his shoulders; his wife followed; then it was up to Joanna and Mrs. Shaw to get safely across.

"You go next, Mother," Joanna said. A young Englishman overheard them and offered his hand in support.

"I am perfectly capable of crossing by myself," Mrs. Shaw told him, her nose in the air.

"Madam, I insist," the gallant young man said.

Reluctantly, Mrs. Shaw gave him her hand. She took a tentative step, then another. As the man stretched his arm across the puddle, trying to keep her steady, Mrs. Shaw lost her grip and fell. She slid down the embankment on her backside, landing in the middle of the muddy water. It reminded Joanna of the day her father had dropped the local baker in the mud, with the woman's arms and legs sticking up in the air. There was a stunned silence around her. The Englishman stood frozen in place, his arms still extended, his mouth opening and closing wordlessly.

The small crowd looked on in horror to see if this frail old woman was all right. They waited for her to burst out in anger, to hurl accusations at the young man. But Mrs. Shaw simply picked herself up and burst out laughing. "I have survived far worse than this," she told them. Everyone cheered.

Doreen was like that right up until the end. She was ninety-four years old when she died, having outlived Dr. Shaw by fifty years and Robert by twenty. She had survived two world wars, an alcoholic husband, abject poverty, five unruly children, and everything else life could throw at her. Even on her deathbed she remained irascible, scolding Joey for looking so glum.

Her dying wish was for her ashes to be scattered in her childhood home of Piggs Peak, Swaziland. For the third time in her life, Joanna left for South Africa, this time taking her younger sister, Wendy, with her, and her two daughters, Jen and Tory, now grown women.

They arrived in Durban and got a taxi to their hotel but discovered the hotel would not allow four people in one room. There were no more rooms available, so the four women were turned out onto the street, dragging their luggage behind them. It was only then that Joanna realized her mistake. This was not the South Africa she had known. The oppressive yoke of apartheid had been lifted, but it had become a very dangerous place for four white women who were traveling alone.

Looking up and down the street, Joanna could see the tension. Everyone was nervous, both Blacks and whites. Concern was etched on every face. She suddenly remembered the stories she had been reading of garrotings and lynchings and burnings. She thought they were isolated incidents—after all, this had been her home, she had helped create this new freedom. But it was still early in South Africa's transition to a representative form of government, and there was unrest in the country.

Joanna recalled how afraid her Zulu boyfriend had been when she was a young woman, how he had been afraid for his life. It did not seem so outlandish any longer. She was now the one in danger, and worse, she had put her family in danger with her. Spotting a tall white South African man nearby, Joanna led the others to him. He clearly wanted nothing to do with them, but it gave her time to look around. Seeing another hotel across the street, she led them to safety and secured rooms for everyone.

The next day, rather than rent a car and drive to Swaziland, Joanna hired a driver. His name was Sam, and he was a very sweet Black African man, highly recommended by the hotel. "Sam will keep you out of trouble," they told her.

During their drive across South Africa, the reality of the situation sank in deeper. They were in a hotel at one point when Joanna got up to have an early breakfast. She found Sam at a table and sat down beside him. Across the room, a white family was eating breakfast, watching them suspiciously. Then the father came over and invited Joanna to join them. At first, she refused, but when she saw the look of fear in Sam's eyes, Joanna pretended she wanted to meet their children.

The following day, while passing Adams College, in KwaZulu-Natal, Joanna said, "Sam, would you mind turning here? I'd like to visit the college where I used to teach."

"No, ma'am," Sam replied. "Too dangerous."

"Sam, I taught there for two years. They will welcome me with open arms."

"No, ma'am," Sam repeated. "Too dangerous."

Joanna said nothing more. She had seen enough to realize he might be right. But then, without warning, Sam stopped the car and turned to her. "How important is this to you?"

"Well . . ." Joanna said.

Before she could finish, they were heading along the road to Aman-zimtoti. Joanna forgot all about the danger and reveled in the familiar scenery. All the beauty of the Drakensberg hills, the memory of riding on buses—it all came back to her. How she missed it! *Remembrance of things past* is how Marcel Proust described it. In his case, it was the taste of the madeleines; for Joanna, it was the sights and smells of Africa.

They found the campus, pulled up to the gates, and were greeted by two men with machine guns who pointed them into the car. Sam spoke quickly in Zulu. Not remembering even the little Zulu she had known, Joanna could not understand what he was saying, but the men lowered their weapons and motioned for Joanna to get out. They took her to another gate, where she was asked a bunch of questions. Everyone seemed very suspicious, but in the end they allowed her to see the campus. Wendy and the girls joined cautiously, and two armed men led them around while Sam stayed with the vehicle.

Adams was very different from her memories. It was no longer the colorful, vibrant, friendly place that she remembered. Rather than students and teachers of all colors mixing on the lawn, it looked more like an army base, with iron bars on the windows and armed men everywhere. Joanna had seen enough. "We're ready to go," she told the guards.

The rest of the journey went along without incident. They found the neighborhood in Piggs Peak where Mrs. Shaw had been born and scattered her ashes in a field. It was more emotional than Joanna expected. Both her parents were now dead. Her older brother was dead. The Shaw family was dwindling.

The next day, there was a service in the local Christian church. Joanna had written to the minister, who had kindly offered to say a few words for her mother. The ceremony was in Swahili, but the minister asked someone to translate so that Mrs. Shaw's family could understand what was being said. The two men stood before the congregation, while Joanna, Wendy, Jen, and Tory sat in the back. Sam sat by himself in a chair by the back door.

The minister began with the Lord's prayer. He was followed by his translator, who spoke in English:

> Our priest is in paradise, blessed is his fame. Your monarchy
> nears, your mind will be done, on dry land as in thin air.

Joanna, Jen, and Tory looked at each other in puzzlement. The minister spoke further, and the translator said:

> Give us each morning our daily rations, and excuse our
> responsibilities but make others do them for us.

Joanna and her daughters began giggling. Wendy smiled nervously. More Swahili followed, and then more English. "Christ tells us that if a man puts out your right eye, you must put out his left eye."

"What is he trying to say?" Jen whispered.

"Something about an eye for an eye, I think," Tory said, struggling not to laugh.

"Shh," Sam said, looking around nervously.

Jen rolled her eyes and giggled some more. Tory shushed her a little too loudly.

More solemn words were spoken in Swahili, followed by: "Jesus was a very wise woman. He tells us that if someone hits you on the right cheek, you must hit them back on the wrong cheek."

Joanna and her daughters had reached the point of no return. Tears ran down their cheeks; their bellies shook; they emitted soft yelps as they tried to suppress their laughter. People turned and stared angrily. "Who are these white women, coming into our service and disrupting everything?" they seemed to be saying. Sam leaped into action. He grabbed the four women and pulled them outside.

"Are you mad?" he hissed, when they were safely in the parking lot. "Why would you laugh in there? Did you not see everyone staring at you?"

He shoved them in the van and sped away. Sitting in the front seat, Joanna felt duly chastened. Sam was right. It was her mother's funeral, and they had been very rude. All four women sat in silence, now sober. Then Joanna turned to Jen and Tory sheepishly. They looked back. And everyone burst out laughing all over again.

"I honestly did not know any of that about Jesus," Jen chuckled.

That was when Joanna knew what was truly important in life. She had spent so much time fighting for causes, struggling to make ends meet, fretting about the endless duties and obstacles before her, but in that moment, it all made sense. The only thing that really mattered was to be with her children and to be laughing with them at the absurdities of life.

When the tears of laughter petered out, Joanna turned back to the front. She watched the African hills roll by: the farms and fields and cows and people. She knew Sam would get them safely back. Then she thought of her mother and wondered what she would say about the day. And with that, Joanna began to chuckle again. After all, being kicked out of her funeral was not the worst thing in life. In fact, her mother probably would have wanted it that way.

Appendix 1

Robert Shaw:
Career Highlights

Actor (Stage)

Apprenticeship: After graduating from the Royal Academy of Dramatic Art (RADA), Robert spent years taking small roles for little pay, mostly with the Royal Shakespeare Company. The result was that he trained with some of the greatest actors of his time:

- *Henry VIII* (1949), with Anthony Quayle
- *Julius Caesar* (1950), with Anthony Quayle and John Gielgud
- *Much Ado About Nothing* (1950), with John Gielgud and Peggy Ashcroft
- *King Lear* (1950), directed by and starring John Gielgud
- *Hamlet* (1951), directed by and starring Alec Guinness
- *A Midsummer Night's Dream* (1952), with Jennifer Bourke (Robert's first wife)
- *Antony and Cleopatra* (1953), with Michael Redgrave and Donald Pleasence
- *The Merchant of Venice* (1953), with Michael Redgrave and Basil Hoskins
- *Tiger at the Gates* (1955), with Michael Redgrave
- *The Long and the Short and the Tall* (1959), with Peter O'Toole

Starring roles: Much of Robert's subsequent acting career was in film, but he starred in several important plays on Broadway and in London's West End:

- *The Changeling* (1961), with Mary Ure (Robert's second wife)
- *The Caretaker* (1962), by Harold Pinter, with Donald Pleasence and Alan Bates
- *The Physicists* (1964), with Hume Cronyn and Jessica Tandy
- *Gantry* (1970), based on the Sinclair Lewis novel, with Rita Moreno
- *Old Times* (1972), by Harold Pinter, with Rosemary Harris and Mary Ure
- *The Dance of Death* (1974), by August Strindberg, with Hector Elizondo

Actor (Film)

Robert made every film he was in better. He turned bad films into good ones, and good films into great ones. A few of the highlights:

- *From Russia with Love* (1963), with Sean Connery
- *Hamlet at Elsinore* (1964), with Christopher Plummer and Michael Caine
- *Battle of the Bulge* (1965), with Henry Fonda
- *A Man for All Seasons* (1966), directed by Fred Zinnemann, with Paul Scofield and Orson Welles
- *Battle of Britain* (1969), with Laurence Olivier and an all-star cast
- *Young Winston* (1972), directed by Richard Attenborough, with Anne Bancroft and John Mills
- *The Sting* (1973), directed by George Roy Hill, with Paul Newman and Robert Redford
- *The Taking of Pelham One Two Three* (1974), with Walter Matthau and Martin Balsam
- *JAWS* (1975), directed by Steven Spielberg, with Roy Scheider and Richard Dreyfuss
- *Robin and Marian* (1976), with Sean Connery and Audrey Hepburn
- *Swashbuckler* (1976), with James Earl Jones and Geneviève Bujold
- *Black Sunday* (1977), with Bruce Dern and Marthe Keller
- *The Deep* (1977), with Nick Nolte and Jacqueline Bisset
- *Force 10 from Navarone* (1978), with Harrison Ford and Edward Fox

Writer

- Novels
  - *The Hiding Place* (1959)
  - *The Sun Doctor* (1961)
  - *The Flag* (1965)
  - *The Man in the Glass Booth* (1967)
  - *A Card from Morocco* (1969)

- Plays
  - *Off the Mainland* (1956)
  - *The Man in the Glass Booth* (1968)
  - *Cato Street* (1971)

Actors who played a role written by Robert Shaw, including stage, TV, and movie adaptations of *The Hiding Place*, *The Man in the Glass Booth*, and *Cato Street* (in order of appearance):

- James Mason
- Trevor Howard
- Richard Basehart
- Kim Hunter
- Dick Cavett
- Sean Connery
- Robert Shaw
- Alec Guinness
- Robert Redford
- Mike Connors
- Donald Pleasence
- F. Murray Abraham
- Abe Vigoda
- Lawrence Pressman
- Jack Warden
- Leonard Nimoy
- Robert Hays
- Vanessa Redgrave
- Bob Hoskins
- Maximilian Schell

Appendix 2

Discussion Questions

Robert Shaw Discussion Topics

- How did your views of Robert Shaw change after reading the book?
- Robert died at 51—do you feel a sense of loss after reading his story? What do you think he might have achieved, had he lived longer?
- What trait do you think Robert is best remembered for? Did he follow his dream?
- What do you think Robert preferred: acting on stage, acting in film, or writing novels and plays? How does each experience compare or differ?
- As a young actor, Robert tended to take the spotlight away from the star of the show, which set his career back. Do you think he benefited from this in the long run?
- What was it about the Orkney Islands, Cornwall, and Ireland that the Shaw family loved?
- What was Robert's relationship with his father (Dr. Shaw)? Do you think alcoholism is the result of genetics, environment, or other factors?
- What made Robert's mother (Mrs. Shaw) such an imposing figure? How did she shape the personalities of her children?
- "Better drowned than duffers" was a popular saying with Dr. and Mrs. Shaw. Do you think it is better to take risks in life, even if they might kill you?

JAWS Discussion Topics

- How did your views of *JAWS* change after spending a week on the set with the Shaw family?
- What was Robert's relationship with Steven Spielberg? With Richard Dreyfuss? How did Robert's family react to the young director and the young actor?
- Do you think *JAWS* is a great movie or just a summer thriller? If a great movie, what made it great?
- How would you compare the USS *Indianapolis* speech in *JAWS* to similar scenes in other movies? To a Shakespearean soliloquy?

Other Discussion Topics

- What did Joanna Shaw find appealing about Nelson Mandela? What did Mandela say was the most important factor in fighting apartheid? Do you think he was right?
- Do you think Joanna was correct in identifying a double standard in which working mothers must also take responsibility for the children and the home?
- Do you think Joanna's lawsuit for gender pay discrimination against her employer of thirty years was justified? What do you think about her lawyer's tactic in winning the case?
- What do you think is meant by the title of Chapter 26, "Show Me the Way to Go Home"? What was it about Robert and Joanna that made them laugh so much together?

Acknowledgments

I first want to thank my uncle, Robert Shaw, without whom this biography could not have been written. Robert was an extraordinary individual, a true Renaissance man, and loads of fun.

I want to thank my mother for sharing her life story with me. To spend any time with Joanna Shaw Myers is to laugh long and hard. She is a gifted storyteller, and it was a rare gift for me to spend so much quality time with her and to hear her stories of the Shaw family. She held nothing back, including their triumphs and failures, their joys and sorrows.

I want to thank my grandmother, whom I still think of as Ouma. When I was a young boy, she terrified me. When I was a young man, she made me laugh. And now, having seen her through my mother's eyes, I am grateful that she instilled in her children so much courage and drive, which have been carried down through multiple generations.

I want to thank my aunts and uncles—Liz, Sandy, and Wendy—who all possess that Shaw charisma, with big personalities and fierce intellects. I want to thank their cousin, Michael Cock— spending time with him at Treworyan while his wife, Margaret, served scones and clotted cream was a lesson in the value of a simpler, more unhurried lifestyle.

I am so grateful to have had Jacques de Spoelberch as my agent. Jacques was one of the most eloquent and joyful people I ever met. While most people begin a sentence with "I think," Jacques would say, "In the view of this aging bookman . . ." Every word he spoke, everything he wrote, was poetry on a grand scale. The last thing Jacques said to me was that he looked forward to celebrating the launch of this book. Unfortunately, he passed away before that could happen, and I will miss him greatly. But like so many others who came under his wing, I will take inspiration from him for the rest of my life.

I want to thank Michaela Hamilton at Kensington Books. Michaela shares my love of Jacques, and she and her team took me under their wing and showed me there is much more to publishing a book than simply writing it.

I want to thank my wife, Colleen, who read more versions of the manuscript than I care to admit and always gave me spot-on advice. I want to thank my inner circle, including my amazing children, Jeff and Lizzie; my good friend and ex-wife, Karen; my brothers and sisters, who shared many of the experiences with me, and especially my sister, Tory, who through her loving care enabled our mother to remain joyful and energetic in her golden years; my best friends, David and Girish, who helped me navigate the many shoals along the way; and everyone else who provided support and encouragement.

I want to thank Bill Guttentag, a childhood friend who became an award-winning documentary filmmaker. Bill taught me to keep the story moving forward, identify the arc in every character, and treat every chapter like a story unto itself, with a beginning, middle, and end.

I want to thank Laurent Bouzereau, another documentary filmmaker, who worked with Bill and me. Laurent has a gift for pinpointing the underlying drama and for creating just the right message to explain it.

I want to thank Mike Greenberg for making me realize that Robert Shaw was much more than just my crazy uncle. When my good friend, Sean Timmins, introduced me to Mike as Robert Shaw's nephew, "Greeny" launched into a half dozen Robert Shaw imitations without missing a beat.

I want to thank Carl Gottlieb, the brilliant *JAWS* screenwriter, whom I met at JawsFest and had several follow up meetings with. Carl corroborated and filled in details on several important backstories from *JAWS*. His own book, *The Jaws Log*, is like a bible for how to make a hit movie.

Finally, I want to thank the people of Ireland, in particular those at Paddy's Bar in Tourmakeady. They shared many stories with me that took me back in time, back to the era when Robert frequented Paddy's. And they showed me why Robert loved the rural corners of Britain and Ireland so much—in Paddy's, no one ever feels the need to say something, yet someone always does.

Most of all, I am grateful to the colorful characters who inhabit this narrative. With this book, I hope to keep their culture, their humor, and their memories eternally alive.

Index